ELECTRIC UTILITY LOAD MANAGEMENT

ELECTRIC UTILITY LOAD MANAGEMENT

Marketing Strategies and Tactics

by

Raymond J. Burby
Nicholas M. Didow, Jr.
Mary Ellen Marsden
Charles F. Hanna
Michele D. Bunn
Stephen A. Johnston

ROWMAN & ALLANHELD
PUBLISHERS

ROWMAN & ALLANHELD

Published in the United States of America in 1985
by Rowman & Allanheld, Publishers
(a division of Littlefield, Adams & Company)
81 Adams Drive, Totowa, New Jersey 07512

85 86 87 / 10 9 8 7 6 5 4 3 2 1
Printed in the United States of America

Library of Congress Cataloging in Publication Data
Main entry under title:

Electric utility load management.

Bibliography: p.
Includes index.
1. Electric utilities—United States. 2. Electric
power systems—United States—Load dispatching.
3. Electric utilities—United States—Rates—Time-of-
use pricing. I. Burby, Raymond J., 1942-
HD9685.U5E535 1985 363.6′2′0685 84-24777
ISBN 0-8476-7383-9

Contents

Tables and Figures

Tables

Figures

Preface and Acknowledgments

This book is a joint product of the six co-authors. Dr. Raymond J. Burby assumed primary responsibility for Chapters 1, 6, and 7 and assisted with Chapters 5 and 9. Dr. Nicholas M. Didow assumed primary responsibility for Chapters 3, 4, and 9. Dr. Mary Ellen Marsden assumed primary responsibility for Chapter 5. Dr. Charles F. Hanna assumed primary responsibility for Chapter 2. Ms. Michele Bunn assumed primary responsibility for Chapter 8. Dr. Stephen Johnston contributed the Logit analysis of consumer participation reported in Chapter 5. We would like to acknowledge the assistance of Asta Cooper, Paul Lauria, John Ingersoll, Diane Brown, and David Boutilier, who provided research assistance on this project; Scott Verner, who provided editorial assistance; and Carroll Carrozza, Barbara Rodgers, Wanda Welch, Debbie Harrington, Mary Perry, Irma Watson, and Linda Wilson, who provided project administrative and secretarial assistance.

The research team was assisted during the course of the study by an Advisory Committee, whose members offered helpful suggestions and provided other assistance on a number of occasions. Members of the committee included Brian Flattery, North Carolina Association of Electric Co-operatives; James McBrayer, Virginia Electric and Power Company; Kay Scott, Duke Power Company, later with Carolina Power and Light Company; W.W. Smith, Carolina Power and Light Company; and William Watson, North Carolina Municipal Power Agencies. We would also like to acknowledge the assistance of Robert W. Taylor, Duke Power Company; Richard Williams and Daniel Oliver, Carolina Power and Light Company; Emmett Toms, Virginia Electric and Power Company; John Moore, Four County EMC; Jimmie Autry, Lumbee River EMC; and Galen Meekins, North Carolina Association of Electric Co-operatives. Finally, a note of thanks is due the more than eighty utility executives from around the United States who responded to our requests for information about their load management programs and the more than 2,800 North Carolina households who took part in our household survey.

The research reported in this book was supported, in part, by the North Carolina Alternative Energy Corporation. The members of the research team wish to thank Jon Veigel, Executive Director of the Alternative Energy Corporation, and Allen Clapp, program manager for the project, for their encouragement and advice throughout the study.

Raymond J. Burby
Nicholas M. Didow, Jr.
Mary Ellen Marsden
Charles F. Hanna
Michele D. Bunn
Stephen A. Johnston

Chapel Hill, North Carolina
November 1984

Introduction

This volume describes the marketing of residential electric load management programs and analyzes factors that affect consumers' decisions about participation. It offers practical advice to utilities about three key aspects of program marketing. First, it identifies load management marketing opportunities and identifies market segments that appear to be particularly promising and worthwhile. Second, it suggests marketing mixes–combinations of product, price, promotional, and distribution characteristics–that are most appropriate for different market penetration objectives. Third, it offers advice about program implementation and monitoring. Drawing on the results of a national survey of electric utility management, in-depth studies of six utilities, and survey responses from more than 2,800 utility customers, it provides the most thorough analysis of residential electric load management marketing available today.

The material presented here will be of interest to several groups of readers. As suggested above, personnel with electric utilities and advertising agencies serving the utility industry will find a wealth of information and suggestions for devising marketing strategies to achieve customer participation goals efficiently, while avoiding costly mistakes. State utility commission members and staff, legislators, and consumer advocacy groups will find data to help them in gauging consumer acceptance of load management and in estimating the potential market for direct load control and time-of-day rate programs. Social scientists interested in consumer decision making in energy-related matters will find a new application of the innovation adoption model and a series of analyses that explore variation in consumer decisions to take part in load management programs and variation in program satisfaction levels after households have enrolled.

The book is divided into nine chapters. Chapter 1 briefly describes the technical operation and benefits and costs of the two major approaches to residential load management: direct load control of water heaters and air conditioners and time-of-day rate programs. Consumer acceptance issues are reviewed, and the ways consumer research can contribute to effective program marketing are described. The chapter concludes by summarizing the data collection methods employed in the study.

Chapter 2 presents a nationwide overview of consumer participation in residential load management programs, highlighting the wide variation in rates of participation achieved to date, and reviews different methods utilities have used to achieve their market penetration goals. Particular attention is given to innovative approaches to the four "P's" of program marketing: product characteristics, price, promotion, and places where the product can be obtained.

Chapters 3 and 4 focus on the program development and customer participation experience of six electric utilities in North Carolina. The utilities studied in depth include three investor-owned companies (Duke Power Company, Carolina Power and Light Company, and Virginia Electric and Power Company), two rural electric membership corporations (Four County EMC and Lumbee River EMC), and the municipal electric system operated by the Town of Tarboro. Chapter 3 describes the load management programs developed by each utility, approaches to program marketing, and rates of customer participation achieved. Chapter 4, based on qualitative analysis of a series of videotaped focus group meetings with utility customers, describes how people react to the utilities, the load management programs, and the different marketing strategies that have been developed.

Chapters 5, 6 and 7 explore household participation in and satisfaction with load control and time-of-day programs based on information obtained through a survey of utility customers. Chapter 5 focuses on households who have enrolled in load management programs, describing motives for participation and comparing the characteristics of program participants and nonparticipants. The chapter concludes with a multivariate analysis of participation decisions in which three groups of predictor variables are compared—customer characteristics, monetary incentives for participation, and promotional methods used by the utilities. Chapter 6 looks at households who have been given an opportunity to take part in a load management program but have decided not to participate. It describes reasons for nonparticipation and suggests how programs can be promoted to convert these households into program participants. Chapter 7 shows how utilities benefit when consumers are satisfied with load management programs. Three major benefits—increased word-of-mouth endorsements, lower drop-out rates, and an enhanced image of the utility—are demonstrated. Chapter 7 also pinpoints the types of households who are most likely to become unhappy with load management and who require positive reinforcement if they are to continue to take part.

The final two chapters recommend approaches to specific program marketing tasks. Chapter 8 focuses on forecasting customer participation in load management programs. It describes how forecasts can be used in integrating general utility objectives with operational plans and procedures and presents a forecasting procedure that most utilities can use. Chapter 9 presents a comprehensive series of recommendations for introducing and promoting load management programs, based on the analyses presented in the previous chapters.

1

Introduction to Residential Load Management and Program Marketing

The United States is in the midst of an electrical energy crisis. After several decades in which building a new generating plant reduced the average cost of generating electricity, in the late 1960s economies of scale ceased to exist for many electrical utilities. In a period of high interest rates, skyrocketing inflation, and long delays in plant construction schedules, each new generating plant needed to satisfy consumer demand brought with it higher rather than lower average costs. Coupled with consumer uncertainty about nuclear energy and concern with the environmental impacts of power plants, the new economics of producing electricity has led to a search for equally new ways of doing business.

This book is about one of the ways utilities are coping–residential load management. Operating on the customer's side of the meter, load management programs have been designed to moderate the peak demands for electricity that have contributed to inefficiencies in generating power and high electricity prices. Because electricity must be produced at the moment it is needed, plant capacity must be adequate to meet peak demand. Some of this generating capacity, however, remains idle during off-peak periods. Peaking is costly for other reasons as well. The power plants many utilities use to meet peak loads operate less efficiently and use more expensive fuels that do plants used to meet base loads. As a result, it costs utilities up to four times more to deliver a kilowatt-hour (kWh) of electricity during peak-load periods than it does during off-peak periods (Office of Technology Assessment 1979). Two methods of moderating peak demands–direct load control and time-of-day rates–have drawn considerable attention from electric utilities and federal and state officials who are charged with regulating the power industry. Direct load control uses automatic on-off switches to limit the use of home electric water heaters and air conditioners during peak-load periods. Utilities have found that by cycling these appliances on and off they can reduce peak electricity demands by about 1.0 kilowatt for each water heater controlled and by about 1.2 kilowatts for each air conditioner controlled (Burby, Didow, and Marsden 1982).

Because load control represents a form of rationing, a number of economists favor an alternative, market-oriented approach to the peak load problem (see Cicchetti and Reinbergs 1979). Called time-of-day or time-of-use rates, the alternative relies on price signals—higher electricity prices are charged during peak periods and lower prices during off-peak periods—to induce consumers to switch electricity use from on- to off-peak. The results of a number of time-of-day pricing experiments sponsored by the utility industry and federal government indicate that in many cases customers will respond to time-differentiated rates, so that potentially this is also an effective method of reducing peak loads.[1]

Over the past decade millions of dollars have been invested in perfecting the equipment and technical procedures needed for load control and time-of-day programs. That investment will have little impact, however, if consumers cannot be induced to take part when programs are introduced. The experience of utilities that have pioneered in load management indicates that customer acceptance cannot be taken for granted. Although some utilities have achieved remarkably high participation rates, others have signed up only a fraction of the customers they hoped would take part (Heberlein 1981).

This book is designed to help private utilities and public agencies achieve their consumer participation goals. In this introductory chapter, the technical operation and benefits and costs of load management programs are described briefly. Consumer acceptance issues are reviewed and the role of consumer research in effective promotion of programs is explained. The chapter concludes by describing how the consumer information and marketing recommendations presented in the eight subsequent chapters were assembled.

RESIDENTIAL LOAD MANAGEMENT IN BRIEF

Residential load management is the deliberate reshaping of households' load curves—the amount of electricity consumed at different times of the day over different months and seasons. Altogether, electric utilities across the U.S. have developed more than forty different ways to shape customers' electrical loads (Gorzelnik 1982). In general, any of these load management activities falls within one of three broad approaches. One approach seeks to directly alter consumers' electrical loads by controlling certain end uses, such as water heating and air conditioning. A second approach uses the price charged for electricity to induce consumers to change the times at which they habitually use electricity. A third approach uses advertising and other means to encourage consumers to conserve electricity. Direct load control and time-of-day pricing—subjects of this book—fall within the first two categories.

Direct Load Control

With direct load control, the operation of customer appliances (loads) is deferred or cycled on and off during periods of local or system peak demand. Typically, one of two methods is used to control appliances: (1) nonremote (local) control devices, such a clock timers located on the customers' premises; or (2) remote-controlled devices, which are automatically activated by utilities. Because they allow utilities to respond to emergency situations and provide more certainty that the desired load has been shed, the remote control method is now favored by most utilities. The more frequently controlled loads are electric water heaters and central air conditioners. Direct load control also has been applied to other residential loads, such as space heating and swimming pool filter pumps.[2]

Direct load control has received increasing public utility attention during the past ten years, but it is not new. The first direct load control patent was issued in 1897. Mechanical time clocks have been used for more than forty years by some utilities to control water heaters. By 1940 New Zealand had initiated a program involving the control of space and water heaters. European utilities have long experienced the factors that more recently have stimulated U.S. interest in load management—escalating fuel costs and high costs of increasing generating capacity—and have long employed both local direct load control with clock timers and remote systems using both radio and over-the-line (ripple) techniques (Mitchell, Manning, and Acton 1978). In the United States, experience with the remote control systems is more recent. The first large-scale use of a radio-control system occurred in 1968, when Detroit Edison converted some 195,000 customers' water heaters from the clock timers it had been using. The first ripple system in the United States was installed by the Central Vermont Public Service Company in 1975, and the first major powerline carrier system was not installed until 1978, when Wisconsin Electric Power Company offered water heater and air conditioner control programs to its consumers.

Spurred in part by federal legislation—the Public Utility Regulatory Policies Act of 1978 (Purpa-PL 95-671) mandates the use of load management techniques that state regulatory commissions find to be practicable, cost-effective and reliable—utilities across the country have been experimenting with load control techniques on portions of their systems. At last count, some 170 direct load control projects had been undertaken by 130 electric utilities, including all sectors of the industry—investor-owned, municipal, cooperative, and large government systems such as TVA. Electric utilities have learned rapidly about direct load control. According to a recent trade publication, *Electric World,* "Top Management has come to believe not only that load control has a beneficial impact on the financial health of a utility, but also that it affects the entire utility organization" (Gorzelnik 1982, 77).[3]

Time-of-Day Rates

At present most utilities charge rates for electricity that are not differentiated by time of day. That is, the same price per kilowatt-hour is charged during all hours of the day throughout the year. Since production costs are higher during peak periods, this practice means consumers who use costly peak-hour electricity actually are not paying for the full cost of that electricity. Their use is being subsidized by those who use electricity during off-peak hours, when production costs are lower. In contrast, with time-of-day pricing, peak-period use of electricity is more costly to the consumer, reflecting the higher costs of providing service during this period. Lower rates are charged for electricity used during off-peak periods, creating an incentive for consumers to shift the times they use electricity from peak to off-peak. In addition, since rates more nearly approximate the marginal costs of production, time-of-day pricing contributes to the goal of charging customers a fair price for service provided.

Time-of-day rates have been used in the past. Detroit Edison had a time-of-day rate in effect in 1913, which it dropped later. Recent interest in this form of load management did not emerge until the early 1970s, however, when a series of generic rate cases in Wisconsin, New York, and California resulted in utility commission orders requiring companies to devise various peak load tariffs. By 1974, the Arab oil embargo and rapidly changing economics of the electric utility industry led the National Association of Regulatory Utility Commissioners to request research designed to find ways of holding down electricity prices, including the use of time-of-day rate schedules. (See Males and Uhler 1982.) In 1975, the Federal Energy Administration (subsequently incorporated into the U.S. Department of Energy) began funding a series of time-of-day demonstration projects designed to measure the effects of various time-differentiated rate schedules and, secondarily, to gauge consumer acceptance of the new pricing schemes. Projects were begun in 1975 in Arizona, Arkansas, Connecticut, California, New Jersey, Ohio, Wisconsin, and Vermont. Subsequently, other projects were funded in California, North Carolina, Oklahoma, Puerto Rico, Rhode Island, and Washington. Together, the studies funded by the regulatory utility commissioners and Federal Energy Administration have provided a wealth of information about time-of-day rates.

In general, these studies found that during peak periods, customers on time-of-day rate schedules used less electricity than customers on non-time-differentiated rate schedules, but that time-of-day rates had little effect on off-peak consumption of electricity. Total daily consumption was typically reduced in response to time-of-day rates as on-peak consumption decreased while off-peak consumption remained constant. In some demonstration projects, weekend consumption also decreased even though the time-of-day rate schedules in effect imposed the same base price during all hours of the weekend period. Thus, it may be that some conservation efforts during peak periods become habitual so that they are carried over to weekend days.

Besides changes in the average daily use of electricity, utilities are interested in the effects of time-of-day rates on days when the entire system is experiencing peak usage, since that determines capacity requirements. Most demonstration projects showed that differences in peak-hour consumption between customers on time-of-day rates and those on conventional rates were greatest during days of systemwide peak usage. In some cases, however, there was evidence of needle peaks during the hours immediately before and after peak periods, particularly if the peak periods used in setting rates were relatively narrow. Also, in some cases, such as in the Carolina Power and Light Company demonstration, there were no statistically significant differences in usage between customers on time-of-day rates and those on conventional rates during the hour of system-wide peak use. Thus, it is difficult to generalize across utilities; each utility must determine for itself whether time-of-day pricing will produce adequate reductions in peak loads to warrant conversion from non-time-differentiated rate structures.

Evaluating Program Options

In adopting load management programs, utilities typically seek to achieve one or more of six possible benefits:

1. Improved economics of system operation.
2. Improved load factor (ratio of average demand to peak demand).
3. Reduced dependence on scarce fuels.
4. Reduced capital requirements for generation and transmission capacity.
5. Improved reliability.
6. Reduced average cost of electricity.

The specific benefits utilities can achieve, however, will vary from one utility to another, depending upon factors such as the mix of electricity generating methods, fuels used, system design and operation, reserve capacity, construction programs, and saturation of loads that can be controlled or influenced (Gorzelnik 1982). In fact, where utilities have excess capacity and the demand for electricity is declining rather than increasing, programs such as load management, where benefits hinge on deferring the need for new generating plants, may have little appeal.

Even where demand is growing, utilities need to be careful that the benefits enumerated above outweigh the costs associated with load management. The costs of these programs to utilities vary, depending upon the load management technique used, but typically include (1) capital costs of the control, communication, switching, and protective devices required by the system, and in many cases, of new meters to measure energy consumed at different times of day or by a controlled appliance; (2) operation and maintenance costs associated with new load management equipment; (3) customer support services, such as customer service personnel, data processing, and billing related to load management programs; and (4) promotional costs related to informing the public about the load management program and persuading people to participate. The relative attractiveness of load management to electric utilities depends on the magnitude of the program's potential costs and benefits, both of which are likely to vary, depending on characteristics of the utility and its customers.

Load management is particularly attractive to utilities with low daily, weekly, or seasonal load factors, since one of the key benefits to be obtained is better use of generating plants. Thus, where utilities experience wide variations in demand over a twenty-four-hour day, between winter and summer, of with extreme weather, they may have a significant opportunity to reduce costs through load management. Some other utility characteristics affecting cost-effectiveness include the utility's generating mix, participation in interchange agreements and power pools, and future generating plant requirements (see Argonne National Laboratory 1980).

Load management tends to be more cost-effective where utilities are using high-cost plants, such as oil-fired generators, to meet their peak power requirements, since these units create more opportunities for cost reduction. Electric utilities with no generating capacity, such as many cooperatives and municipal systems that purchase wholesale power, also have a strong incentive to adopt various load management techniques. Typically, the price they pay for electricity includes a demand charge based on their peak requirement for electricity during a given period. The demand charge may be based on peak demand during the month power is purchased, but often purchase contracts include ratchet clauses that set the demand charge at up to 100 percent of the highest peak demand during the previous year. In either case, these utilities can usually reduce their costs substantially through load management programs that cut peak electricity use.

Where utilities participate in interchange agreements and power pools, their generating capacity requirements are determined by the load characteristics of the pool rather than of the individual utility. In addition, where pooling agreements include sharing of savings achieved in exchanging power, the marginal costs of any given utility participating in the pool are not the critical criterion for judging the merits of load management. In many cases, for example, utilities will split the savings achieved by sharing power (half to the seller and half to the buyer) so that the potential benefits from load management are sharply reduced (Argonne National Laboratory 1980).

Besides the shape of the load curve, generating mix, and participation in pools and interchanges, a fourth utility-related factor affecting the potential cost-effectiveness of load management is the utility's future expected costs of additional capacity. Where the costs of adding capacity are substantially higher than current costs of generating electricity, load management should become increasingly attractive over time.

The feasibility of particular load management options depends on both the nature of the loads to be controlled and the willingness of consumers to take part. For example, before a utility can determine whether direct control of air conditioners is cost-effective, it needs to know how many customers have central air conditioners, the size of the individual loads, and how air conditioner saturation will change in the future. Only then can it determine the potential size of the controllable load and benefits from controlling it. Of course, since load management programs are voluntary now, whatever potential benefits they offer will not be achieved unless consumers are willing to participate.

The initial round of utility- and government-sponsored research on direct load control and time-of-day rates focused on development of the technical systems needed and the question of cost-effectiveness. Customer acceptance of load management was apparently taken for granted, although various analysts have expressed some concern. Ferrar, Clemente, and Uhler (1979) and Uhler (1981) have observed that residential customers' acceptance of utility-sponsored load management programs is difficult to predict and suggest "customer information programs will be crucial in achieving customer acceptance of both load controls and time-differentiated pricing" (Ferrar, Clemente, and Uhler 1979, 128). An Argonne National Laboratory (1980) study of the costs and benefits of load management concluded that until it is shown that giving up control of space and air conditioning equipment does not create an unacceptable burden, consumer acceptance will be slow. More recently, Gorzelnik (1982, 71) summarized industry feeling by noting in *Electric World* ". . . there seems to be a nagging feeling that utilities must be cautious in their approach to customer acceptance." (Also see "Time-of-Use Rates" 1981 for another review of industry experience.)

THE ROLE OF CONSUMER RESEARCH

If consumer acceptance and program marketing are to move to center stage in the evolution of electric load management programs, utility efforts must be supported by carefully conducted consumer research. In particular, research is needed on factors that determine whether consumers take part in or reject utility-sponsored load management programs and also to inform specific marketing tasks. Marketing decisions that can benefit from consumer research include the selection of market segments as the targets of program marketing efforts, development of effective load management programs for market segments, formulation of communication objectives and tactics, selection of program participation objectives, retention of program participants over time, and calculation of market penetration forecasts.

Understanding Program Adoption and Diffusion

Theories regarding the adoption and diffusion of innovations provide useful perspectives for exploring consumer decisions about load management. A detailed conceptual model of the consumer adoption process is provided in Chapter 5. In this introductory chapter it is sufficient, first, to note that since load management programs are unique, new ideas to most households, it is appropriate to view them as innovations and, second, to mention two key concepts: the innovation adoption process and the diffusion process. (Also see Roberson 1971; Rogers and Shoemaker 1971; Midgely 1977.) The adoption process describes the psychological steps (awareness, interest, evaluation, adoption) through which a consumer must pass to be a participant in load management programs. The diffusion process reflects the fact that eventual participants agree to enroll in load management programs at different points over time. That is, not every consumer decides to participate in the programs as soon as they are introduced. Both processes have a number of important implications for program marketing decisions.

The adoption process can serve as a useful planning and tactical framework for utility management. For example, knowledge that a consumer household is at a particular stage in the adoption process suggests that different marketing objectives are appropriate. If households in the target market segment are aware of the load management program innovation, will they be motivated sufficiently to find out more about it? In the evaluation stage, how does a utility talk about the innovation to achieve target levels of subsequent adoption? Are consumers thinking about load management programs as alternatives to existing conservation programs, or are load management programs distinctly unique? The nature of the evaluative criteria and the competing alternatives determine consumer information requirements that utility marketing management must address.

The diffusion process describes the spread of innovation adoption over time and space. As noted above, innovations are not suddenly adopted by all potential consumers at one time. Instead, new products such as load management programs initially are adopted by a relatively small group of innovators. "Innovators," who typically comprise about 2.5 percent of the potential market, are the first households to become knowledgeable about the new product and decide to try it. The next group of consumers to adopt the product is known as the "early adopter" group. They typically comprise 13.5 percent of the potential market. Once this group decides to join the program, other groups are sure to follow. "Early majority" (34 percent of the market) and "late majority" (also 34 percent) are the next groups to join. Finally, the innovation will be adopted by a small group of consumers known as "laggards" (16 percent of the market).

These distinctions among eventual program participants are important for several reasons. First, if the innovators and early adopters can be reliably identified by the use of sociodemographic and psychographic characteristics, then this group can be treated as a target market segment for the initial promotion of load management programs. In fact, the total market for load management programs can be divided into segments based on the diffusion process and the resulting groups of participating households. Second, the innovators and early adopters are important market segments because there is little prior knowledge in the marketplace about the new product. The new product information available at this stage is largely controlled by the utility. Third, however, the innovators and early adopters are important influences themselves on subsequent groups of adopters, who tend to rely less on media sources and more on word-of-mouth and interpersonal factors in learning about and deciding to adopt or reject new products.

Research on the adoption and diffusion of load management programs can provide useful inputs for a number of marketing tasks. Marketing is more effective if target groups (market segments) can be identified and used as a basis for designing information programs, incentives and other promotional material intended to foster consumer participation. As noted above, innovators and early adopters make up especially important market segments; the rate at which these groups enroll in load management programs can affect the overall success of the program. A key task of market research is to identify the characteristics of load management innovators and early adopters.

Reaching Target Consumers

In each market segment, utility management must communicate with potential participants to move them through the steps in the adoption process. Market research provides insights into the distribution of residential consumers in different market segments across the steps in the adoption process. Awareness, interest, evaluation, and adoption all imply different communication objectives and tactics.

Utility marketing management needs to know what to say, to whom, by what communications methods, and at what time in order to produce desired results. Many utilities, however, do not now have enough information to make these decisions. A number of different types of information are needed. For example, how do different types of consumers (particularly innovators and early adopters versus later adopters) become aware of load management programs? Are different channels of information used by each group? What factors do different groups of consumers (market segments) take into account in evaluating load management programs? How important are incentives to each group? The type of incentive (monetary, peer regard)? The size of the incentive? How important is personal comfort? How accurately informed are people about load management? Answers to those and related questions are essential in formulating appropriate messages to communicate to potential load management participants.

There are also a number of tactics available to utility marketing management to achieve awareness and interest in load management programs in a particular target market segment. For example, the utility may provide speakers to civic clubs, use bill stuffers, organize community energy conservation meetings and exhibitions, develop displays for home shows and fairs, run announcements on radio and television, offer residential energy conservation audits, or organize and enlist employees, Boy Scouts, Girl Scouts, and PTAs in making door-to-door calls on residential customers. Some of these communications tactics will be able to reach some target markets. Other target markets will require different tactics for awareness and interest or for other adoption process objectives. Consumers' evaluation of load management programs may be aided by tactics such as published reports on energy-efficient technologies, testimonies from satisfied users, and providing a toll-free "load management" hot line. Although utilities have used all of these techniques in the past, the most appropriate tactics for promoting load management are not known. Thus, market research may reduce many of the uncertainties involved in communicating with target consumers.

Maximizing Consumer Retention

Consumer retention in load management programs, like initial consumer participation, has varied. In general, retention has been highest in water heater control programs, somewhat lower in air conditioner control programs, and lowest in time-of-day programs. The task for marketing management is to maximize residential retention. One set of influences on retention is the set of attributes that embody the specific load management program. For example, is retention enhanced by the magnitude of the financial incentive? A second influence on retention is the follow-up by the utility after a residential customer enrolls in the program. For example, how often should participation be reinforced by the utility and in what manner should participation be reinforced?

Forecasting Market Penetration

Forecasting market penetration is a final example of a marketing management decision that can be aided by market research. Utility management needs to have insight into the time and eventual magnitude of load management program participation, given selected marketing programs and market area characteristics. Reasonably accurate forecasts enable utility management to make more productive inventory and staffing resource allocations. Penetration forecasts also enable management to consider issues such as the impacts of different load management programs on the utility's financial performance and generating capacity requirements. Finally, forecasting ability enables the utility to know when and how to implement the next phase of load management programs to meet future participation objectives on schedule.

HOW NEEDED CONSUMER INFORMATION WAS DEVELOPED

The following eight chapters of this book provide data needed for effective marketing and promotion of direct load control and time-of-day rate programs. This unique information was developed from three primary sources: a national survey of utility marketing and load management personnel; case studies of six utilities in North Carolina that have introduced load management programs; and, viewing those direct load control and time-of-day rate programs as "test markets," responses from 2,804 households who returned a mail questionnaire. Each of these data sources is described briefly here. Readers who would like additional information, including copies of the survey instruments used, are referred to the appendices.

The National Load Management Marketing Survey

In order to more accurately gauge electric utilities' success in enrolling customers in load management programs and to identify effective marketing techniques for these programs, telephone interviews were conducted with personnel from eighty-three utilities. This nationwide sample was selected from information provided in the *1980 Survey and Evaluation of Utility Conservation, Load Management, and Solar Land-Use Projects,* Vol. 3 (January 1982), the most recent national compilation of utility load management programs. The sample of utilities queried includes each major type of electric utility: investor-owned (24 utilities), electric membership corporation (27 utilities), and municipal (32 utilities). They operated a variety of load management programs, including water heater load control (44 programs), air conditioner load control (55 programs), and time-of-day rates (15 programs). The telephone interviews were conducted in late spring and early summer 1982. The resulting data on utility load management programs, participation rates, and marketing practices are reported in Chapter 2.

In-Depth Case Studies of Six Utilities

Six electric utilities in North Carolina were selected for in-depth case studies. They comprise all of the state's investor-owned utilities that have initiated load control or time-of-day rate programs (Duke Power Company, Carolina Power and Light Company, and Virginia Electric

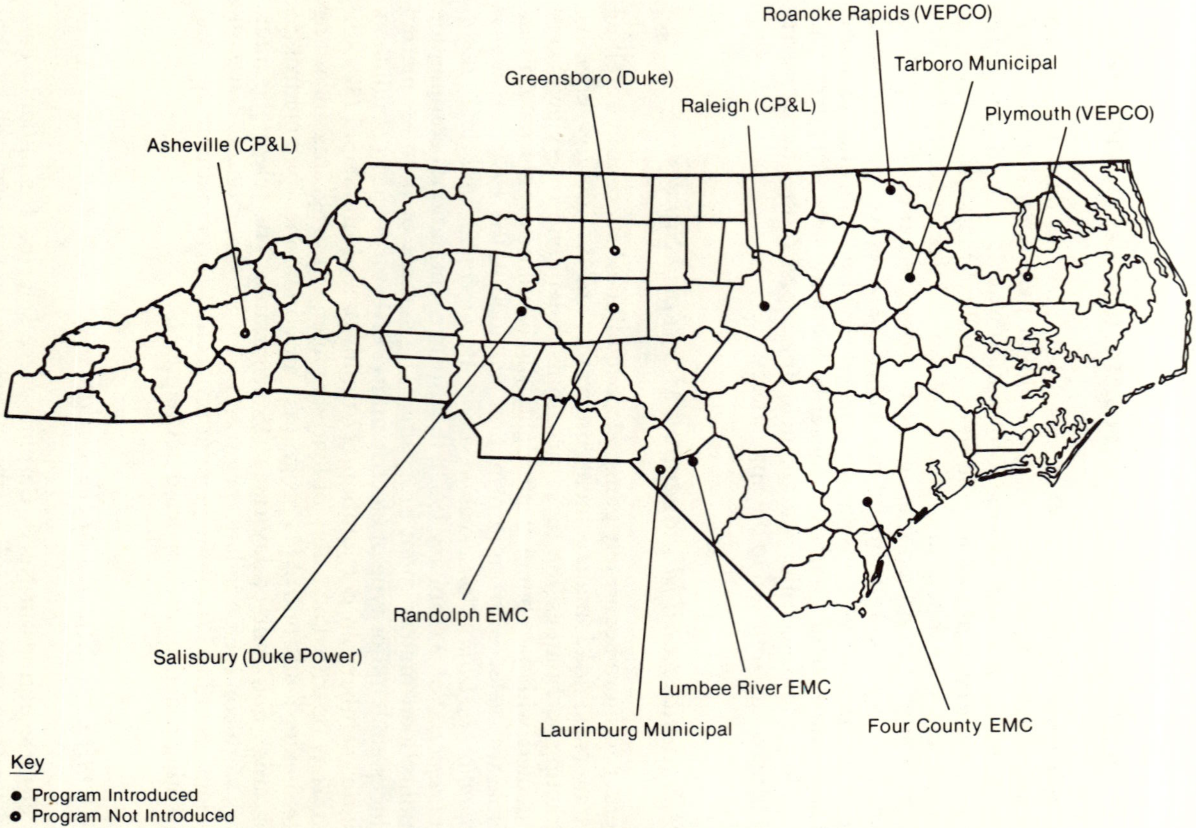

Figure 1.1 Utility Study Areas

and Power Company); both of the rural electric membership corporations with load control programs (Lumbee River EMC and Four County EMC); and one of seven municipal systems that have load control programs (Tarboro). The locations of the utilities and market areas studied are illustrated in Figure 1.1.

The case study method involved two major data collection techniques. First, personal interviews were conducted with the marketing staff of each utility during early summer 1982. These marketing audits produced information regarding the characteristics of the load management programs that had been developed, reports of customer participation in the programs, and detailed descriptions of the marketing efforts that had been mounted in support of the programs. Second, focus group meetings were held with groups of six to twelve customers of each utility to explore in-depth consumer perceptions of load management and reactions to the utilities' programs. The method used for the marketing audits and focus group meetings is presented in Appendix C.

Each of the six utilities offered a direct load control program and three—Duke Power, CP&L, and VEPCO—had time-of-day rate schedules approved by the North Carolina Utilities Commission; however, only the Duke Power time-of-day program was being actively marketed.

As of June 1982, Carolina Power and Light Company had succeeded in enrolling 8,600 customers (18 percent of those eligible to take part) in a water heater control program that was introduced in the Raleigh area in June 1980. The program involved shedding and cycling water heater loads up to four hours per day during peak periods.

Duke Power Company offered its customers their choice of time-of-day rates or direct water heater and/or air conditioner load control. The company employed a powerline carrier system in its load management program, which it was introducing systemwide in incremental steps as the appropriate equipment was installed in substations. In contrast with CP&L, Duke did not cycle appliances in its load control programs but used the system only to shed load during emergency situations. The program was introduced in the Salisbury area, which was nominated by Duke for inclusion in this study, in February 1981. By the summer of 1982, program participation included 184 customers in the time-of-day rate program, 1,497 in water heater control, and 610 in air conditioner control. Penetration rates for the load control programs were about 25 percent of those eligible to take part; in the case of the time-of-day program, about 1 percent or 2 percent of those eligible were taking part.

Virginia Electric and Power Company has experimented with a variety of load management techniques. At the time of this study, the company had enrolled 1,412 customers (19 percent of those eligible) in a water heater load control program in the Roanoke Rapids area, which it nominated for inclusion in this study. VEPCO shed and cycled water heater loads up to twelve-hours per day.

The Lumbee River EMC initiated a direct load control program in December 1976 and by June 1982 had enrolled 6,500 customers in water heater load control (54 percent of those eligible) and 2,500 in air conditioner load control (88 percent of those eligible). The Four County EMC introduced load control in November 1977 and by June 1982 had enrolled 7,556 customers in water heater control (88 percent of those eligible) and 1,827 in air conditioner control (59 percent of the eligible customers). Both electric membership corporations shed and cycled off water heater loads up to four hours per day and air conditioners seven-and-one-half minutes per half-hour during peak periods.

Finally, the Tarboro municipal system introduced water heater and air conditioner load control programs in June 1979. By 1982, 1,366 electricity customers were taking part in water heater control (65 percent of those eligible) and 977 were participating in air conditioner control (75 percent of the eligible population). Tarboro used the same water heater and air conditioner load shedding and cycling strategies as did the electric membership corporations we studied.

Of the six study areas, the Raleigh area served by CP&L is the most urban, with a metropolitan area population in excess of 300,000. Income and educational levels also are higher than the other utility study areas. The Duke Power, VEPCO, and Tarboro study areas are small towns with populations between 10,000 and 30,000. Income and educational levels rank between the highly urban population served by CP&L and the rural populations served by the two electric membership corporations studied. The EMCs serve rural areas with much higher-than-average minority populations and much lower-than-average incomes and educational attainment.

Consumer Surveys

A mail questionnaire, reproduced in Appendix A, was used to obtain information about consumer attitudes and decisions related to load management programs. Three groups of households were sampled: (1) households participating in load management programs; (2) households eligible but not participating; and (3) households in areas where the programs had yet to be introduced. The sampling strategy was designed to produce 100 respondents for each of the load management programs offered by the utilities studied, 100 nonparticipants who were eligible to take part in each utility's programs (households with electric water heaters and air conditioners), and 100 respondents from areas served by each utility where programs were not yet available.[4]

The sample design and responses obtained in each utility study area are summarized in Table 1.1. Overall, 3,997 households were surveyed, and 2,804 responded, a 70 percent response rate.[5] As shown in Table 1.1, response rates varied somewhat by utility and by sample strata. In general, the best response came from program participants and the poorest from nonparticipants; the response from areas without programs fell in between.

books as sampling frames. Thus, these samples produced a cross-section of utility customers including both program participants and nonparticipants. (Of course, the program participants obtained in these samples were excluded from analyses of nonparticipating households.) In the case of the Tarboro municipal system and the two electric membership corporations, lists of nonparticipating households were available and could be used by the research team to select random samples.

Each utility (in the case of the municipal and EMC systems, the state associations representing groups of the utilities) was asked to suggest a study area where programs had not been introduced. The areas nominated included Greensboro (Duke Power); Asheville (CP&L); Plymouth (VEPCO); Laurinburg (municipal electric system); and the Randolph EMC (EMC systems). The first two are metropolitan cities with populations similar to Raleigh; Plymouth and Laurinburg are small towns with populations similar to those of Roanoke Rapids and Tarboro; the Randolph EMC serves a predominantly rural area. In each area, a random sample of 150 households was selected. The locations of these samples are illustrated in Figure 1.1.

The mail survey was conducted as follows. Personalized cover letters with copies of the questionnaire and a postage-paid business reply envelope were mailed to the entire sample on July 20, 1982. One week later, a postcard follow-up was mailed to the entire sample, thanking those who had responded and urging nonrespondents to return the questionnaire. Three weeks after the original mailing a second personalized letter with replacement questionnaire and business reply envelope were mailed to nonresponding households. Finally, seven weeks after the initial mailing a third personalized letter was sent by certified mail to households who had not returned a questionnaire.

SUMMARY

The changing demand for electricity over each twenty-four-hour day is a major factor contributing to the electrical energy crisis of recent years. Typically, customer demand peaks one or more times daily at several times the average daily rate of consumption. Additional peaks occur seasonally, corresponding to the winter heating season and the summer cooling season. Because electricity must be produced at the precise moment it is needed, plant capacity must be adequate to meet demand even though much of this generating capacity will remain idle during off-peak periods. If peak demand for electricity can be moderated, the need for expensive new generating capacity can be reduced with consequent savings for electric power consumers.

This introductory chapter has described two of the more promising approaches to reducing peak loads—direct load control and time-of-day rates—and noted the factors that utilities must consider before deciding to begin a load management program. Over the past decade, utilities have paid particular attention to the design of effective technical systems for implementing load management programs. Now attention needs to be given to the issues of customer acceptance and effective program promotion to ensure that consumer participation goals are attained.

A well-thought-out marketing program backed by adequate consumer research is essential to the successful promotion of load control and time-of-day rate programs. Consumer research can contribute to rapid program adoption and diffusion by identifying key market segments, providing insights about appropriate messages and ways of reaching consumers, formulating measures to limit the number of program dropouts, and preparing market penetration forecasts.

NOTES

1. Much of this work is summarized in *Load Management: Issues, Objectives, Options,* The Final Report to the National Association of Regulatory Utility Commissioners (Males and Uhler 1982).

2. Three techniques for control of customer loads have been developed and are commercially available: radio, ripple, and powerline carrier systems (see Gorzelnik 1982; Argonne National Laboratory 1980). Each of these systems has four basic components or subsystems: (1) a central controller, which initiates commands to shed or restore load; (2) a signal transmitter (radio system) or injection device; (3) a communications link, which carries the signal to a receiver; and (4) a receiver, which decodes the incoming message and activates a switch to turn off or on the controlled appliance. With radio systems a signal is broadcast over a load management allocated frequency (most often 154 to 174 MHz). Ripple and powerline carrier systems use the electrical distribution power line to transmit the signal; the primary difference between them is the frequency at which they operate. Ripple systems use lower frequencies (200-1,500 Hz) than powerline carrier systems (5-300kHz) and as a result require more signal injection power. A fourth technique, telephone systems, is still experimental. They are similar to the other systems but use existing telephone lines as the communication link between the central controller and the receiver located on the customer's property. Besides controlling customers' appliances, direct load control systems—particularly those such as powerline carrier systems that can operate in two directions—have several other potential uses that are attracting utility attention. Two-way communication allows utilities to read meters automatically, verify that on-off commands have been carried out, and automate the distribution system to the substation level. This latter feature has the potential for greatly improving the reliability of the distribution system and electric utilities' ability to respond to emergency situations.

3. The primary argument against the use of load control has been made by economists, who have pointed out that because load control is a form of rationing, in which the utility rather than the customer determines when electricity is used in the household, consumers may have an incentive to beat the system. For example, customers participating in load control programs could reset their thermostats, raising water heater temperatures and lowering air conditioner settings, to ensure a given level of comfort. Or, over time, customers may begin oversizing appliances (Reinbergs and Harlan 1980). Thus, some concern has been expressed that the benefits from direct load control could be transitory; utilities may find that after they spend large sums of money, the intended reductions in peak period demand are not being achieved (Cicchetti and Reinbergs 1979).

4. The original study design called for the inclusion of only one electric membership corporation. Based on discussions with the North Carolina Association of Electric

Membership Corporations, both EMCs that had developed load control programs were included in the study. The consumer survey was split between the two EMCs, so that each sample was designed to produce fifty program participants and fifty nonparticipants per EMC. Only one EMC-served area without a load management program, the Randolph EMC, was included, however.

5. If 305 questionnaires returned by the Postal Service as undeliverable are excluded from the original sample, the overall response rate obtained increases to 76 percent.

2

Load Management Marketing in the United States

Customer participation in residential load management varies greatly. Some utilities have enlisted the participation of nearly all eligible residential customers, while others have signed up only 1 percent of those who might take part. Why do some utilities achieve high rates of participation while other utilities do not? Market penetration levels depend on the manner in which programs are marketed, the characteristics of the programs, and the characteristics of the population served. This chapter focuses on the first of these dimensions—the manner in which load management programs are marketed by electric utilities in the United States—and is based on findings from telephone interviews with representatives of eighty-three utilities.

MARKET PENETRATION EXPERIENCE

Heberlein (1981) studied fifty-four load control programs in the United States and found that market penetration was quite high in older and vigorously marketed programs such as Detroit Edison's load management program but substantially lower in newly introduced programs such as Wisconsin Electric Power Company's water heater control program. Participation, Heberlein found, was linked to both marketing and the date of introduction of the program.

Almost half the utilities queried for the present study (48 percent) had signed up fewer than one-third of their eligible customers in a load control or time-of-day rate program. As shown in Table 2.1, time-of-day programs in particular have had difficulty penetrating the market. Only two of thirteen utilities with time-of-day programs had signed up 60 percent or more of their customers. On the other hand, utilities offering water heater and air conditioner load control have had greater success. More than 40 percent of the water heater programs and more than one-third of air conditioner programs had penetrated 60 percent of the market.

TABLE 2.1

LOAD MANAGEMENT MARKET PENETRATION IN THE UNITED STATES
(percent of programs)

	Penetration Rate (percent of eligible households)			
	Low	Moderate	High[a]	
Type of Program	Under 30%	31% - 59%	60% or More	Total (N)
Water Heater Control	39	18	43	100 (38)
Air Conditioner Control	45	19	36	100 (47)
Time-of-Day Rates	85	0	15[b]	100 (13)
Average for All Programs	48	16	36	100 (98)

[a]High rates of participation also includes those utilities which achieved complete participation of their target group.

[b]Customers using 2000 kWh or more per month were required to participate in these programs.

PROGRAM MARKETING EXPERIENCE

For the present study, utilities' successes in marketing load management were examined in terms of four marketing concerns: (1) program or product characteristics; (2) price of the product; (3) place the product can be obtained; and (4) promotion of the product (Markin 1982). For each of those four "P's" interviews with utility personnel probed for marketing techniques, especially unique strategies used, and results obtained.

Program

Program characteristics include physical attributes of the particular product, e.g., a load control switch and its cycling strategy, the manner in which the program is intended to be seen by utility customers, and incentives offered to induce participation. Marketing approaches by utilities across the nation place primary emphasis on levels of financial incentive and the technical features of the program. They ignore the physical attributes of the product and whether customers should view the program as an energy conservation techniques or merely an innocuous piece of hardware.

Only six of the utilities queried gave customers an opportunity to examine the physical attributes of load control devices before deciding whether to enlist in the programs. These six utilities provided mockups of water heater or air conditioner control devices at billing places or at other places where heavy customer traffic could be expected. Some mockups were nonfunctioning units displayed at county fairs or shopping malls. Other mockups were functioning units and could be demonstrated to interested customers. The demonstrator learned whether the interested customer was eligible to participate; for example, whether he possessed a big enough water heater or air conditioner. The potential participant, in turn, became aware of the program and could evaluate how load control fit into the welter of energy related products and programs and whether his household might try load management. This process of awareness, interest, and evaluation is thought to be critical to the adoption of innovations (Rogers and Shoemaker 1971). How the device looks and operates is, no doubt, important to some households; cosmetic features may dissuade some and persuade others to participate.

More important, how is the program viewed by customers? The national marketing data assembled for this book cannot directly answer that question, but they tell about the impression utilities wished their customers to have about load management programs. The name given to load management programs supplies a clue as to how the program is to be viewed. Program name is important for two reasons: (1) the name provides recognition and identity; and (2) some names are easily incorporated into advertisements, thus integrating the "program" and "promotional" dimensions.

Mainly, utilities called their programs by some variant of the phrase "load management," such as load management program or load management system. Other utilities provided their programs with unique names. These unique names fell into three distinct categories. Each category tended to highlight a particular feature or function of the load management program. First, some names emphasized the switch or hardware. "Remote switching," "water heater switch," "air conditioner control switch," and "time-of-day metering program" are examples. Second, some names emphasized savings to the customer, such as "cycle and save," "silent saver," and "summertime break." Utilities that emphasized savings in their program name also rewarded customer participation with direct financial incentives. Third, some names emphasized peak demand and conservation. One utility highlighted the conservation emphasis by telling its customers to "Be a good neighbor, be a load shaver," while another warned "Watch your watts." A third told its residential users to "Plug into off peak," and a fourth asked customers to join the "peak corps." A few program names combined the emphasis on savings with hardware; "saver switch," "dollar saver switch," and "switch makes cents" are examples. While these names are clever, are easily recognizable, and can be incorporated into promo-

TABLE 2.2

FINANCIAL INCENTIVES AND PROGRAM PARTICIPATION
(percent of utilities)

	Participation Rate			
Monthly Incentive	Low Under 30%	Moderate 31% - 59%	High 60% or More	Total (N)
		Water Heater Control Programs		
No Money	42	8	50	100 (12)
Under $2	80	20	0	100 (5)
$2 - $2.99	25	50	25	100 (4)
$3 or More	29	29	42	100 (7)
		Air Conditioner Control Program		
No Money	21	8	71	100 (14)
Under $5	75	25	0	100 (4)
$5 or $6	67	22	11	100 (9)
More than $6	67	22	11	100 (9)

tional materials, it is impossible to determine their impact on rates of participation, since very few utilities used catchy names.

Incentives

Incentives or inducements are an important characteristic of programs. Table 2.2 portrays the relationship between levels of monetary incentive and participation in direct load control programs. These data are suggestive if only because they question the folk wisdom that says people participate in load management only for the incentives offered to them.

Financial incentives or inducements do have an impact on participation, but incentives alone do not assure high rates of market penetration. For example, more than 40 percent of the water heater and air conditioner control programs did not offer direct financial incentives for households, yet a majority of these achieved high participation from eligible households. Of the utilities that offered direct financial incentives, more than 70 percent achieved only low to moderate rates of customer participation. Further, the utility offering the highest monthly incentive for control of an air conditioner claimed that only 1 percent of the eligible residences were controlled. Finally, only three of the eleven programs that claimed that nearly 100 percent of eligible households were participating in a load control or time-of-day program offered direct monetary incentives. Monetary incentives, no doubt, influenced some households to participate in load management programs, but how and why incentives work is more complex than it would first appear.

Utility representatives also mentioned some nonfinancial and social conditions related to participation. One observed that customers may receive "psychological comfort from doing something to conserve." Several others spoke of "a sense of satisfaction" or a feeling of "community spirit" from participation. Others appealed to households' sense of community by showing how load management "holds down wholesale costs and keeps rates from rising too quickly."

A sense of satisfaction and holding down rate increases are indirect appeals, while monetary incentives are a direct appeal for participation. The indirect appeals usually were made by utilities serving small towns and rural areas. There was often much contact between utility representatives and townspeople. As one man put it, "In a smaller community you can communicate better than in a city. If I were in a city and doing this, it would never work . . . people come up to me and ask if load management is a good thing. I tell them it is and they go ahead [sign-up]." Thus, indirect appeals to residential customers can be an effective marketing strategy.

Price

Price influences participation rates since it means a cost to the consumer. Very few utilities (only 18 of the 98 programs) charged households to participate in load management programs. When charges were made, they were either service charges, ranging from $1.35 to $12.50 monthly, or installation and other charges, ranging from $10 to $120. Electric utilities tried to reduce the burden that high installation charges place on the consumer by offering low-interest loans or by offering payment options, such as a low monthly charge over a period of many years. Of the eighteen programs that charged households for their participation in load management, only two claimed high rates of participation. This suggests that costs to the consumer act as disincentives to participation.

To the extent that costs act as disincentives to participation in load management programs, they probably influence the adoption process in the evaluation stage (Rogers and Shoemaker 1971) in which the household forms attitudes and behavioral intentions about load management. If members of the household perceive the service charge or installation charge as a significant cost, it follows that they may not participate. This problem is discussed further in Chapters 5 and 6.

Costs are not solely financial. If households are not given the opportunity to try a load management technology without penalty, they may be disinclined to participate. The vast majority of load management programs permitted households to try load management then drop out without penalty. Only six utilities required customers to sign contracts that required participation in a program for a specific period of time. This is not to say utilities did not have participation "agreements." Rather, most utilities allow customers to discontinue participation without incurring an additional cost.

Paradoxically, price or costs to the consumer may even lead to increased participation. A representative from a generating and transmitting cooperative mentioned that one of his distributing co-ops charged members who were *not* participating in the co-op's water heater control program. They claimed to be successful, too. It should be noted, however, that when the North Carolina load management program participants queried for the household survey (reported on in Chapters 5–7) were asked whether they would favor charging nonparticipants extra for electricity, most did not think that was a good idea.

Place

"Place" refers to the channels through which a load management program is distributed and the kinds and numbers of outlets through which a product such as a load control switch may be merchandised (Markham 1982, 288). Channels of distribution may be viewed as pipelines through which products flow on their way to consumers. Given this metaphor, numerous pipelines and outlets for the distribution of load management technologies should be associated with higher rates of consumer adoption. Channels of distribution influence the adoption process by increasing awareness, stimulating interest, and culminating in adoption or rejection of the load management program (Rogers and Shoemaker 1971).

In effect, increasing the number of distribution channels leads to more opportunities for participation, thus making it easier for households to take part. With only a few exceptions, however, utilities did not use multiple channels to distribute load control and time-of-day rate programs. Households could not participate unless they went through the utility directly. Typically, they could not purchase a load control switch or time-of-day meter from a local energy conservation shop, a building contractor, or a heating and air conditioning contractor. Indeed, more than 80 percent of the utilities said households became participants solely through utility-initiated contacts.

Only two utility representatives mentioned that their utility had attempted to increase the number of places at which households could sign up for a load management program. Each reported that they had augmented participation rates by giving a bonus or incentive to independent heating and air conditioner contractors who enlisted households in load management programs. This additional channel of distribution works as follows. An independent contractor is hired to install an air conditioner control device on a home in a particular neighborhood. While installing the device, the contractor observes that neighbors on both sides of the house have central air conditioning. The contractor can obtain a $5 bonus (in addition to the installation fee the utility normally pays) if he enrolls either neighboring house. The contractor knocks on the door, explains load control to the resident, and, with the resident's permission, installs the device. The utility representative who described this scenario also noted that when out on service calls, contractors who were involved in selling load control switches usually did not disconnect switches from customers who were having problems with their air conditioning units.

Channels of distribution or "place" describes the process by which products move from producer to consumer. Thus, place considerations represent an interlocking network of organizations and groups (Markham 1982), which include the manufacturer of load management devices, utilities, and ultimately, consumers. Smooth and coordinated action between manufacturers and utilities that market their load control devices affect the ease with which a household can participate. Many utilities reported, for example, that they carefully timed their promotional activities with the availability of load control switches and opportunities for installation. One utility representative noted that his utility deliberately waited until it had a large surplus of switches and no backlog on their installation list before unrolling a multifaceted advertising campaign designed to increase participation. Another representative observed that his utility had produced ill will because it did not have sufficient switches for all households who signed up for load management programs. Although it was the manufacturing agency that was lax in delivering the switches, the utility bore the brunt of antagonism from the households.

A few utilities had tried to encourage participation by making it simple and direct for the customer to enroll in load management. Most utilities that had attended to that simplified the "letter of agreement" or contract the household had to sign in order to participate. A modification used by thirteen load control programs was to supply a box on the electric bill that could be checked by customers who wished to participate in load management programs, rather than an imposing contract.

In general, "place" may be the most overlooked marketing dimension. A single distribution channel typically had to serve all residential customers who wished to adopt a load management program. To the extent that "place" considerations permeate the entire process and directly affect rates of consumer participation, utility marketing managers must address the kinds and numbers of outlets through which their programs find their way to residential consumers. Neither can they ignore time schedules and transactions with the interlocking network of manufacturers, wholesalers, retailers, and installers that are part of the distribution channel for load management.

Promotion

Promotion concerns the way utilities communicate load control programs to households; literally, how the programs are "pushed" before the public (Markham 1982, especially chap. 13). In the broadest sense, promotion consists of coordinated activities intended to create channels of information and persuasion in order to sell a good or service or idea (Markham 1982; Brink and Kelley 1963).

It is reasonable to assume that effective promotional activities are based on knowledge of the potential buyers. Sixty-five percent of the utilities contacted tried to determine which households had electric water heaters or air conditioners or high usage of electricity before creating these channels of information and persuasion. In other words, utilities typically conducted "saturation surveys" before promoting programs so that their promotional efforts would be targeted to households that were eligible for load management programs. It was not typical, however, to further delineate this targeted group by learning their attitudes and preferences with respect to load management programs. Nor was it common for utilities to research the factors that might lead household members to participate in particular load management programs. Indeed, fewer than one-third of those interviewed attempted to assess customer attitudes, and about one-fourth tried to tease out factors that might increase participation. Thus, some utilities undertake their promotional activities knowing only which households have loads that might be controlled or which households, according to kWh usage, might benefit from time-of-day programs.

Given that relative lack of information, it is not surprising that a plurality of utilities used trial-and-error procedures in which they varied their promotion over time. Other utilities avoided traditional advertisement and simply contacted potential adopters of load management programs in person. In fact, more than half the direct load control programs and 46 percent of the time-of-day programs were promoted in a nonsystematic fashion or relied primarily on personal contacts.

Trial-and-error promotional activities or nonsystematic promotion occurred when, for instance, the utility attempted something like a bill insert, then monitored the response to it, then modified or abandoned it. Even with those nonsystematic approaches, many electric utilities achieved high rates of participation. Table 2.3 shows that nearly one-third of direct load control programs with high rates of participation were promoted nonsystematically as compared to one-fourth of these programs with high levels of participation that were promoted in the most comprehensive fashion.

TABLE 2.3

TYPE OF PROMOTION AND CUSTOMER PARTICIPATION
(percent of utilities)

Type of Promotion	Participation Rate (percent of eligible households)[a] Low Under 30%	Moderate 31% - 59%	High 60% or More	Average
Primarily, Personal Contact	18	31	17	20
Nonsystematic	50	13	30	35
Comprehensive	24	44	27	29
Comprehensive[b] (research & Personal contact)	9	13	27	16
	100	100	100	100
Number of Utilities	34	16	30	80

[a]Includes both water heater and air conditioner programs.

[b]The most comprehensive promotional activities began with a saturation survey to determine eligibility, then a questionnaire to determine interests and preferences, then a barrage of information from the utility including direct mailings and bill inserts, followed by advertising in the newspapers, on the radio and television. These effort would be followed by personal contact, i.e., going door to door. Somewhat less comprehensive were those promotional strategies that included the information barrage through bill inserts, direct mailings, radio, etc. but excluded personal contact and, usually, attitudinal questionnaires.

Table 2.3 also shows that of the load control programs with low rates of participation, fully one-half were promoted nonsystematically while only one-third were promoted comprehensively. Additionally, more than half the programs with high rates of participation were promoted by activities that reflected some degree of comprehensiveness. This suggests that comprehensive strategies may have a strong impact on rates of participation in direct load control programs.

SPECIFIC PROMOTIONAL ACTIVITIES AND PERCEIVED EFFECTIVENESS

Utility representatives were asked whether they had attempted some commonly used promotional activities and the extent to which these were effective in increasing participation rates in their various load management programs. Their responses are summarized in Table 2.4.

As the table indicates, there was uniformity across utilities in the types of promotional activities used. Bill inserts were popular ways of promoting water heater control programs and time-of-day programs. Half the utilities used direct mailings in promoting all types of load management programs. Publicity for load management programs, especially direct load control programs, was typically generated during civic club presentations. Indeed, more than half of the water heater programs and more than 40 percent of the air conditioner control programs were promoted at civic club meetings. In addition, newspaper advertisement was commonly used to promote direct load control programs. Finally, several utilities used personal contacts in an effort to increase participation. In fact, nearly all of those interviewed contended that personal contact was either very or moderately effective in increasing household participation in load management programs.

Direct mailings and bill inserts were perceived as effective by nearly four out of five utility representatives. One man noted, "Every time we do a bill insert activity we get [a positive] response." Mass forms of advertisement (radio, television, and newspaper ads), in contrast with more targeted approaches (direct mailings, personal contacts), were not seen as either very or moderately effective by as many representatives. The perceived effectiveness of each promotional activity should not mask the fact that many utilities employed various combinations of these activities.

Several utility representatives were quick to point out that the entire package of promotional activities they employed determined the effectiveness of each specific activity. For instance, media activities alert potential participants to a bill insert or direct mailing. As a result, it is sometimes difficult to determine the relative effectiveness of a specific promotional technique, since consumer responses are influenced by previous and subsequent marketing activities. Addressing this point, a representative from an investor-owned utility said, "It takes a combination of things with each in the proper amounts [and] what works in what amount is going to be different for each utility."

Personal Contact

Nearly every utility representative claimed that direct personal contact was effective in promoting direct load control programs. Newspaper and radio and television promotion, on the other hand, had mixed effectiveness ratings. Only a few representatives based their ratings of the effectiveness of personal contact on quantitative information. But nearly everyone interviewed claimed that customers almost never refused an invitation to participate from a utility representative who came to the household.

By going door to door the utility can create awareness, stimulate interest, answer questions the household may have, and persuade the

TABLE 2.4

PROMOTIONAL ACTIVITIES AND THEIR PERCEIVED EFFECTIVENESS FOR VARIOUS LOAD MANAGEMENT PROGRAMS
(percent of utilities)

Type of Promotional Activity	Water Heater Control		Air Conditioner Control		Time of Day	
	Use Method	Rate Method Very or Moderately Effective	Use Method	Rate Method Very or Moderately Effective	Use Method	Rate Method Very or Moderately Effective[a]
Bill inserts	49	81	34	79	a	a
Direct Mailings	51	81	53	80	a	a
Telephone Contacts	43	77	32	75	a	a
Personal Visits	49	94	41	94	a	a
Radio	37	36	33	64	a	a
Television	18	67	23	57	a	a
Newspaper	55	62	56	50	a	a
Civic club presentations, etc.	57	80	42	77	a	a

[a]The data base for time-of-day program (N=13) is too small to even suggest the effectiveness of specific activities.

household members to participate in load management. Moreover, the consumer survey conducted in conjunction with this study found that a large percentage of people claimed they would participate in load control if they were asked (see Chapter 6).

Unique Promotional Activities

Utilities were not wedded to the more traditional promotional activities. Several representatives believed that the most effective ways of increasing residential participation involved unique promotional activities. Increasing employee involvement, maximizing personal contacts with customers, using special bills, and working with installers and contractors led to impressive gains in residential participation, according to spokesmen in a minority of electric utilities. A handful of utilities offered prizes or cash to individual employees or departments who enlisted the most residential customers. One utility offered employees a $2 incentive for each household they recruited. A by-product of this tactic is that it increases interest and awareness among employees who also may be eligible for load control or time-of-day pricing.

By making the most of customer contacts, utilities may contribute to the word-of-mouth process that appears important in the diffusion of load management. Utilities often explain load management options to households through employees who routinely or periodically come in contact with customers, such as customer service representatives and energy auditors. More than 60 percent of utilities trained their staffs about load management. Obviously, those utilities were aware of the importance of having knowledgeable employees who can answer questions that potential participants may ask.

For very little additional cost, several utilities manipulated their bills or billing procedures so as to stimulate interest and participation in load management programs. One of the most interesting of these approaches is the three-line bill. The first line contains the user service charge, the second line the kWh usage and charge, and the third line a "O" for nonparticipants and the word "credit." Households call the utility to find out how they can get the "credit" and the representative tells them about load management.

Intuitively, these unique promotional strategies make a great deal of sense. They stimulate interest and awareness and increase the channels through which households can evaluate and try load management. Moreover, utilities engaging in these unique promotional activities usually used more traditional promotions, too. When viewed as a total promotional package, these utilities appear to be successful because they employed comprehensive, aggressive strategies that maximize personal contact. Of course, comprehensive strategies that use personal contacts are also expensive. Utilities must not lose sight of the fact that net benefits can decline if promotional costs become excessive.

SUMMARY

No single marketing strategy can guarantee high rates of participation in residential load management programs. Ultimately, residential customers decide whether or not to adopt the program. (See Chapters 5 and 6 for an analysis of this process.) If utilities' marketing management staffs are sensitive to the characteristics of their load management programs, the price households must pay to participate in load management, the places load management can be obtained, and the promotion of these programs, however, utilities can enhance their success in penetrating the market.

Mindful of "program" characteristics, some utilities have increased customer interest and awareness by providing water heater and air conditioner control mockups at billing places, shopping malls and county fairs. Others have given unique names to their programs that are easily recognized and incorporated into promotional campaigns.

Costs to the consumer—either monthly service charges or installation fees—tend to be associated with lower rates of household participation. Only slightly more than one in ten load management programs that charge households for participation claimed high rates of market penetration.

Place considerations—"pipelines" through which load management programs flow on their way to residential households—were the most overlooked marketing dimension. Typically, a single distribution channel served all residential customers who wished to adopt a load management program. More than 80 percent of the utility representatives reported that households become participants through utility-initiated contacts. A handful of utilities, however, tried to increase the number of distribution channels and opportunities for residential customers to participate by offering bonuses to independent contractors who enlisted households in load management programs.

Aggressive and comprehensive promotional activities were positively related to participation in load management programs, even though nonsystematic promotion was very common. Direct personal contact, whether part of comprehensive set of promotional activities or the main staple in a nonsystematic type of promotion, was rated as very or moderately effective by nearly all utility representatives. Bill inserts, direct mailings to customers, and telephone contacts with households were given high effectiveness marks by three-fourths of those who used them.

Perhaps the most surprising finding is that financial incentives are not clearly related to high rates of residential participation. More than 70 percent of the utilities that offered direct financial incentives had low or moderate, rather than high, rates of participation. Just over one-fourth of those utilities that achieved complete participation of their target groups or 100 percent of eligible households offered direct monetary incentives. Yet, when household members were surveyed (see Chapter 5), a clear and direct relationship between level of economic incentive and stated willingness to participate was found. This paradox is more fully discussed in Chapter 9.

Customer participation repays utilities' efforts both financially and nonfinancially. Chapter 1 listed three interrelated economic benefits from load management: reduced peak loads and associated reductions in needed generation, transmission, and distribution capacity; improved daily load factor and decreased use of peak-load generating plants and fuels; and, as a result, reduced cost of electricity supply. When asked about the magnitude of these savings, two-thirds of the utilities that had tabulated program impacts reported net savings of at least $100,000 per year, and one-fourth had saved more than $1 million. In addition, several utilities reported that capital outlays for new generating facilities had been deferred because of successful load management efforts.

Significant nonfinancial benefits, including improved systems operations, better public relations, and general employee education, also were attributed to load management programs. Among the most commonly mentioned technical advantages were increased system flexibility, increased ease of maintenance, and decreased probability of power shortages. Fully one-third of the utilities cited improved public relations. Addressing the public image of electric utilities, one utility representative said, "For electric utilities, friends are hard to come by and easy to lose."

Utility management also saw benefits to the communities they served. Load management programs increase awareness of electricity use and the need for conservation. Also, local income is generated when local people are hired to install load control devices and to sell load management to households. To the extent that people participate in load management programs because they perceive benefits to their community (see Chapters 5 and 6), it is reasonable to assume that community benefits may lead to higher rates of participation and potentially higher financial benefits to utilities and their customers.

3

Load Manangement Programs in Six Utilities: An In-depth Look at Program Marketing

This chapter provides a descriptive and objective history, or marketing audit, of the residential direct load control and time-of-day rate programs in six selected utility service areas up to the summer of 1982. The study areas and load management programs are (1) Duke Power Company (Duke) and its time-of-day rate program and water heater and air conditioner control programs in the Salisbury service area; (2) Carolina Power and Light Company (CP&L) and its water heater control program in the city of Raleigh; (3) Virginia Electric and Power Company (VEPCO) and its Roanoke Rapids water heater control program; (4) the water heater and air conditioner direct load control programs marketed by the town of Tarboro; (5) Lumbee River Electric Membership Corporation and its water heat and air conditioner direct load control programs; and (6) the water heater and air conditioner control programs marketed by Four County Electric Membership Corporation. The marketing audits are briefly discussed for each utility.*

DUKE POWER COMPANY LOAD MANAGEMENT PROGRAMS IN SALISBURY

Duke Power Company introduced three load management programs in Salisbury in February 1981. About 184 Salisbury households were participating in the time-of-day rate program by the summer of 1982. About 1,497 Salisbury households, or 26 percent of a potential market of 5,670 households, had direct load control devices installed on their water heater by that date. Likewise, some 610 households, representing about

---

* Many utilities provided detailed information and illustrative materials from their load management marketing experiences. This information is available in a two-volume publication, *Compendium of Load Management Marketing Materials,* by Charles Hanna, Nicholas Didow, and Asta Cooper, on file with The North Carolina Alternative Energy Corporation, Research Triangle Park, North Carolina.

a 27 percent penetration of an estimated potential market of 2,240 households in the Salisbury service area, were participating in the air conditioner direct load control program some seventeen months after program introduction.

Duke Power marketing personnel estimate the potential market for load control on water heaters or air conditioners by multiplying appliance saturation rates (percentage of customers who have the appliance) times the number of residential customers in the service area. Estimating the potential market for time-of-day rate programs, however, is more difficult. Marketing management does not yet have a satisfactory procedure for estimating the size of the potential market for this program.

At the time of this study Duke had received few complaints from participants in these load management programs. Fewer than 1 percent of households who signed up for the program had requested removal of the control devices from their houses later. Any complaints or requests for removal, however, should be cause for concern among marketing management, since water heaters and air conditioners had not been frequently cycled off in the Salisbury service area. The Duke Power service interruption plan is to use direct load control only as needed in severe system emergencies, rather than to control on a daily basis during the summer or winter system peaks.

The economic incentive for households to participate in time-of-day rate programs varied from household to household. With respect to the direct load control programs, though, the original financial incentive was a billing credit of $1 per month per appliance controlled. In 1982 the economic incentive for participation in the water heater program was a billing credit of $2 per month granted throughout the year. Participation in the air conditioner program resulted in a billing credit of $2 per kilowatt-day per month, granted during the months of July, August, September, and October. A restriction on the economic incentives offered in the Duke direct load control program was that the total monthly credit granted could not exceed 35 percent of a household's current monthly electric bill. In general, then, the typical annual credit for the household that participated in both the water heater and the air conditioner programs was about $50.

Eligibility requirements for participating in any of the three load management programs were that the household (1) be the owner of the premises or have the permission of the owner or manager to participate and (2) be located in the Salisbury substation service area. Households seeking to participate in the water heater load control program had to have an approved water heater with at least a thirty-gallon capacity. Air conditioner program participants had to have an approved central air conditioner. (The latter two eligibility requirements eliminated virtually all mobile homes from participation.)

A qualifying household had to sign a formal contract in order to participate in either of the direct load control programs. The contract was valid for an initial period of two years. The contract also included provisions whereby the household could be charged $25 if the household asked that a direct load control device be removed within the first year of participation.

The Duke service agreement for participating in the time-of-day program was simpler. This service agreement consisted of a brief card that the residential customer had to sign. The time-of-day agreement involved no initial commitment or removal/withdrawal fee provision.

Duke arranged installation of the load management equipment in participating households by private contract electricians. Each household participating in load control was required to pay a substantial installation fee. The installation fees generally were $35 for a water heater or air conditioner control device, or $50 if devices were installed for both appliances during the same service call. The load control devices generally were mounted outside the home at some distance from the appliance to be controlled. Where special wiring was not required for installation, however, the installation fee could be as low as $10 per device.

Duke allocated several personnel positions for load management marketing activities. The Salisbury load management program was staffed by a customer service/residential marketing staff of five: four whose responsibilities included the direct load control programs and one who was primarily responsible for the time-of-day program. All five were located in Salisbury. Supporting personnel and marketing area specialists also were available to the Salisbury marketing staff from Duke's corporate headquarters in Charlotte.

The load management programs in Salisbury were promoted primarily through direct sales to individuals and groups. The Salisbury promotional program made little use of advertising, including both print and broadcast media.

In February 1981 the Salisbury marketing staff identified an initial group of about 200 heavy-user households and sent them a direct mailing. The letter invited the household to send someone to a forthcoming "Time-of-Day Energy Seminar." The household was given a Duke Power telephone number to call to make reservations to attend the seminar. Accompanying the letter was a brochure titled "Duke Power's Time-of-Day Rate Can Mean Savings for You." The brochure was designed to introduce the household to the time-of-day rate program and provide some detailed information about energy usage by several popular electrical appliances. If a household was interested in finding out more about the load management program, but was unable to send anyone to attend the scheduled seminars, an appointment would be scheduled for someone from the marketing staff to meet individually with the prospect at the residence or at the local Duke Power office. The basic strategy was to use a personal, direct exchange between the household and the Duke representative to examine the possibility of adopting the time-of-day program. If a household seemed inappropriate for the time-of-day program, the marketing representative would introduce the water heater and air conditioner control programs to the household.

Each "Energy Seminar" followed a standard format. The seminar was conducted by a Duke consumer education representative. Each household was given a number of handouts at the meeting, including a brochure titled "How to Get Paid For Helping Hold Down The Rising Cost of Energy." The seminar typically began with a slide show designed to introduce the time-of-day and load control programs. Next, households would examine the feasibility of time-of-day rates by calculating a break-even point for demand on the time-of-day rate compared to existing rate structures. The household would then look at a demand sheet that itemized average kilowatt ratings for various electricity-consuming tasks around the home. If the household believed that enough tasks could be scheduled during off-peak hours, the household was qualified for the time-of-day rate program. If it appeared that the household electricity consumption patterns would be unlikely to shift to accommodate time-of-day rates, the discussion would move on to load control devices.

Duke marketing personnel were able to obtain participation agreements from many households who were represented at the meetings. There were generally eighteen to twenty-five people present at a typical Energy Seminar. Thus, through this direct contact and through some initial door-to-door solicitation the utility was able to obtain participation in load management programs by many key people in various neighborhoods.

By July 1982 every residential customer in the Salisbury substation area had been sent a letter about the Energy Seminar. Follow-up letters also were mailed to potential load control households. The letters mentioned that nearly 1,000 Duke Power customers in the Salisbury area already had decided to participate in direct load control programs. Like other direct mail pieces, the letter also gave a utility telephone number as a source of further information. Some follow-up letters included a preaddressed, postage-paid card that could be returned to the utility to request more information about the load control program. The general theme of all letters was that the household was eligible for a credit on its electric bill in exchange for giving the utility permission to interrupt service to the electric water heater and/or central air conditioner during an emergency power shortage.

The utility made considerable use of door-to-door solicitations within the neighborhoods in Salisbury. Marketing staff members often referred to participating neighbors by name in order to persuade a prospect household to join in a load management program. Staff members also made frequent appearances and speeches at local civic club meetings.

CP&L AND THE RALEIGH WATER HEATER PROGRAM

In June 1980, CP&L introduced a voluntary water heater direct load control program in the Raleigh service area. Two years of marketing activity by this investor-owned utility resulted in about 8,600 enrolled households from a potential of about 48,000 households, representing an 18 percent penetration of the estimated market.

The total potential market estimate of 48,000 households was determined by estimating the number of eligible water heating customers within the Raleigh load management transmitter range and then eliminating an estimated number of households for which installation would likely be impractical or objectionable for the household or property owner.

Up to the time of this study the utility had received relatively few complaints from participants, even though water heaters were frequently cycled off. The CP&L service interruption plan involved shedding and cycling off water heater loads for up to four hours a day. The plan anticipated 100 to 200 hours turnoff per year in each participating household. CP&L management has conducted several field experiments to determine the effect of various water heater interruption strategies on complaints. The findings from these experiments, held during the summer and winter of 1981, are that there are many control strategies that result in virtually no complaints telephoned in to the utility. At the time of this study removals also were minimal, estimated at fewer than 1 percent of the enrolled households.

CP&L established system-wide goals for its load management programs. The formally adopted short-term load management goal was to have 92,000 households participating in load management by the end of 1985. The utility wanted to achieve a 630-megawatt reduction in system residential demand by the end of 1995. To meet this demand reduction goal, the utility would need roughly 175,000 participating households. This target number of households represents about a 25 percent market penetration level system-wide for load management programs.

The Raleigh water heater direct load control program originally included an economic incentive of a $1 credit per month for each participating household. In November 1981 the amount of credit was raised to $2 per month. The credit was applied monthly to the participating household's electric bill. In May 1982 the utility added an additional incentive of a free water heater insulation wrap for each new and existing participant.

Households had to meet three major requirements to qualify for the program. First, the household had to have an approved electric water heater with at least a forty-gallon rated capacity and either one or two self-contained, non-simultaneously operating heating elements designed to require less than 5,500 watts per element. Second, the household had to be the owner of the premises in which the load control device was to be installed. Renters qualified for the load control program if they could obtain written permission from the owner or manager of the property. Third, the household had to be located within a twenty-mile radius of the load control radio frequency transmitter site on the Meredith College campus.

A representative from an eligible household was required to sign a brief contract card to participate in the program. The contract card originally included a provision for a $25 removal fee, should the household decide to withdraw from the program within one year. This provision had been dropped from the contract card by the summer of 1982.

CP&L used private contract electricians to install load control devices in participating households. There was no installation fee for the household. Neither was there any household fee for the equipment itself. The utility preferred that someone from the household be present during installation, a process that typically took one to two hours. Since the radio-controlled devices were generally mounted on the outside of the residence, however, it was not necessary for someone from the household to be present during installation.

CP&L allocated several staff positions to its load management program. The program was managed by a staff that included a corporate program director, a district coordinator for each service area involved in load management, and a communication specialist. The staff was supported by access to a variety of other specialists, including an in-house marketing and market research expert and a private advertising agency.

The Raleigh water heater program was promoted using a variety of advertising, publicity, and group sales tactics. The mix of these tactics changed frequently.

The utility promoted its water heater control program with considerable advertising after the program was introduced in the summer of 1980. CP&L frequently used radio spots, newspaper ads, television ads, bill inserts, employee check inserts, and direct mailings to household prospects with follow-up letters. The promotional theme for most of the advertising was that load management could save the household money and that the participating household could help control future electric costs.

The brochures were generally colorful and included a self-addressed, postage-paid contract card. The brochures also identified a CP&L telephone number where the prospect could call for further information.

Radio and television advertising copy was typically designed to explain the basic problem of electrical system peaks and the logic of load management.

Magazine and newspaper advertisements in the Raleigh area also were heavily oriented toward a theme of saving money. Some print advertisements referred to the load management program as a "Home Energy Rebates" program in which the household could get a bill credit and reduce its energy usage while helping CP&L reduce the peak demand. This advertising copy, like most used by the utility, also counterargued the objection that the load control program might be inconvenient for the household.

The CP&L Raleigh water heater program enjoyed considerable publicity, especially when it was first introduced. The program was the focus of many newspaper, radio, and television feature articles. The utility provided a load management speaker for appearances at many civic clubs and other community functions.

The utility made little use of direct sales tactics. CP&L did not attempt any door-to-door solicitation for load management participation. Neither did the utility attempt to identify and obtain participation from qualified prospects when they came into CP&L offices to pay bills or request various utility services.

VEPCO AND THE ROANOKE RAPIDS WATER HEATER DIRECT LOAD CONTROL PROGRAM

Virginia Electric and Power Company (VEPCO) introduced a voluntary water heater direct load control program in most of the Roanoke Rapids service area in June 1980. The program was developed to meet an established system-wide objective of 25 percent load management saturation. By the summer of 1982 the utility had enrolled about 1,412 households in the program. Those households represent a 19 percent penetration rate in an estimated potential market of 7,544 households. The total number of potential load control households was estimated using appliance saturation data and other demographic data pertaining to the Roanoke Rapids service area.

After two years of field operation, the utility had received few complaints from participating households. Requests for removal of installed load control devices had come from fewer than 1 percent of the participating households. This low level of complaints and removal requests may reflect the fact that, although the service interruption plan was for rotated interruption on a daily basis as needed up to a maximum of twelve hours total per day, the cycling off of water heaters rarely approached the maximum described in the plan.

The VEPCO water heater load control program originally included an economic incentive of a $1.85 billing credit per month. The rate for the monthly incentive later was changed to $2.34.

There were two basic eligibility requirements. First, the household had to have an approved electric water heater with a capacity of at least thirty gallons. Second, the household had to live in a single-family residence or in a mobile home on a stationary foundation. Any mobile home also had to have a 240-volt water heater.

The utility did not require a household to sign any contract card or service agreement to participate in the program. The water heater direct load control program included no provision for a removal fee, should the household seek to stop participating. Households seeking to participate in load management were asked informally to agree to stay in the program for at least one year.

The utility used private contract electricians to install the load control device in the household. The household was not charged a fee for installation or for the equipment itself. VEPCO load control equipment could be installed at the water heater itself or on the outside of the structure. Consequently, the customer had to be present during installation to allow access to the water heater circuit. Installation of the equipment usually took about thirty minutes.

A large staff was involved in the marketing of the VEPCO direct load control program. The staff included four supervisory personnel and ten other staff employees. These fourteen people also had other responsibilities within the utility. Supporting personnel and specialists also were available to the marketing staff as needed.

The utility promoted the water heater direct load control program in Roanoke Rapids by use of direct mailings, telephone follow-ups, and bill inserts. Radio spots and newspaper advertisements also were used to help establish program awareness in the service area.

The utility used several bill inserts and direct mailing materials. The early bill inserts used a theme of saving the household money each month by participating in the water heater program. The yellow insert was a preaddressed and prestamped reply card by which the household could indicate an interest in the water heater program. The household was asked to enter their name, address, phone number, and account number on the card and mail it to the VEPCO office. Later the household would be called by a member of the local district customer service staff. During the call the staff member would explain the program and seek a verbal agreement to participate. The utility representative then would attempt to schedule a convenient time for equipment installation. (The installation contractor, however, confirmed the final appointment time.) Another early brochure used the single theme of the water heater program as "a chance to save on electric water heating costs." This brochure had a drawing of a water heater on the cover and a simulation of the financial credit for participating stamped over a standard VEPCO bill. Inside, the brochure answered a number of questions about the program. The household could enter their name, address, and other information to receive further details about the program.

The VEPCO water heater program was featured in several articles in the local newspaper. The articles were generally introductory pieces that described the basic benefits and requirements of the load management program.

THE TOWN OF TARBORO DIRECT LOAD CONTROL PROGRAMS

The Tarboro Electric Department introduced a water heater direct load control program and an air conditioner direct load control program to its residential customers beginning in January 1979. As of the summer of 1982, 1,366 households were enrolled in the water heater control program, representing a 65 percent penetration of an estimated potential market of 2,100 participants. The air conditioner program had achieved a similar penetration level at that time: 977 households were participating in air conditioner direct load control, for a 75 percent penetration of the 1,300 potential households. These penetration levels were encouraging to the town, particularly since the goal of the programs was to install as many as possible in order to reduce the summer peak demand charge from VEPCO, the source of electricity for the town's municipal system. The size of the potential market was estimated from Electric Department appliance surveys.

Town personnel noted few complaints or requests for removal of the controls. Fewer than 1 percent of the participating households had contacted the Electric Department to ask for removal from the programs by the summer of 1982. That was the case even though the utility actively managed demand using load control during the hottest summer months.

The town program originally provided for a bill credit of $15 per control device per year for the participating household. The credit was lumped and posted during the months of June, July, August, and September. In 1982, the credit was increased to $20 per device per year.

Mobile homes were not eligible to participate in the programs. An approved water heater with at least a thirty-gallon capacity was required for a household to join the water heater load control program. The air conditioner program required that a household have an approved central air conditioner.

Households had to sign an authorization card to participate. The authorization card indicated that the household could at any time request removal of the device.

Installation of the load control device was performed by town electrical crews. No installation fee was charged to the household, nor was there a household fee for the equipment itself. Someone from the household had to be present during installation, since the radio controlled device was mounted at the appliance itself. Most devices were installed and field tested within about a one-hour period.

The marketing staff for the Tarboro load management program consisted of only one full-time person to oversee and coordinate the program. The program received much direct support, however, from numerous city officials and community leaders.

The Tarboro program followed an initial promotional strategy that used direct mailings, some radio spots and newspaper ads, many press releases, and frequent appearances at the speaker's stand of local civic and community clubs. By 1982, however, the marketing staff used only informal word of mouth communication to obtain new participants.

The direct mailings initially were aimed at potential air conditioner load control households. A letter was sent to all 1,200 Tarboro central air conditioning households who could be identified from city records and observation by meter reading personnel. The theme of the letter was that the load control program was a specific step Tarboro and its citizens could take to reduce the amount of money paid to VEPCO for demand charges. The letter also cited a number of other social and economic benefits for becoming one of the Tarboro "Peak Shaver" households. Included in the mailing were a descriptive brochure about the "Peak Shavers" program and an authorization card for the household to complete to join the Tarboro Peak Shavers team. More than 600 completed authorization cards were received from the first mailing to the 1,200 target air conditioner households. Later direct mailings to water heater program prospects resulted in a similar initial response.

This high immediate response probably resulted from a number of factors. One major factor was that there had been much public discussion and outrage concerning increases in demand charges and the price of buying electricity from VEPCO. After much debate in the city council, civic clubs, the local newspaper, and other public forums, load management was identified as the most promising alternative for the community to fight back. The load management program still is often cited publicly as a community action that brought direct, demonstrable benefits to all members of the town.

THE LUMBEE RIVER EMC DIRECT LOAD CONTROL PROGRAM

In December 1976 Lumbee River Electric Membership Corporation introduced a voluntary direct load control program to its residential customers. By the summer of 1982 about 6,500 households were participating in the water heater load control program. Those households represented a penetration rate of 54 percent of the estimated 12,000 potential households. The air conditioner program had achieved about the same penetration level. It stood at 57 percent, representing participation by 2,500 households out of the estimated potential residential market of 4,380 households. The number of potential households for each program was estimated using demographic information about the service area and appliance saturation data.

Complaints from participants were few. Similarly, requests for removal of the load control devices also were few, even though the utility followed a service interruption plan involving some control each month, particularly during the summer months. Water heaters were cycled off in rotation for the duration of peak demand. This generally was for two to three hours, though on occasion the control episode lasted as long as six hours.

The utility established a formal goal of having 10 percent of system demand under control. This translated into original objectives of 6,000 water heater devices and 2,000 air conditioner devices among households in the service area. By 1982, the utility believed it had met its load management goal and was seeking to increase the amount of demand under control in rough proportion to the annual growth of the entire electrical system.

The Lumbee River program originally involved no direct economic incentive for a participating household. Company records suggest that about 1,000 devices were installed in Lumbee River EMC households in the early months of the program without any billing credit for participation. Early in the program, however (August 1977), a monthly billing credit of $1.25 per switch was established.

An interested household had to meet minimal eligibility requirements to qualify for the program. The household had to have an approved water heater with at least a thirty-gallon capacity to join the water heater direct load control program. An applicant to the air conditioner program had to have an approved central air conditioner or heat pump. Devices were installed in mobile homes only if the mobile home was permanently mounted in one location.

The Lumbee program originally required the household to sign a brief authorization card. The agreement involved no term for the contract. Neither did it include any reference to a fee for removal of the device. The card was dropped later, and the utility began to install direct load control devices upon only a simple verbal request, perhaps by telephone, from the household.

Load control devices originally were installed by private contract electricians. These electricians were reimbursed $15 for every switch they installed. By 1982, however, the devices were being installed by Lumbee River EMC electricians. The participating household was not charged a fee for installation of the device.

The utility originally staffed the load management program with one full-time supervisor. A second full-time person was added to the marketing staff in early 1982. Though there was but one person directly responsible for supervising the program, the utility marketing strategy involved using almost every Lumbee employee and subcontractor as part of a massive direct sales force.

The Lumbee marketing strategy was to rely heavily on direct selling to achieve participation by households. Lumbee River EMC employees were involved in an employee incentive program to promote load management. An employee was awarded one dollar for every new residential consent form that the employee obtained. Meter readers were encouraged to identify prospects and obtain consent as they traveled throughout the service area. Contract electricians carried extra load control devices with them as they went out on installation calls. They were encouraged to stop at nearby houses after an installation to try to obtain consent from the new participant's neighbors. One contract electrician loaded up his service truck with direct load control devices and made "cold calls" on households throughout the service area to try to obtain participation.

The utility supported the direct sales strategy with limited use of radio spots and newspaper advertisements. Direct mailings also were sent to household prospects. Much publicity surrounded the Lumbee River EMC load management program. It was within this utility's program that the first direct load control device was installed in North Carolina. The installation was a "media event" and was covered by numerous radio and television stations, and newspapers.

The utility used no bill inserts about its program. Instead, every member's bill shows a load management credit. Thus, a nonparticipant's bill shows $0.00 credit.

The *Lumbee River EMC News* was the primary vehicle used to promote load management participation. Virtually every issue of this EMC newsletter included some article about load management and a telephone number and reply coupon for further information. The newsletter articles often discussed the benefits load management provides to the member households and answered a number of frequently-asked questions about the direct load control program.

The theme for the Lumbee River program was primarily that load management was a specific way for the EMC to reduce power costs for wholesale purchases of electricity from generating utilities such as CP&L. The Lumbee River marketing program enjoyed a favorable reception from many households because of the community interest in the early days of the program to do something to reduce the rise in electricity costs for households and other service categories within the EMC. During and after the late 1970s there was continuing local public pressure on the utility board of directors and management to contain members' costs.

FOUR COUNTY EMC LOAD CONTROL PROGRAM

In November 1977, Four County Electric Membership Corporation introduced its water heater and air conditioner direct load control programs to its general membership at the annual meeting. Consent cards were handed out and collected at the meeting from attending general members, officials, and staff personnel. Some 7,556 households were participating in the water heater direct load control program by the summer of 1982. They represented an 88 percent penetration of the estimated potential market of 8,546 residences in the service area. The air conditioner direct load control program had achieved a 59 percent penetration of the estimated market at that time: 1,827 households out of a potential market of 3,076 households were participating. The size of the potential market for each direct load control device was estimated using appliance saturation data and other demographic information pertaining to the utility service area.

These relatively high levels of market penetration were in keeping with the formal goals established by the utility for its load management program. Four County EMC always has marketed its load management program with the goal of installing as many load control devices as possible in residences in the service area.

Four County EMC's load management program experienced some awkward initial years. The utility originally required that a household representative sign a consent card to participate in the program. Some 500 consent cards were obtained at the initial Annual Membership Meeting in November 1977. By the end of 1977, the utility had collected more than 1,000 consent cards. Shortly after that time it was discovered that the load control switch itself failed to pass a required test for Underwriter's Laboratory approval. The problem was corrected by installing the load control switch in a waterproof metal box, which was furnished by the manufacturers. The utility adopted a maintenance marketing effort for many months while the metal enclosures were being manufactured and UL approved. The utility ended up with about 3,000 consent cards in hand before the first device was installed in the service area in April 1980.

Four County had received few complaints and requests for removal of the devices by the summer of 1982. The utility keeps detailed information about complaints and requests for removal. Through the two years of the program operation Four County had received 415 member complaints about the power being off too long and 333 complaints about equipment problems. Within the latter category only 35 complaints turned out to be instances of direct load control equipment failure. The remaining 298 complaints turned out to be caused by problems with the member's air conditioner or water heater itself, completely unrelated to the direct load control switch. About thirty-nine air conditioner switches and seventy water heater switches had been removed by household request by the summer of 1982. Thirty-two of the requests to remove air conditioner switches came after the first control session, as the utility personnel were still experimenting with optimal cycling patterns. Utility policy was for personnel to write letters to all households who withdrew from the program. The letters were designed to maintain good consumer relations and to give the utility a chance to regain the participation of the household in load management.

The Four County service interruption plan involves active direct load control in the summer months. The first control session was held in the summer of 1981, after most of the currently installed switches were actually in place. Control sessions varied in duration of off time, sometimes up to six hours off at a time for water heaters. The normal cycling strategy for air conditioners is about eight minutes off and twenty-two minutes on.

Debugging the ripple direct load control system has identified some potential problems for which the utility now has safeguards. For example, at the end of a control episode during the early days of the system operation, the operator threw the switch to send out the signal for all controlled water heaters to again receive power. The operator had no way of knowing that a minor electrical problem had occurred in the ripple signal device just before the control session ended. Thus, the operator left the control room late that Saturday afternoon and headed home. By Saturday night and early Sunday morning several thousand households in the Four County service area were completely without hot water. The major topic of conversation at church gatherings Sunday morning was that everyone had had to bathe in cold water. To complicate matters, the direct load control equipment service technician at that time lived in the Midwest and could not get to North Carolina to fix the problem before Monday. The utility later mounted several direct load control devices on the wall of the control room in order to verify positively that the devices were working as intended.

The Four County water heater direct load control program originally offered each participating household a billing credit of $1.25 per switch per month, posted on electric bills each month. The credit later was raised to $2.00 per water heater switch, posted monthly. The air conditioner direct load control program also included an economic incentive. Households participating in that program received a billing credit of $3.75 per air conditioner switch for each of the four summer months. Other economic incentives, arising from reduced peak demand charges for the system as a whole, were passed along to each household, regardless of its participation status.

Mobile homes were excluded from Four County EMC's direct load control programs, unless the mobile home was permanently mounted upon a stationary foundation. Other eligibility requirements were that the household have an approved water heater with at least a thirty-gallon capacity, to qualify for the water heater program, or an approved central air conditioner or electric heat pump, to qualify for the air conditioner program.

At first the Four County program required a household to sign a simple consent card in order to participate in load management. That was dropped later, and a verbal request by a household was sufficient to initiate participation in one or both direct load control programs. The utility no longer requires any agreement form, consent card, or formal contract.

Initially, the switches were installed by private contract electricians. No installation fee or removal fee was charged directly to the participating household. The EMC paid installers $35 for the first switch and $20 each for any additional switches installed at a residence. The switches were inspected by the county electrical inspector before they were operated. The utility paid the inspection fee of $10 per switch. The equipment cost for the switch itself, also paid by the utility, was estimated at about $100 per switch.

Three full-time conservation and load management program advisers were hired in 1977 to market these programs within the Four County service area. As is noted later, the EMC marketing effort also was partially staffed by many of the other utility employees and private electricians hired primarily to install the switches. Thus, the Four County marketing staff included just about every EMC employee and subcontractor.

The promotion strategy involved a heavy emphasis on personal selling. The utility attempted to motivate every employee and subcontractor who came into contact with a residential customer to obtain program participation for that customer's household.

The utility initially sponsored an employee contest to name the direct load control program. More than 100 suggestions were received from about seventy participating employees. The name selected in the contest was "The Switch For Tomorrow." The Four County direct load control program operated under that general name for several years.

Four County employees were encouraged to participate in "The Switch For Tomorrow." Employees also were involved in a contest that offered them a finder's fee for new residential customers they could sign up for the load management program. The private electricians who installed the switches also were offered finder's fees, besides incremental installation fees, for new participating households. Thus, a private electrician often would take additional switches along on an installation service call and stop at nearby houses to solicit participation from neighbors.

The three-person conservation staff acted as lobby sales people as they intercepted customers coming into the utility to pay their electric bills the first week of each month during the early years of the program.

As a result of the emphasis on direct personal sales contact, the utility estimates that most household EMC members had been contacted personally about "The Switch For Tomorrow" at least twice by some utility representative.

Four County supported the direct sales strategy with considerable advertising and publicity. The primary theme was "Defeat the Peak," and the argument that this was a specific way for members to reduce the EMC's wholesale power costs was repeated time and time again. The advertising and publicity also often included personal testimony from identified, local participants. The testimony covered a variety of questions typically raised about water heater and air conditioner direct load control programs. Radio spots, newspaper ads, television ads, and direct mailings targeted to a group of 350 community opinion leaders often identified Carolina Power and Light Company rate increases as the source of higher wholesale power costs that would have to be passed along to EMC members.

SUMMARY

Table 3.1 summarizes various characteristics of the selected load management programs from the date of their introduction to the summer of 1982. As discussed in the narrative and summarized in Table 3.1, no two programs were alike. They were designed in different ways to meet different, or unspecified, load management program objectives. Many programs were changed over time to incorporate different economic incentives and promotional tactics. Furthermore, the programs all experienced different participation rates, even where the program penetration objectives were similar.

Several dimensions can be identified, however, to generally characterize and contrast these programs. One of these dimensions is the "trialability" of the load management program. Other dimensions pertain to the way the program was promoted. The extent to which the utility used mass media and personal direct selling are examples of the latter.

Trialability

Several researchers (e.g., Rogers and Shoemaker 1971; Rogers and Stanfield 1966) have identified the importance of "trialability" as a product characteristic associated with the adoption of innovations. "Trialability" refers to the extent of effort and resource commitment required to try out the innovation and the extent to which trial is irrevocable. The general finding is that new products high in trialability are more likely to be adopted and to spread throughout a market. Alternatively, products low in trialability will be slower to spread through a market, since poor trialability hinders initial trial and subsequent adoption.

Looking across the load management programs reviewed in this chapter suggests that the Four County and Lumbee River programs were relatively very high in trialability; the Tarboro, VEPCO, and CP&L programs were moderate in trialability; and the Duke Power program was relatively low in trialability.

A simple, verbal request was sufficient to participate in the Four County and Lumbee River programs. Similarly, participation in the VEPCO program could be accomplished by verbal request, but participation involved an informal, one-year commitment. The other three programs all required a household to sign either an authorization card or a formal contract in order to participate. The Duke Power participation contract was very formal and extended for two years. Trialability was reduced to the extent that participation required a formal contract over an extended period of time.

The Duke Power program is the only program that required a household to pay an installation fee. None of the other programs required a fee for installation. The household installation fee charged by Duke Power reduced the trialability of the load management program, since it represented a financial expense to the participant.

The Duke Power program was also uniquely expensive for households to terminate if they chose to stop taking part. At the time of this

TABLE 3.1

SUMMARY OF SELECTED LOAD MANAGEMENT PROGRAMS AS OF SUMMER 1982

Customer Response	Duke Power-Salisbury			CP&L-Raleigh	VEPCO-Roanoke Rapids	Tarboro		Lumbee River EMC		Four County EMC	
	(TOD)	(Water Heater)	(A/C)	(Water Heater)	(Water Heater)	(Water Heater)	(A/C)	(Water Heater)	(A/C)	(Water Heater)	(A/C)
Potential House-holds (summer 1982)	-	5,670	2,240	48,000	7,544	2,100	1,300	12,000	4,380	8,546 (e)	3,076
Enrolled House-holds (summer 1983)	184	1,497	610	8,600	1,412	1,366	977	6,500	2,500	7,556	1,827
% Penetration (summer 1982)	-	26%	27%	18%	19%	65%	75%	54%	57%	88% (e)	59%
Date of Program Introduction	February 1981			June 1980	June 1980	January 1980		December 1976		November 1977 *(April 1978 program stopped pending UL approval of switch) *(April 1980, first switches installed, 3,000 consents cumulated)	
Complaints	Few			Few	Few	Few		Few		Few (35 Equipment failures) 298 member-caused problems (non-switch problems) 415 member complaints re: power off too long	
Removals	Few, less than 1%			Few, less than 1%	Few, less than 1%	Few, less than 1%		Few		Few: 32 A/C switches removed after 1st control session, 70 w/h disconnected to date. Write letters to disconnects to maintain good customer relations	

TABLE 3.1 continued

SUMMARY OF SELECTED LOAD MANAGEMENT PROGRAMS AS OF SUMMER 1982

	Duke Power-Salisbury	CP&L-Raleigh	VEPCO-Roanoke Rapids	Tarboro	Lumbee River EMC	Four County EMC
	(TOD) (Water Heater) (A/C)	(Water Heater)	(Water Heater)	(Water Heater) (A/C)	(Water Heater) (A/C)	(Water Heater) (A/C)
Goals & Objectives System Control (Residence)	Not ascertained	System wide 92,000 HH by 1985 175,000 HH by 1995 630 MW demand reduction by 1995 25% system saturation by 1995	25% system saturation	Install as many as possible	10% of demand under control Original goal of 6,000 water heaters and 2,000 air conditioners under control	Install as many as possible
Service Interruption Plan	As needed in system emergencies	Up to 4 hours per day per water heater Typically 100-200 hours turnoff per year	Rotate interruption on daily basis as needed Maximum of 12 hours total per day	Rotate interruption in summer peak to reduce annual system peak demand	Rotate interruption daily if needed Control some each month but primarily in summer Cycle off water heaters for duration demand; generally 2-3 hours, occasionally 6 hours	1st control in summer 1981 Control in summer varies in length of off time to as much as 6 hours at a time in water heaters 8 min off/22 min on strategy for A/C's

TABLE 3.1 continued

SUMMARY OF SELECTED LOAD MANAGEMENT PROGRAMS AS OF SUMMER 1982

	Duke Power-Salisbury			CP&L-Raleigh	VEPCO-Roanoke Rapids	Tarboro		Lumbee River EMC		Four County EMC	
	(TOD)	(Water Heater)	(A/C)	(Water Heater)	(Water Heater)	(Water Heater)	(A/C)	(Water Heater)	(A/C)	(Water Heater)	(A/C)
Discounts, Credits and Incentives	Variable	$2.00 per month billing credit each month	$2.00 per KWD per month billing credit for July, Aug., Sept., Oct.	June 1980–November 1981 $1.00 per month credit		Originally, $15.00 per year as credit during June, July August, and September		Originally, no financial credit or incentive		Originally, $1.25 per switch credit per month	$3.75 per switch credit per summer month
		total monthly credits ≤ 35% of current monthly bill		November 1981–$2.00 per month credit		Raised to $20.00 per year as credit during June, July, August, and Sept.		August 1977 to present: $1.25 per switch per month credit		Raised to $2.00 per switch credit per month	
		typical annual credit for participation in both DLC programs ≃ $50.00		May 3, 1982–free water heater insulation wrap	$2.34 credit per month						
					Originally, $1.85 credit per month						
		Originally $1.00 credit per month									
Eligibility Requirements		Have an approved water heater ≥ 30 gallon capacity	Have a central air conditioner	Have an approved water heater ≥ 40 gallon rated capacity with either 1 or 2 self-contained non-simultaneous operating heating elements ≤ 5500 watts per element	Have an approved water heater ≥ 30 gallon capacity	Have an approved water heater ≥ 30 gallon capacity	Have an approved central air conditioner	Have an approved water heater ≥ 30 gallon capacity	Have an approved central air conditioner or heat pump	Have an approved water heater ≥ 40 gallon capacity	Have an approved central air conditioner

TABLE 3.1 continued

SUMMARY OF SELECTED LOAD MANAGEMENT PROGRAMS AS OF SUMMER 1982

	Duke Power-Salisbury	CP&L-Raleigh	VEPCO-Roanoke Rapids	Tarboro	Lumbee River EMC	Four County EMC
	(TOD) (Water Heater) (A/C)	(Water Heater)	(Water Heater)	(Water Heater) (A/C)	(Water Heater) (A/C)	(Water Heater) (A/C)
Eligibility Requirements (Cont.)	Be the owner of the premises or have the permission of owner or manager of premises Be located in substation service area	Be owner of the premises, or have written permission of owner or manager of premises, if rental house or apartment Be located within 2 mile radius of transmitter located at Meridith College	Single family residence or mobile home on stationary foundation with 240 volt water heater	No mobile homes	No mobile homes, unless permanently mounted	No mobile homes, unless permanently mounted
Contract	Household must sign 2 year contract form	Household must sign brief contract card	No, informal agreement to stay in at least 1 year	Household must sign authorization card	Originally, household had to sign brief authorization card; changed to verbal request (e.g. by telephone call)	Originally: household must sign simple consent card changed to verbal request
Removal Fee	$25 removal fee for program withdrawal within 1 year	Initially included provision for $25 removal fee for program withdrawal within 1 year Provision dropped	No	No	No	No

TABLE 3.1 continued

SUMMARY OF SELECTED LOAD MANAGEMENT PROGRAMS AS OF SUMMER 1982

	Duke Power-Salisbury	CP&L-Raleigh	VEPCO-Roanoke Rapids	Tarboro	Lumbee River EMC	Four County EMC
	(TOD) (Water Heater) (A/C)	(Water Heater)	(Water Heater)	(Water Heater) (A/C)	(Water Heater) (A/C)	(Water Heater) (A/C)
Installation Practices	Installation by private contract electricians	Installation by private contract electricians	Installation by private contract electricians	Installation by city crews	Installation by private contract electricians ($15 per switch for installation	Installation by private contract electricians ($35 for first switch, $20 for others per residence)
	$35 water heater or AC installation fee	No installation fee/ equipment fee for household	No installation fee	No installation fee	No installation fee for household	Must be inspected by county electrical inspection @ $10 switch (paid by EMC)
	$50 water heater & AC installation fee	Prefer customer be there at installation, which takes 1 to 2 hours	Installation at water heater or at outside of structure	Installation at appliance	Changed to installation by Lumbee River EMC electricians	
	Only $10 per DLC device if special wiring not required	Installation at outside of house	Customer must be at home for installation which takes about 1/2 hour	Customer must be at home for installation		
Marketing Staff	Customer service/residential marketing staff (with other responsibilities also); 4 people DLC 1 person TOD (all located in target city)	Corporate program director	14 people with other responsibilities 4 supervisory 10 staff	1 full-time supervisor	1 full-time supervisor; second full-time person hired in 1982	3 full-time conservationist and load management advisors hired in 1977 also use installation electricians as door-to-door sales force
	Supporting personnel from corporate headquarters	District coordinator	Supporting personnel as needed	City and local officials and leaders support	Use meter readers and other employees as direct sales force	
		Communication specialist			Installation electricians also used as door-to-door sales force	

TABLE 3.1 continued

SUMMARY OF SELECTED LOAD MANAGEMENT PROGRAMS AS OF SUMMER 1982

	Duke Power-Salisbury	CP&L-Raleigh	VEPCO-Roanoke Rapids	Tarboro	Lumbee River EMC	Four County EMC
Advertising	(TOD) (Water Heater) (A/C)	(Water Heater)	(Water Heater)	(Water Heater) (A/C)	(Water Heater) (A/C)	(Water Heater) (A/C)
Radio Spots	No	Yes, since July 28, 1980	Yes	Yes, in early months of program only	Limited use	Yes
Newspaper Ads	No	Yes, since July 30, 1980	Yes	Yes, in early months of program only	Limited use	Yes
Television Ads	Yes	Yes	No	No	No	Yes
Bill Inserts	Yes	Yes	Yes	No	No, but show load management credit on all bills	No
Employee Check Inserts	No	Yes	No	No	No	No
Direct Mailings	Yes, multiple letters followed up by door-to-door solicitation	Yes, multiple letters and follow up letters	Yes, with telephone follow up	Two each to potential control households and water heater control households	Yes	Yes, especially to "opinion leader" groups of 350 persons
Newsletters	No	No	No	No	Yes, extensively	Yes
Publicity Tactics						
News Releases	No	Yes	Yes	Yes	Yes	Yes
Stories in Newspapers & Magazines	No	Yes	Yes	Yes	Yes, especially when 1st switch was installed, since 1st direct load control device installed in N.C.	Yes

TABLE 3.1 continued

SUMMARY OF SELECTED LOAD MANAGEMENT PROGRAMS AS OF SUMMER 1982

Direct Sales Tactics	Duke Power-Salisbury (TOD) (Water Heater) (A/C)	CP&L-Raleigh (Water Heater)	VEPCO-Roanoke Rapids (Water Heater)	Tarboro (Water Heater) (A/C)	Lumbee River EMC (Water Heater) (A/C)	Four County EMC (Water Heater) (A/C)
Door-to-Door Solicitation	Yes, primary target = "key person in neighborhood"	No	No	No	Use meter readers to identify prospects and obtain consent Employee incentive of $1 per new residential consent Contract electricians encouraged to solicit agreements from neighbors after an installation	"Tickler" survey in limited area for initial rollout Yes, most members contacted twice by conservation staff Employee contest to obtain consent cards
Other	No	No	Follow-up telephone calls to landlords if tenant requests switch	Relied heavily on word-of-mouth from other participants and civic leaders	Lobby display of load management switch	3 person conservation staff as lobby people at first week of each month
Group Sales Tactics						
Civic Club Presentations	Yes	Yes	Yes	Yes	Yes	Yes
Fairs & House and Gardens Shows	No	Yes	Yes	No	Yes	No
"Prospect Meetings"	Yes	No	No	No	No	No

TABLE 3.1 continued

SUMMARY OF SELECTED LOAD MANAGEMENT PROGRAMS AS OF SUMMER 1982

	Duke Power-Salisbury	CP&L-Raleigh	VEPCO-Roanoke Rapids	Tarboro	Lumbee River EMC	Four County EMC
	(TOD) (Water Heater) (A/C)	(Water Heater)	(Water Heater)	(Water Heater) (A/C)	(Water Heater) (A/C)	(Water Heater) (A/C)
Other	No	No	No	No	Annual meeting of EMC	Annual meeting of EMC Obtained 500 consent cards at initial annual meetings
Promotional Theme	"How to save money on your electric bill"	June 1980–December 1980 "Here's how to save $12 a year on your electric bill" Jan 1981–present "You can help control future electric costs" and "save $64 a year on your electric bill"	"A chance to save on electric water heating costs"	Lower the peak demand for Tarboro as a way to fight VEPCO price increases "Tarboro Peak Shavers will Stretch Tarboro Electrical Dollars"	Reduce the EMC's wholesale power costs No slogan or theme other than "Load Management"	Reduce the EMC's wholesale power costs economic theme: "Defeat the Peak" Employee contest to name switch–"The Switch for Tomorrow" Promote it as "free" why not sign up? Use personal testimony by local residents about having the switches

study the Duke Power program contract still included a clause about a $25 removal fee for program withdrawal within the first year of participation. While this may have reduced the number of requests for removals, it also inhibited the trialability of the program.

Personal Versus Mass Promotion

The use of direct, personal sales provides an effective opportunity to introduce a new product to a prospect, explain the product benefits, and obtain trial and adoption. Mass media advertising is generally an effective way to achieve awareness within a market but is usually less effective in getting people to try the product (Kotler 1980).

Lumbee River, Four County, and Duke Power used door-to-door personal selling as a primary tactic in their load management marketing mix. These utilities used many different types of utility personnel, besides the load management marketing staff, as sales representatives. Some of the people used included meter readers, customer service representatives, installation contractors, and other employees and subcontractors. Tarboro, VEPCO, and CP&L, on the other hand, made little use of direct sales tactics.

CP&L and Four County depended heavily on mass media advertising to promote participation in load management programs. Duke Power, Tarboro, and VEPCO used far less television, radio, or newspaper advertising. Lumbee River used only a limited amount of advertising to promote its load management program. Extensive use of mass media advertising is probably less effective than direct selling after general product awareness has been achieved in a market.

4

Consumer Reactions to Program Design and Promotion

Qualitative research is one method for identifying and understanding how households react to various load management programs. This chapter summarizes the results of five focus group discussions held across North Carolina during the summer of 1982. A load management program had been operative in each of the locations for at least eighteen months. Focus group participants were randomly selected adults who were asked to represent their households in a group discussion of several energy usage and energy conservation topics. Included among the discussion topics were several items pertaining to electric utilities and load management programs.

This chapter identifies the major motivations, reactions, and themes that were expressed in the focus groups. The results are presented in a number of sections. The sections begin with consumer reactions to different aspects of the design and implementation of load management programs available in North Carolina. Other sections focus on general issues that affect the successful marketing of load management programs. Consumer reactions are summarized across the five focus group sites. Most motivations, reactions, and themes identified by the researchers are illustrated by a few quotations from the focus group discussions.

REACTIONS TO LOAD MANAGEMENT

How have North Carolina consumers reacted to load management programs that were made available in the state? Had most people heard about load management? Did they understand load management programs? How did they react to various aspects of current and potential load management programs? Households participating in the focus group discussions were drawn from utility service areas in which load management programs had been available and widely promoted for a number of months. Many of the consumers at the focus group discussions were participating in those programs. Others were not participating. All consumers at the focus groups, however, would meet the eligibility requirements for at least one of the load management programs that were available in the state.

Program Awareness

Most consumers had heard of load management. However, many consumers whose households would have qualified for existing load management programs in their service area thought the programs were not yet available to them. Even after the extensive program promotions that were undertaken in each of the focus group locations, some consumers were simply not aware of the programs' availability in their area.

MODERATOR (M): Look at two things in particular on [this newspaper advertisement], then if you would. One is called the time-of-day rates. Have you heard about that before?

CONSUMER (C): Said something in the paper about it. We called the [Duke Power Company] office out here to ask about it. They said, well, that it was being tried, but it was not in this area.

* * *

M: Now load control. Let's check that out a minute. Has anybody heard about load control?

C: None other than reading it here . . . When was this ad run? I doubt that you can get it here.

Understanding Load Management Programs

Most consumers understood the general logic of existing load management programs. They generally had an accurate comprehension of how direct load control works and the benefits that it provides to the utility. There was still some confusion, however, about the details and mechanics underlying water heater and air conditioner direct load control.

M: What is this water heater direct load control program about?

C: It has to be on a certain transformer, too. I think over 35 gallons. If it was more, if just wouldn't conserve.

M: What kind of deal did they give you?

C: A lower rate—much lower. It's very small. About $2.65 a month is what they estimate. Something like that. See, that's a lot to pay. That's what they did do.

I just thought it was a credit. A couple of dollars.

M: What does the box do, anyway?

C: It's supposed to heat your water during the non-peak hours. You know at lunch and things in the afternoon. Probably heats your water from, I'd say, seven o'clock at night until the next morning.

* * *

C: Years ago they [the utility] had this. It changed and nearly everybody had it.

M: Here?

C: Well, I say I had it. Mother had it. You had two meters, actually, and when quick recovery come on the market and did away with it [they] took all the [other] meters off. [Then,] you just had one meter, but [the old system] regulated when you heat your water.

I think it's a lot the same thing. You just put them back on and most people who took them off, I think their light bill went up so, I think, a lot of people kicked on it and didn't want them taken out.

* * *

M: Tell me a little more about these shutoff devices.

C: Radio controlled. Remotely controlled by the power company. They can fit on any number of devices on air conditioners and hot water heaters. It's a peak load control monitor, in order to keep peak load costs from being so high. You have to drop the peak consumption. To drop the peak consumption, when their controls indicate the peak is coming, they will cut off remotely some of the hot water heaters or whatever for seven minutes of an hour. I believe, now, isn't it? Small portion of an hour's time. So small it's not even noticed when it happens. Your bell curve becomes very flat during the peak load and that helps to save. I don't understand why it costs so much more for power for peak load power. Here's the way it was at one time. REA was charged by CP&L for the peak load in June or July for the whole year. That's what the cost to Lumbee River was based on. So they installed these devices to cut down this peak load, which occurred in June or July. I forget now, they said at one time how many thousands of dollars it saved.

M: And what do you get?

C: $1.25 credit each device. So we have two. Most people have two. They only put them on hot water heaters and air conditioners. Homes and not trailers. They didn't put them in trailers.

M: Why do people put these on?

C: For the credit. That's why I put them on.

The reason for it, as we were talking a minute ago, is to trim the peak load that REA is pulling from Carolina Power and Light. CP&L talks on TV about the peak. The REA's power charge from CP&L each year is based on their peak load in June or July. If they use one million watts at peak rate, they'll pay for a million watts for the rest of the year.

And another reason [we participated in DLC] was that the power company puts them on for you. It doesn't cost you anything, and they'll come and check them and service them. They're only off about seven minutes an hour. You don't even know they're there. There's no reason not to have them.

M: You've not been inconvenienced at all?

C: No.

* * *

M: What is the [direct load control] savings now?

C: They don't guarantee you, but they say when you register if you're on the town electricity when you go in to pay your bill, there's a sign there that says, "Inquire about a $15 a month savings during certain months of the year on your electricity bill." It's a device where the town can monitor the outflow of electricity. They have the control of your hot water heater and your air conditioner. They don't just turn it off and leave you there to get hot.

M: But they turn it off and leave it off for seven or eight minutes?

C: I've never noticed it yet to be inconvenient.

* * *

M: Do you understand the time-of-day-rates? That deal that they're offering is that if you can change your lifestyle like [he] was saying, that basically, you're paying more for using electricity while everyone else is using it. You pay less at times when not many people are using it. So the time of day that you're using your appliances determines how much you're going to be charged for it.

C: Like he was saying a while ago about running his clothes dryer at night instead of using it at eight o'clock in the morning when everybody in the world is using theirs. I believe that I won't want to get up at three o'clock in the morning to do the things I would have to do to save that energy. I suppose some people would feel like, you know, if this were successful it would be the same old thing. There'd be a peak load at three o'clock, you know.

* * *

M: What's this called? What's this program like?

C: It turns your air conditioning off in [summer] according to their load. In other words, you don't have any say over when it's shut down. They will do it by radio transmission into your house. It can only be off for a maximum of two hours. And then it can resume. It might not ever happen. I dare say it would happen, though. It might happen two or three times [a summer]. There's another program whereby they turn your hot water heater off. It doesn't go off for more than, again, something like two hours. Only when it peaks again, but it may not peak at all—what [the utility] considers a peak.

* * *

M: Let's go back a minute to something she talked about. You said that one thing the power companies do is this peak . . .

C: Peak load.

M: How many people have that?

C: We called to have it and they never got back in touch with us. It was my understanding that they're doing it primarily for the summer, for the use of the air conditioner. But they haven't gotten back to us. I called them. They couldn't quite tell me anything. I think what they've done is they got their quota.

The people just asking them for the water heater part of it, they're not getting the service first. The people doing the air conditioning and the water heater are first.

Well, we wanted both.

Well, you ought to be getting something.

M: How long ago did you call?

C: Let's see, three weeks.

You've got a long wait.

Well, we wrote down the little sheet that you send back. We did that last month, two months ago . . . You got this little information card. If you're interested, you kind of fill it out. We did that. It was probably two months ago. Then we heard several of our friends mention that their neighbors had gotten this little red light thing. It kind of reminded us, "Yeah, we haven't gotten ours put on," so we called. They didn't and I didn't honestly pursue it again. Since we got a lukewarm response, and we're going to be gone most of the summer, but that's irrelevant.

M: Did you call your customer service representative?

C: Yes, the CP&L Building . . . they moved me to another person and another person. Finally it was getting kind of old. They weren't mean.

We don't have it yet. My friend says it's $2 off her bill.

Every month in the year?

Plus, I have no way to measure it, but I would imagine it would save a little bit in power depending on how often they turn it off.

* * *

C: I got the water heater thing over a year ago. They weren't doing the air conditioning, I guess, at that time. I had them come out and do that at my house. I've never even been able to tell any difference. I don't know whether it goes off or not. Well, they say often it won't go off. . . A friend of mine found out somehow, I don't know how she found out, that it went off once when she was at work. When she came home, and it was on again, she couldn't tell the difference, cause doesn't water stay hot?

They come in and hook up a couple of little radio receivers. When they have a peak period, they shut power off to your water heater and the air conditioner now, I guess. I asked them to do that also. I haven't seen them either.

They put a regular water heater blanket around it to keep the water hot.

M: Does it make a difference in your bill?

C: A friend of mine has it and he said so far he hasn't had any problems. They hook it up where it turns off the compressor but it doesn't turn off the fan so your air is still circulating. I understand from him, I don't know where he got the information, but they can alternate areas of town so they wouldn't really have a peak load at all. They can shut down in one area, for let's say, thirty minutes, bring them back up—shut down another during peak load time.

Why Were People Participating in Load Management Programs?

Consumers generally had diverse reactions to various characteristics of existing load management programs. Stereotypical homogeneous reactions to any given program characteristic were few and far between. Rather, the picture that emerges is one of many substantively different yet somewhat overlapping market segments in any utility service area. There is little support for the concept that all households in a service area will react similarly to program characteristics and promotional tactics and therefore form a single mass market.

The answer to why consumers decided to participate in load management programs varies from one household to the next. In general, however, financial credits seem to be effective incentives for many North Carolina households to participate in the program. There is some question about the level of credit at which the economic incentive becomes sufficiently motivating for many households to participate. Most consumers saw relatively little difference between economic incentives of $1 per month versus $2.25 per month. Economic incentives of less than about $10 a month were not recognized as particularly different in their motivating appeal. When the economic incentive was $10 a month or more, though, those consumers who appeared to be motivated by the use of economic incentives began to express considerable interest in joining the load management program.

Other consumers believed they would not participate in load management programs regardless of the amount of economic incentive offered to them. Those consumers appeared to be people who valued their ability to control their environment to whatever extent control is possible. They saw participation in direct load control programs as an incremental loss of control. The air conditioning direct load control program, in particular, was a troublesome concept for those people. In fact, most consumers had a different response to the idea of participating in air conditioning direct load control than was the case with water heater load control programs. In general, consumers seemed to have many more reservations about air conditioner programs. Maintaining control over the cooling capability of the air conditioning system was viewed as more critical and important than maintaining control over the water heating system.

Still other consumers would have participated readily in load management programs if they had simply been asked to participate. Many households would gladly have participated in load management, particularly if other neighbors and friends had already decided to take part.

Most consumers would have no objection whatsoever if load management were mandated by state or federal decree. Consumers would view load management programs that involved the installation of several direct load control devices in the residence as just as legitimate a part of having electrical service as the demand meter mounted at any service site.

Installation fees are clearly a disincentive for participation in load management programs. Most consumers had difficulty understanding why they should pay an installation fee, particularly since the benefits from the household participating in load management accrued to many parties other than that specific household. Installation fees, formal contracts, and removal fee clauses all act as disincentives for participation. The logistics of getting load control devices actually installed are also a hassle for many households.

C: I talked with several people [at my utility about getting a direct load control device on my water heater]. They just never did anything. They said, "We'll be there," and they never came by. . . .

M: So you're telling us that you called them?

C: Several times. I called my customer representative and told her that I wanted a little thing on my hot water heater and I wanted her to check out my insulation. Well, the guy didn't show up twice and I took off from work so he could come look at it twice, but he didn't show up twice.

* * *

M: Suppose they said, "Well, we are not going to give you $2.65 a month credit. We'll give you a dollar." Would it still be a good deal if they only gave you one dollar a month?

C: If every time you turn your hot water on, you can't get nothing, you would rather pay that dollar.

M: What if they would pay you ten dollars a month credit?

C: I would just keep calling them. . . . Sure would!

* * *

C: They're saying you can hold that peak down or raise my light bill in order to generate more electricity. They're getting the most out of the price they have. Maximum benefit out of the price that way.

M: All right. Is that ok?

C: Definitely, it's holding my cost down and then again I'm trying to hold their cost down.

M: Well, if that's the case then what if they came to you and said simply, "We want to put one of these on your water heater. We're not going to give you any credit, but we just want to put one on?"

C: They'd have to give me a good reason.

M: Well, the reason we just talked about.

C: Not if they make my rate several times more.

It would still help us. Save you money.

Fine with me.

M: Let me push it a little bit further. What if they came to you with that story and said, "We want to put one of these on your water heater and this device does cost us money. So, not only do we want to put it on your water heater, but because it's a good thing for everybody to have, we are also going to charge you a one-time installation fee of $20? "

C: If they made it mandatory, you would have to take it. You don't have any other choice about it. But I can't see them coming in and charging me for the device that they say is going to cut it down.

M: In a year's time you would probably get your $20 back. Say, if they did give you your $2.65 off per billing, like I said in a year's time [you would get your $20 back].

C: So I guess in that case I probably would go along with it. But, if they just said they're not going to give me nothing flat [and] I've got to pay them $20 to install this device without any off the deal, then I can't see it.

M: Well, now we just went through this story about how it's going to keep, you're telling me, going to keep [electricity costs] down and let them make good maximum effective use of the plant and not have to build other plants, other capacity, and you're going to say even with all of that, you're not going to pay them $20 one time to let them install it in your house?

C: I probably would, because if they've got to, they'd get my neighbors going and say, for another box we're going to charge you $20 more or less for installation so I'd pay this amount.

M: So if your neighbor went along with it you'd go along?

C: It's hard to say in a case such as that. I really don't know what I'd say if I was actually confronted with it.

Well, what's the alternative. They'll turn your lights out?

I couldn't pay. $20 is a big hunk out of my monthly budget, what little of it there is. If they charged me $20 in one month that would really mess me up a lot.

* * *

M: What objections might people have to this load control thing? These devices? What kind of problems would maybe people say they cause?

C: I'm just not going to fool with it.

They don't want the inconvenience. They don't like anything.

But like, if [my neighbor] knows that I'm inconvenienced the same time he is, then it's not as bad.

It does make a difference.

M: Kind of like if everybody were [participating in direct load control]?

C: They could put these devices in every house if it would save a $6 billion plant from going up down here on the river. Then, when [my neighbor's] power and my power went off, I might say, damn it, you know that's inconvenient, and it would be. But I would at least have the satisfaction of knowing that every other citizen in Rowan County had the same problem.

* * *

C: I was somewhat hesitant [about direct load control] at first. He assured me I would never know that the thing was on anyway.

M: What was your concern?

C: My main concern was someone coming into my house and putting a little foreign gadget on my hot water heater. I really didn't know what it was going to do. I was afraid I might run out of hot water. I guess I don't know when I would need it, but they assured me that that would never be the case and it has not been. Plus, they said if you were dissatisfied with it, they would take it off upon your request. I believe that's what they told me.

M: They'd come back and take it off?

C: Yeah, I thought I'd try it a month or two and if I didn't like it, they'd come and take it out.

* * *

M: So suppose, let's stay on this load control, let me ask you this, I come to you, I'm working for Duke Power, and I've told you here that I'm going to pay you up to $50 a year for having these devices on your house, and now I'm going to come up to you and say, but it does cost us to install and so I'm going to ask you to pay a $35 installation fee, but I'm going to save you $50 a year once they're installed.

C: I'd think about that. Since I've already read this [ad], I'm prejudiced. I feel it's going to be saving Duke Power a lot more money than it will me.

* * *

M: What if the utility asked you to pay small installation fee for the direct load control device? Say, $10 or so?

C: I believe I would have to say, "I'm going to have to think about that a little longer."

They'd have to be a little shorter of electricity before I'd want to pay more than I'm paying now.

M: I'll just put it on your electric bill next month. You don't have to write me a check when we install it, but I'll put it on your electric bill next month.

C: I don't believe that's quite right. I don't think it would make much difference if it's $1 or $35 [installation fee]. It would be the same thing.

I'm perfectly willing to help them save electricity. I'm not willing to pay them more than I'm paying them now.

* * *

C: [Reading from utility advertisement] "Load management can play a large role in your future electric bill but in order for it to work for all of us we're going to need the cooperation and participation of all of our customers." I wouldn't mind doing that if you're going to save something, $50 a year or more, or $50; $60 a year would be $5 a month.

M: You were telling me about here they were saying they would pay you up to $50 or $60, which you are saying, is maybe $5 a month? Does that seem like an ok deal?

C: I would. Well, it depends on what your family uses you know.

M: [Suppose the utility said], "We'll give you $1 a month." Would most people [say] "All right, put them on?"

C: If it's going to help the country in general, I'll do it for nothing.

* * *

M: We talked about the deal on the water heaters where they come and put a device in that they shut off from time to time. Suppose they wanted to put one on your AC?

C: That is the peak load when you need it.

M: The deal would be that you let them put one of these devices on your AC and they'll pay for installation and they'll give you [a monthly credit]. It's really a way to beat the peak. To keep the peak down.

C: My first question would be what I would [have] to do to take it off.

M: Ok. So in order to have better control over that peak VEPCO wants to come to your house and put a device on your AC.

C: And charge you installation. (*Laughter*) Well, I would have to say "no" under that situation.

M: Well, it's important. It helps keep the peak down for everybody and if you're not using that electricity in your AC, which we said was probably a pretty heavy user of electricity, if you're not using it in your AC, then you'll have it available to use it in other places.

C: Yea, but who would it benefit? I mean, would the average [electricity savings] be better in big business?

M: So are you telling me that that's unfair?

C: Well, uh, possibly to a certain extent, of course, because you've got to take into consideration that not all of us still have families at home. I mean, I wouldn't want to go off, say on a 90 to 100 degree day, and leave my wife and family in a house that would be just about as hot without an AC, because that's what I bought and paid for the AC for. Just for that reason.

M: Suppose the shutoff device just shut off the compressor and the fan would still work so you would still circulate air in your house.

C: What would be the difference from that and an AC that had a thermostat control to come on when you needed it and cut the entire system off when you didn't?

M: Like a central air conditioner?

C: Like a central, yeah.

That's what mine does. That's what I bought it for.

M: Let's go back a minute. Let's go back to this idea about our neighbors. Suppose our neighbors had one of these on their AC and here comes the VEPCO person to your door and your neighbors over here have one and your neighbors over there have one and we'd like to put one on your AC.

C: I suppose I'd listen and let them explain to me when they're going to cut my AC off and they'd tell me that they'd probably never need to cut it off because it would probably never get that high, but they'd probably want to do it anyway. I would probably try it and I'd probably put up with the inconvenience for probably two or three times and then I'd be giving them a call back and tell them to come and remove the device.

M: But you'd probably be willing to try it?

C: Sure. But you know you couldn't go but so far with it, I mean.

* * *

M: Suppose instead of giving you $2 a month credit, they gave you $5 a month credit. Would that be a better deal?

C: Yes.

M: Suppose they gave you $1 a month? Would you still have it?

C: Sure.

* * *

M: So you'd be willing to do this? For $15 a [summer] month? What if they weren't going to pay you anything? They just wanted to try to control this peak? They wanted to put it on and not pay you anything, would you do it then?

C: I don't believe I would. I don't think I would cause, honestly, they're [the utility] saving money. They're passing their savings on to the customer, so I want to get in on that, too.

They come to your house and they put this device in it. I'm not overly pleased with this meter that's in the room with our hot water heater even though it's in a room enclosed for the hot water heater. It's fine if it helps, but I wouldn't be excited about someone coming out and controlling my use unless I had something to gain from it.

M: You think you did it because of conserving?

C: No, it's because of the cost of electricity. We didn't do it with the thought of conserving electricity except that it relates directly back to your dollar bill—your money.

* * *

C: Well, I noticed Carolina Power and Light or Duke, one of them, was putting them in. They give $2.50 credit. Why should they get $2.50 and we [in the EMC] get only $1.25?

M: Suppose we said we want to come put one of these on but we're not going to give you credit? Would most people still put them on?

C: Yeah.

Yes, because it's reducing that peak load. It's reducing our [EMC] light bill a little bit each month.

* * *

M: Suppose someone knocked on your door and said, "We're here to install the switch for your water heater and your air conditioner. Could you show us the way to your air conditioner? "

C: It would become very academic.

So you say, "Here it is."

* * *

C: We would've still attempted to find out about it. I think right now they'll [CP&L] get about the same response if they didn't offer you money.

I don't think I agree. Some of my friends told me you get $2 off. That seemed to be a big selling point with them. I mean that's fine. That $2 off, but I think that if it weren't there, they wouldn't have bothered.

It wouldn't have made any difference to me. Really they [CP&L] put on quite an advertising campaign on peak load. The guy stacking up the little blocks before they come out with this. That's basically the thing that caught my eye. They show you a stack of these building blocks and up here is the amount of power that they must produce and do that twenty-four hours a day or have the capability of doing that twenty-four hours a day. Even though it's only used short periods of time. That was basically the reason.

* * *

M: So the deal is they'll cut it [the compressor of your air conditioner] off every now and then if they need to?

C: They'll cut it off for a maximum of two hours. They tell you that is the maximum that you'll go without. They're very careful to say now that doesn't mean you'll have no air coming into your home. You'll get a circulation of air because your blower's still on.

M: Would most of you take that air conditioning deal? Is that a good deal?

C: I think it depends. Like she says, she lives in a nice wooded area. Hardwood, they're fantastic air conditioners themselves. She hasn't been hot. I live in a brick home in one of the newer developments. They come in and just mow everything down and put the streets down and throw those cracker boxes together. That place is hot. I haven't used my air conditioner and I've been sweating in there. And I still keep my bill down. I would like to leave my air conditioner compressor intact and turn it way down.

* * *

M: You say you asked them to do the same thing with your air conditioning?

C: Yeah, that worries me a little bit. I imagine they turn it off when it's hottest and everybody is using the most power. I'm scared it's broken. You know I'll sit around waiting and "is it really broken?" thinking that they've turned it off or something . . .

* * *

C: They come and put a similar kind of thing on the compressor of your air conditioner?

M: Is that a reasonable deal?

C: That's one I'm a little leery of. I don't have it yet but why do I need to sit around there at eight o'clock in the evening and the air conditioner go off and knowing I've got to sit there for two hours and fry?

* * *

M: What happened to his argument here about the peak and shifting the peak and how that was good for the whole system?

C: I would go with the hot water heater but not the air conditioner.

M: Social responsibility stops somewhere between the water heater and the air conditioner?

C: Yeah, because you think about your family personally. What's it going to do to me? It unfortunate, perhaps, if there's a sick child or if there's a pregnancy there which you're going through. It becomes a personal thing. A hot water heater's not as personal, because it's down there and you don't see it. The hot water stays reasonably hot.

I don't think that this is the solution to the problem doing what they're doing right now, but it's a step in the right direction, and one day those costs are going to kill us. It's getting to be more people. More industry. More uses of electrical power. One day something's going to have to be done. They won't be able to produce enough power.

* * *

C: We were on the fence before and I'm going away feeling a little bit more inclined against it [air conditioning direct load control]. I don't want it there because what I really felt was that, as far as the air conditioning, I think I'd like to turn it down myself. Now that someone else has validated it, that's ok. I think I wouldn't do it regardless of the money. We haven't had our air conditioner on for any period of time.

M: Even if they offered you $20 a month?

C: Yes, as he pointed out, you can do that yourself by conservation and other measures and it's still there at times that you need it most.

M: Suppose they said we'll give you ten [dollars for participating in the air conditioner program]?

C: Well, I don't know. I don't think I would do it. I think I'd rather be able to switch it off myself and save more than ten bucks and turn my fans on. I've got some reservations about doing it.

It doesn't appeal to me.

* * *

M: If it's a good deal, why are not all of your neighbors on?

C: I don't think the program will really fly unless we start having brown outs. Things of that nature. Something that will really prompt people to participate in it. Two dollars a month is nothing. I question if you're really saving any money.

I do, too.

Turning it off and turning it on.

Right, all the time your water heater's off, you're losing temperature and you're helping CP&L out during the peak. When their peak's over, they'll turn your water heater back on, and you have to heat that water back up, and it's not free.

I would imagine it comes pretty close to balancing out. It depends on how well insulated your water heater is, how many calories you lose, because you have to replace them to get to the temperature setting again. If it happens often, I don't think you'd be ahead. If it doesn't happen often, perhaps you would. The break point, I don't know where that is, you'd have to calculate it. You'd have to know something about the efficiency of your heater.

* * *

M: So why else might people not have it? Why did it take you so long? Why does it take people so long to fill in the little card?

C: Fear. We had just gotten our air conditioner. Fear that it would be non-usable, but also fear that you've got somebody invading your territory, your home and sticking a little light, a red light, on it. It's kind of like Big Brother watching you. You've lost control. You no longer have control over your utilities. It's your home and all of a sudden, it's not.

I find a lot of people don't know about it, and I'm sure they're paying electric bills.

They don't read the little bulletins.

They throw that over there and pay the bill.

Who Makes the Decision to Participate?

There appear to be at least two ways in which the decision to participate or not to participate is reached in most households. In a traditional household the decision to participate is likely to be made by the husband, with little or no discussion or input from other family members. Alternatively, in less traditional households the decision is likely to be a subject for general discussion over a meal or at a household meeting. The latter method for reaching the decision allows every family member to potentially influence the decision. Although the proportion of each of these two types of decision settings is difficult to estimate, it is likely that the latter form of decision-making predominates in this instance.

M: At your house, would you get the rest of the family together to discuss it or would you say, "Good deal. Let's do it"?

C: Just tell [my family] why. Most of them would agree on it, I think, if they were to look into it.

M: So basically, you would [make that decision to participate] on your own?

C: Yeah.

M: If they called up while your wife was there and not you, would your wife do it on her own?

C: I don't know. She would probably listen to them and tell me and we would discuss it. Before I'd do it, I'd discuss it with her. I wouldn't do it till I discussed it with her.

We didn't have a family meeting. My wife pays all the bills. She handled this [direct load control] thing, too. She said, "What do you think about that? " "It looks all right to me. Go ahead." That was all of the conversation.

* * *

C: Ours was a bit more [family discussion] because we were concerned again, taking a shower . . . gee, what does this really mean? Well, we had to think about it. In fact, we thought about it for a year, because when it first came out we thought it sounded like a good idea but we were wary.

M: You heard about it the first time around from a bill stuffer?

C: Right. It didn't come up again for several months so I guess they got their quota. But when it came out again, we thought, "Gee, we're ready to take this."

Were Participating Households Satisfied with Direct Load Control Programs?

Most households who were participating in direct load control programs were quite satisfied. These consumers viewed participating in load management as an agreeable experience. No consumers in the focus group discussions had encountered bad experiences with load management, once the devices were installed. There were no reports of a household experiencing discomfort or inconvenience from being cycled off by direct load control. The general satisfaction with direct load control among participating households implies favorable word of mouth among neighbors, friends, and work peers concerning load management programs. It appears, however, that most households were not sufficiently motivated by their satisfaction with direct load control programs to initiate word-of-mouth discussions with other households who might have been prospective participants. In fact, it may be more accurate to describe the experience most households reported while participating in direct load control as an absence of dissatisfaction, as opposed to an experience that leads to strong feelings of pleasure and gratification. In summary, most direct load control participants could best be described as not dissatisfied with the program, yet also not overwhelmed with missionary zeal to initiate conversations with others about direct load control.

GENERAL ATTITUDES ABOUT ELECTRIC UTILITIES

Reactions to load management may be affected by what people are saying generally about their electric utilities. Suspicion and distrust of the utilities characterized the general attitudes of most people. This was the case regardless of whether the utility is an investor-owned company (IOU), a municipal utility, or an electric membership corporation (EMC). The litany of complaints about utilities is quite long and is growing. On the other hand, the list of good things that the utilities are doing is quite short according to the people attending the focus group meetings.

Excessive Salary Levels and Raises

Many households were concerned about what they believed were excessive salary levels and raises for utility management. Most households failed to see any justification for high executive salary levels and large periodic salary increases for utility management. Utility personnel were viewed generally as being overpaid and underworked. Consumers were personally resentful of this.

M: Imagine for me. Imagine that you're looking at the president of VEPCO. What does that person look like?

C: He drives a Rolls Royce.

I'd say it's a big position with low pressure.

My way of seeing it, low pressure.

Title job.

[He] just calls up and says, "I won't be in until about three o'clock this afternoon. Hold all of my calls."

* * *

M: What do people say about your electric company?

C: Well, you know a short time not a long time ago there was a comment someone wrote in the *Wall Street Journal* about Carolina Power and Light having a reputation of being a very efficient operation. Well now, of course, it's all focused on the salaries of the executives. What bothers me most is the 50 percent increase they got. Now I know executives get big salaries—you can get them all the time—but when you see something like a 24 percent increase one year and 28 percent increase in salary the next year, it makes people wonder where their money's going. And then of course I think the Shearon Harris [nuclear] plant and all the uncertainty about those nuclear units and the cost of them. This is what I think is what is bothering people more than anything. Especially what the electricity is costing.

People are becoming very wary of what are they actually paying for, and of course the media is contributing to that wariness but you know, it allows us to feel a little . . . am I paying part of the salary? Am I paying for a nuclear plant that wasn't built? What am I paying for? So you break down your bill [and see] the little explanation, in kind of an apologetic tone, "We hiked the rates a little bit." It's becoming repetitive and you don't even believe them anymore. I get very angry. I get to where I don't really remain open-minded. I am anti-CP&L right now. I've had friends who've actually worked there and quit just because it seems to be against their goodness—the part of them that's good right now. They see [CP&L] as being negative and overbearing. Correctly or not we have begun to assume that the company is gaining an inordinate profit. When I go into Ivey's and buy a dress, I assume that when I buy there some of it is paying not only their cost of keeping the store open, but paying the employees, the president of the company or whatever, but I don't feel really ripped off. The public is beginning to wonder, I think, just what is the profit that CP&L is gaining from this? Is it inordinate, or one that is unfounded? Are they electricity barons?

* * *

C: Tonight, the guy from Carolina Power and Light was on television saying that they've got to have more raises in prices so they can provide us with better service. I thought to myself, "Young man, if you would take a cut in salary . . ."

Resentment of Monopoly Position Guaranteed Utility

Consumers seemed to understand the monopoly position of a utility in any given service area because of the economics of the distribution of electricity. They also believed, however, that the monopoly position afforded little incentive for the utility to be productive. Most consumers resented not only the monopoly position of the utility, but also the idea that the utility should be guaranteed an "acceptable" return on investment in rate hearings.

M: Are any of the utilities doing anything to help you save money or help anyone save money?

C: Why should they? They make more money than we do. They're not competitive, so why should they?

* * *

C: We've sort of legislated ourselves into a situation where electricity is going to cost us more. It's one of the industries where we, the consumer, pay in advance for their growth.

They're building these nuclear plants. We're paying for that right now. [Electric utilities] and the telephone company. You know how the telephone company is governed by legislature. I feel like when you pay, the customer is taking the risk. [Give] people an avenue that is easier than the average business risks . . . for expansion. They're going to utilize it of course. You would expect them to, but I can't think of many businesses that we pay for their problems. Take the Three-Mile Island thing. We're all going to pay for that sooner or later. There was a lot of conversation when it happened. They wanted to raise their bills to compensate for their losses.

* * *

C: I think that many of these companies are overstaffed, and I think that many of the staff are overpaid in both the electrical companies and the telephone companies. All the utilities [are], because they have no competition. They don't have to go out into the marketplace and buy steel and compete with 1,000 other people to do the same thing we do. I don't think it's [just] the executives. I think it's the entire organization. I wouldn't want to point out the president or the top five staff. I'm talking about the system itself.

* * *

C: Why should utilities operate at 15 percent when most of the rest of the industries operate at 2 percent or less?

M: Who's 15 percent now?

C: That's what CP&L said they needed on their return on money: 15 to 17 percent. What's Burlington Industries doing, 2 percent or less? Why should [CP&L] and it's a stockholder-owned company, when you put stockholder-owned companies on the line, why should it be way up and the others be way low?

Uncertainty about Nuclear Power Plants

The construction and operation of nuclear power plants were also topics for anxiety among consumers. Construction costs of new power plant facilities were considered exorbitant by many consumers. Other consumers were quite worried about design faults and construction problems in new nuclear power plants, as well as the long-term problems involved in the disposal of nuclear waste from those facilities.

Lavish Buildings

Many consumers complained about the physical facilities in which their utility and its operation were housed. Utility buildings were often characterized as excessively lavish, particularly since the utility was expected by most consumers to try to do all that it could to keep operating and capital costs at a minimum. The concern about overbuilding and unreasonably pleasant surroundings for utility personnel was not restricted to just the investor-owned utilities. Rather, many of the EMC facilities also were viewed as too large and too nice.

C: [People used to be thankful to the] REA to the extent that they got us out of the dark back in the forties when nobody in the country had electricity. And we were so thrilled to get it. If you had one light in the center of the house which pulled the cord and turned on. We were delighted to have a refrigerator for the first time. And so, it's meant much to the people in the country. The farmers and so forth. That's why it was good. But now, see, they're trying to be like Carolina Power and Light. They've got those fancy buildings and all that help down there [at the EMC]. You know, when you go down there, you see there is too much overhead.

* * *

C: Well, I think the . . . problems are buildings. Buildings. Fifteen years ago we mailed our bill to [the utility]. Then they moved into a little trailer over on Lake Reed. They had a little trailer over on Lake Reed where you could go and pay your bill. Ok and they read the meter. We didn't do that. Now they have a real big, fancy building with original oil paintings in it.

Metering and Billing Confusion

Metering devices, meter reading, and utility billing practices concerned many consumers. Consumers generally distrusted metering devices and questioned the accuracy with which meters were read. Furthermore, many consumers had difficulty understanding their electric bills. They often questioned whether their electricity use in a given period had much to do with the electric bills they subsequently received for that period. Some consumers reported that they had gone so far as to join with others in their service areas to independently monitor the accuracy of meter readings and subsequent billings.

C: [There is] a basic mistrust amongst the general public. . . . I've been involved in this where we've even monitored houses in different parts of town—not mine, we stopped doing it before we ever got over to get this monitoring device on my house—that is where you actually run a survey in front of the light meter, because there have been people who feel like rates are adjusted, are controlled—our metering devices can be tampered with. You know, there was a group about two years ago that thought about having a campaign and going out canvassing the entire country to find out that [the] meters were actually measuring accurately.

* * *

M: Well, you buy your electricity from the town. Do you feel mistrust toward them or toward VEPCO or toward whom?

C: The distrust in that case would be toward people who were controlling the installation and involvement with the meter itself, and is it properly being read? Now let me tell you what creates this. The general public does not, in every case, understand how the averaging of bills works and how the accrual charges of different times of the year works . . . then you get into your fossil fuel, uh, whether it be a charge or a credit.

And then we hear last year that if you are on the town electrical system, you got a nice rebate because of the overcharge. You see all of these things create distrust in people when a company comes back and says we owe you $100 for last year that we overcharged you. And you say, "Hey, do they owe me $100 or do they owe me $500?"

* * *

C: There's not one person . . . including myself, unless I go back and read the [rate] book and the letter again and get myself up to date, that can tell you in any given month, how that bill is figured for that month. Not even people that work for the town. I think that some of the engineers would have a difficult time explaining it to you. There are various things that are best not to explain to the user.

A Few Good Things

Many consumers could identify a few good things they believed their utility was doing. The list of good things that utilities were doing is very brief, though. Consumers cited the low-interest home improvement loans, available through many utilities, as a primary example of something good that the utility was doing. Load management programs also were identified by some consumers as a good utility activity. Although consumers could cite the loan program and the load management program as examples of good utility activities, they did not talk about these good activities with the same level of fervor and personal involvement that was present when they talked about the bad things the utilities were doing.

M: Is the electric company doing anything good? Anything people like?

C: Well, I don't know cause it doesn't concern me, but what is this 6 percent interest loans on, what is it? Installation, home improvements, on things like that . . . But I don't know, I would think it would appeal to some people to get 6 percent interest loans, but they can't get more than, what, $600.

Even I, who am not real fond of the electric company per se, was pleased to see them take some sort of step to say, "Look public we realize we need to do something, even though $2 back on your heating bill for the winter [isn't a lot]." It's something [at least].

* * *

C: But I like the deal [by which] the house is insulated, and there's this little thing with the water heater.

INTERPERSONAL CONVERSATION ABOUT ELECTRIC BILLS

Many consumers appeared to have shared information with each other concerning their electric bills. In fact, several consumers in the focus group discussion reported that the electric bills had periodically been a subject of much discussion between friends and neighbors. The discussion about electric bills generally focused on how unbelievably high the bill was for the most recent period. Some consumers even kept very detailed records about electricity use and charges for respective billing periods. Many consumers reported keeping records that extended over years and years, starting with the date they moved into their present residence.

C: The people do not talk to me so much about energy like they used to, except every three months when they see in the paper that Duke Power wants to raise the electric rate or the public gas company wants to raise their rates. Then they're sore about it for a few days. But they're just sore about the price, they're not sore about conserving energy. But they will say, damned if they're going to conserve it because Duke Power will just get it out of you some other way.

* * *

M: You really do talk about the price of power and the price of energy and things like that?

C: I have a neighbor who has kept his electricity records in this particular neighborhood since 1942. Since he has retired, and is something of a statistician by nature, he takes great pleasure, I think, in seeing how much he is paying for wattage in air conditioning this summer versus when he first put it in . . .

* * *

C: Like I told them, I brought my book I kept since I built my house out there. I've got every month—the highest and the lowest.

HOUSEHOLD ELECTRICITY CONSERVATION

Participating in direct load control programs or time-of-day programs was rarely mentioned as something the household was doing to conserve electricity. That is, load management programs were not perceived as conservation programs. Many North Carolina households, however, appeared to be doing a number of things to conserve electricity. Some of these things involved retrofitting, while others attempted to change electricity consumption by modifying household member's behavior.

Many consumers reported that their households had purchased or were considering purchasing some equipment or one-time service designed to conserve electricity. Items consumers mentioned frequently include the following:

Adding fireplace inserts
Adding wood stoves
Adding timers to the water heater thermostat
Installing attic fans, ceiling fans, and window fans
Modifying the vent to the clothes dryer so that the warm air is directed into the house during the winter and outside the house during the summer
Adding storm windows and storm doors
Having extra insulation placed in areas subject to heat and cooling loss

Replacing existing light bulbs with lower-wattage bulbs or florescent fixtures

Many consumers reported that their households were attempting to change their basic electricity consumption behavior in order to conserve electricity. These behavior changes included:

Turning off unnecessary lights
Cutting off the water heater when no need for hot water is anticipated
Not using the electric dishwasher
Turning the thermostat down in winter and up in summer
Wearing extra clothes inside the house during winter
Running the ventilation in the kitchen while cooking during the summer time and not running the ventilation fan during winter
Lowering the thermostat on the water heater
Washing clothes with cold water or warm water rather than hot water
Closing off unused rooms in the house
Raising and lowering window shades and draperies to correspond with the season and position of the sun with respect to the house.

Many consumers appeared to be very committed to making one-time modifications to their homes and adopting behavior that would lead to electricity conservation. Commitment and motivation to achieve electricity conservation within the household often permeated the whole family. Many parents seemed to be rearing their children to be much more sensitive to electricity conservation practices than their own parents had been. This suggests that North Carolina utilities may soon see a cohort of residential customers who are quite comfortable with and willing to pursue behavior that will lead to electricity conservation.

UNDERSTANDING THE PEAK

Did people understand the peak? Did they understand what the peak is and when the peak is? There appeared to be a general understanding of the concept of the peak. There was considerable misunderstanding, however, about whose peak it is, when the peak occurs, and what causes it.

Generally, consumers seemed to understand the concept of the peak and peak electrical demand. The use of the name "peak" is very descriptive and communicates well to most consumers. Most consumers easily understood that the demand for electricity is not at a constant level over time. There was much confusion, however, about whose peak it is. Consumers could think of peaks in demand for their own household. They saw those peaks as being the times at which they were active in their own electrical energy consumption at home. Alternatively, consumers also could see peaks in the electrical use for a given community. Furthermore, the time frame for the peak also was a matter for various interpretations.

Consumers also appeared to be uncertain about the causes of peaks in electrical use for their communities or larger electrical service areas. Many consumers attributed the peak more to variation in the demand from commercial and industrial uses, rather than to residential customers. There was much uncertainty and confusion about the extent to which electrical demand for a North Carolina community is a function of residential customers' electricity use versus demand from other classes of users. Residential consumers were generally unaware of anything that commercial and industrial users were doing to help conserve electricity.

M: Well, when is the peak?

C: Depends on demand for electricity.

Weekends.

Especially on weekends. When I turn on my air conditioner. Weekends.

10:00 in the day and 5:00 in the afternoon.

It would be more than that.

I would say air conditioning, wouldn't you?

About 10 to 4 is peak time.

M: When? Seven days a week?

C: Yeah, Possibly seven days a week.

Well, I would say the industry is going . . .

M: Yeah, so probably the peak time then is when?

C: Probably, say, from 10 to 2 and then 4 to 8. Everybody's coming home for lunch. Then in the afternoon when everyone's coming home again for dinner.

* * *

M: So what time do you think the demand is higher?

C: Eight in the mornings. A lot of people wash in the mornings. Wash their clothes. I think it would be in the mornings. The demand is also pretty high around supper time on up. About 4 o'clock to 8 o'clock. Looks like to me as many people that work that probably from 5 o'clock to 9 o'clock . . . but I don't know, that would be my assumption. 9 o'clock sticks in my mind.

M: At night? Like what time?

C: From the time you turn on the lights until about 11 o'clock.

I think it depends on what you're actually doing. I think a house with an air conditioner in the summertime with a thermostat keeps [the air conditioner] on during the day [and] will maintain a balance during the day. At night, and if you decided not to use the thermostat in the summertime and just turn it off until they got home at 4 o'clock, we know that people are taking showers, or baths, or cooking. All of the things that you do in the afternoon from, I think, from 4 from 5, maybe 4 to 9 at night, would be the peak load. I think that your peak load, if you cook with electricity, would have to be when you cook or heat water.

* * *

M: You mentioned that you use your dryer at a particular time. You try to watch when you run the clothes dryer?

C: Yeah.

M: When do you run it?

C: I run it a lot of times at night, in the evening, and Saturday mornings. [From] 6 to 9 [o'clock in the evenings].

M: And Saturdays. You mean Saturday mornings?

C: Yeah Saturday mornings. You see, the mills always shut down and you don't use so much.

I particularly try not to use it in the middle of hot weather. During the hottest middle part of the day when the air conditioners are on.

* * *

M: How often would they shut it off?

C: They say they do it only during peak load periods in the evening when everybody is fixing meals.

Well, I got the understanding that the actual, what they considered, the peak, not per day, their peak but the peak is like brown-outs or whatever. You know, rather than you expect your air conditioning to go off. And what they're trying to do is [to] balance out the daily load where they can level the peak off.

Really, they put on quite an advertising campaign on peak load, you know. . . . Stacking up these little boxes before they come out with this.

That's basically the thing that caught my eye was [stacking] these building blocks up. Here was the amount of power that they must produce and they have to be able to do that 24 hours a day. The capability of doing that 24 hours a day even though [the system] don't [need it all the time].

The individual consumer is not the peak maker. The peak people are these government buildings and organization corporations' buildings. You never see a peak problem on the weekends.

They never talk about cutting power by 5 or 10 percent saving on the weekends.

WHAT ABOUT UTILITIES ADVERTISING ON RADIO AND TELEVISION?

The propriety of utilities' advertising, even for conservation programs, was a troublesome question for most residential customers. Most consumers believed that through their electric bill they were paying some portion of the air time or print space for any advertising tactic used by a utility. Most consumers viewed this type of expenditure with resentment. The only type of advertising content that most consumers did view as reasonable was that designed to address conservation themes.

Most residential consumers seemed to react very negatively to utility advertising for any other purposes.

IS THERE ANY WAY FOR THE CONSUMER TO "WIN"?

A final theme emerging from the focus group discussions was that many households saw no way to "win" in the fight to contain rising electricity costs. The dominant view of those consumers who stopped to consider the future implications of conservation behavior was that, regardless of their own electricity conservation and participation in load management programs, they would be paying more per kilowatt-hour for electricity in the future. Many households believed that the more they conserved, the more they would end up having to pay for the electricity that they used in the future. Thus, many households were not convinced that any of the conservation efforts they might undertake today would be reflected in real economic savings to them in the future. The belief seemed to be that the major burden for maintaining and increasing utility revenues and return on investment rates would fall upon the residential customer.

C: The average American citizen is going to get stuck, regardless, no matter what they do. If they're encouraged to conserve, they get stuck anyway. I guess it's the economy. I have people tell me, "Well, I could try to cut my energy consumption in half, but Duke Power would double consumer rates because they said they had to make so many billion [dollars] a year."

M: So you try to cut back on what you use and end up paying double?

C: Yes, I think that's what discourages a lot of people. Say, if you were using 100 gallons of gasoline and you cut back to 50, you'd pretty well guess that the oil companies, through the aid of state or federal government, is going to double the amount of the cost so they'd get just as much money out of you. The average person is not given the incentive to conserve. You can save money by conserving electricity, but their track record on this thing hasn't been that good.

The average person, I think a lot of people are saying, "Why should I try to conserve, because it doesn't do me any good in the end!"

* * *

M: Is there such a thing as an energy crisis these days or is it all over with? Do people talk about it?

C: They just don't talk about it. I think they complain more about it like when you see it on TV—they talk about the prices and stuff like that, but as far as trying to deal with it, they just accept it because they've got the high cost of it.

You've got the thankless thing when they ask you to conserve and the more you conserve the higher the prices go. Instead of that being an advantage to either the prices staying the same or going down.

SUMMARY

The focus group discussions suggest that marketing load management programs is by no means an easy task. Most consumers reacted with suspicion and distrust toward their utilities, particularly if the utility was an investor-owned company. Consumers had a lengthy list of complaints and questions about their utilities and the provision of electricity to households. The advantage in good will from their customers that electric membership corporations enjoyed for many years after the Rural Electrification Act was eroding quickly. Municipal utilities and electric membership corporations, however, were subject to less consumer criticism and distrust, because of the blame and complaints that consumers readily had at hand for investor-owned utilities. Thus, promoting any utility program, including programs such as load management, begins with a market that is fairly homogeneous with respect to negative consumer attitudes about the utilities. Consumers also generally talked about their utilities as if they were impersonal entities.

The focus group discussions also suggest that consumers were ready and willing to talk with each other about their complaints regarding their utility. Perhaps much of this underlying frustration came from the feeling that many households were indeed trying to do their part to conserve electricity in a variety of ways. At the same time, however, consumers generally believed that their energy conservation activities at best could provide only temporary economic benefits to the household.

There appeared to be a growing awareness about load management programs among the households represented in the group discussions. There remained many households who were either uninformed or misinformed about the basic logic underlying load management and the particular programs utilities were offering. Households appeared to be heterogeneous with respect to their motives for agreeing to participate in load management programs. Many households were motivated by economic incentives. Others said they would participate in load management programs if they were simply asked to do so. Still other households would be even more ready to participate if they knew their neighbors were already enrolled in a program. If the load management programs were changed from voluntary to mandatory participation programs, the vast majority of North Carolina households would simply accept the load management programs as a *fait accompli.*

Air conditioner direct load control programs apparently were viewed by many consumers as dramatically different from water heater direct load control programs. Consumers were more troubled by the idea of losing control over their cooling systems than they were about losing control over the heating of hot water in their homes.

Time-of-day rate programs also generated uncertainty in the minds of many consumers. Although most consumers liked the concept of differential pricing based on the time electricity was used, few households could envision ways to change their behavior sufficiently to benefit from a program like this in the long run.

In many North Carolina households the decision about participating in load management programs involved virtually every member of a given household. Thus, the marketing communication task is even more difficult because of the large number of people likely to be involved in the decision.

Households participating in load management programs generally were not dissatisfied with the program. They did not view it as a negative experience, although this may reflect the relatively limited use of service interruption by most North Carolina utilities up to the time of the focus groups. Few households were sufficiently motivated by participation in direct load control to go out on their own and favorably promote participation to their friends, neighbors, and other peers. Thus the potentially favorable word-of-mouth program endorsements remained largely unmotivated by utility marketing programs. Paid mass-media promotional tactics, such as radio, newspaper, and television advertising, were likewise problematic, because many households believed it was generally inappropriate for a utility to advertise.

Qualitative research methods such as focus group discussions are intended to capture the diversity of motivations, reactions, and themes pertaining to an issue. This diversity was strongly reflected in the perspectives that emerged from the discussions. The frequency with which these various perspectives occur among North Carolina households can best be estimated by a rigorous consumer survey. The results of such a survey are highlighted and discussed in the following chapters.

5

Consumer Acceptance

Consumer participation rates directly affect the total amount and timing of load that can be shed and thus the potential value of load management programs to utilities. Most residential load management studies conducted to date have examined the level and timing of electricity use among participating households. Studies of factors that increase the rate of customer participation, generally referred to as studies of customer acceptance (Task Force Report No. 10 1977), are less common.

Previous consumer acceptance research has focused on three issues: (1) consumer knowledge and understanding, (2) consumer attitudes, and (3) consumer perceptions of electricity consumption (Hellman 1980; Males and Uhler 1982). The research reported in this chapter builds on that earlier work and goes further to look directly at consumers' decisions to take part in or reject utility-sponsored load management programs. Issues related to consumer participation also are addressed in Chapter 6, which focuses on the participation intentions of households who have been slow to enroll in load management, and Chapter 7, which examines consumers' satisfaction with programs and their intentions to continue participating in, or drop out of, load control and time-of-day programs.

A MODEL OF CONSUMER ACCEPTANCE

Various models have been used to depict the process by which consumers adopt new products, behavior, or programs. By describing the stages through which consumers may pass in making their decisions, researchers can better understand the adoption process and the reasons it may stall before final adoption for large groups of people.

Three models borrowed from the social and behavioral sciences are appropriate to the study of consumer acceptance of load management programs: models of adaptation to change; decision making and choice; and the adoption and diffusion of innovation (Burns 1980, 5–23). These models describe different processes and issues in consumer adoption. In models of adaptation to change, consumers react to changed social situations, such as scarcity or technological and social change. The models depict processes of overcoming resistance to change. Decision-making and choice models depict the stages through which consumers progress in decisions, from the identification of a problem to its active resolution. Models of the adoption and diffusion of innovations are related to decision-making models but describe the processes by which new, rather than familiar, products become adopted.

The innovation adoption model is the most widely used of the three and is especially appropriate for the study of new energy products and programs. The model hypothesizes that the adoption process begins when a consumer hears about an innovation and ends when the consumer finally adopts or rejects the product or program. The process consists of the following steps: awareness; interest; evaluation; and adoption (see Robertson 1971; Shama 1981; Williams 1982). It may be shortened, however, by rejection at any stage (Havelock 1971, 10–30; Robertson 1971, 75). For example, the consumer after reflection, may not develop sufficient interest in or may negatively evaluate the innovation. Marketing management can enhance rates of adoption to the extent that it can move an individual decision maker through the various steps to the point of adoption. Each step implies a different mix of marketing objectives and tactics. Thus, it is important for utility managers to have an accurate understanding of the adoption process, how many consumers are at each of the different stages of the process at any given time, and the factors that induce consumers to move from one state to the next.

The first step in consumer adoption of a load management program is *awareness.* Here the consumer becomes informed that the new product or program exists and is available to the household, but he has little additional information about the product or its attributes.

The second step is *interest.* Now that the consumer is aware of load management, will he or she be sufficiently motivated to pursue further information about it? Or will consumers lack sufficient interest to investigate it further? Consumers who move through the interest stage of the process gain knowledge about load management, understand its functions, and begin to form opinions about its potential usefulness.

In the *evaluation* stage, the consumer develops specific attitudes about a load management program. These attitudes consist of affect, beliefs, and behavioral intentions pertaining to the program, i.e., to give the program a try, to reject it, or to wait and see. Some of the information available to consumers at this stage is subject to the control of marketing managers, such as the themes and content of promotional messages in newspapers, bill stuffers, radio and television announcements, or speeches and presentations by utility employees. Other information is less subject to control by utility marketing managers. The latter category might include word-of-mouth information from existing or former participants in load management programs or consumer misperceptions about participation in the programs.

The consumer becomes a user of the new product in the *adoption* step of the process. Some consumers may decide to try a load management program and then drop out if they are not satisfied. In this case, the innovation is put to a personal test before it is completely accepted by the household.

The adoption process can serve as a useful planning and tactical framework for utility management. For example, knowledge that a household is at a particular stage in the process suggests that particular marketing objectives are appropriate. If households in the target market segments are aware of the load management program innovation, will they be motivated sufficiently to find out more about it? In the evaluation stage, how does marketing management talk about the innovation to achieve target levels of subsequent adoption? Are consumers thinking about load management programs as alternatives to existing conservation programs, or are load management programs distinctly unique? The nature of the evaluative criteria and the nature of competing alternatives determine how much and what kind of consumer information utility marketing management must try to provide.

Marketing researchers who have investigated the adoption and diffusion of innovations (e.g., Robertson 1971; Midgely 1977; Midgely and Downing 1978; Rogers 1976) have come to several conclusions about these two processes. These conclusions are summarized by Burby, Didow, and Marsden (1981):

> First, innovative behavior differs from one product class to another. For example, the typical length of time to go through the adoption process and the type and amount of information needed at various stages are different for various categories of innovations.
>
> Second, there appears to be no precise set of Innovator, Early Adopter, and Early Majority characteristics across different product classes. An Innovator for one type of new product is not necessarily an Innovator with respect to another type of new product. Rogers and Thomas (1975) and Rogers and Stanfield (1966) reviewed over 2,700 research publications on the diffusion of innovations and concluded that Innovators and Early Adopters are generally of higher education and higher income than later adopters. They are also more likely to think of themselves as cosmopolitan and to have greater exposure to information from both mass media sources and innovation change agents. However, marked exceptions to the generalizations are frequently found in innovation and diffusion research.
>
> The third general finding, however, is that within product classes reliable adoption patterns and general adopter characteristics can often be identified.

In sum, although previous research on the adoption and diffusion of innovations cannot be transferred directly to help identify characteristics of key groups in the diffusion of load management programs, market research undertaken for this specific purpose can uncover characteristics of adopters that can be generalized within this specific class of consumer products and programs.

A modified version of the innovation adoption process, which will be used to guide analyses presented in Chapters 5–7, is illustrated in Figure 5.1. The tendency of consumers to try new products before becoming committed to their use is represented by the "satisfaction/continued adoption and dissatisfaction/discontinuance" steps at the end of the adoption process. A distinction is made between "adoption" and "later adoption" because some consumers are likely to enroll in a load management program shortly after it is introduced, whereas others may take some time before deciding to take part. Thus, a nonparticipant at any point in time is recognized as a potential later participant and cannot be ignored in program marketing. Factors affecting whether a consumer passes through the stages of the adoption process also are delineated in Figure 5.1. They include consumer characteristics, program characteristics, and program marketing and promotion.

Analyses based on this model of adoption can help to identify factors that result in acceptance or rejection of load management programs, such as attributes of the program; attitudes, information levels, or personality characteristics of the potential adopter; and market characteristics (Shama 1981; Darley 1977–1978). Furthermore, identification of market segments whose members are likely to enroll in a program early can help to predict initial and later levels of adoption.

PREVIOUS RESEARCH

This chapter documents factors that affect whether and how consumers move through the awareness, attitude formation/interest, evaluation/decision, and adoption stages of program participation. These stages are shaded in the diagram presented in Figure 5.1. Subsequent chapters consider the issues of satisfaction/continued adoption, dissatisfaction/discontinuance, later adoption, and continued rejection. Although the field is not well developed, some previous effort has been devoted to explaining customer awareness, interest, and adoption of load management programs. Before turning to the findings of this study it is useful to review the current state of knowledge in terms of the stages outlined in Figure 5.1.

Awareness of Program

Although load management programs are relatively new in many areas, a few households are likely to have heard of load management even before programs are formally introduced in their communities. Elrick and Lavidge found in a 1978 survey (cited in Hellman 1980, III-22), for instance, that one-fourth of the customers of a certain utility had heard of time-of-day rates. Similarly, Van Liere (1982) found that in two

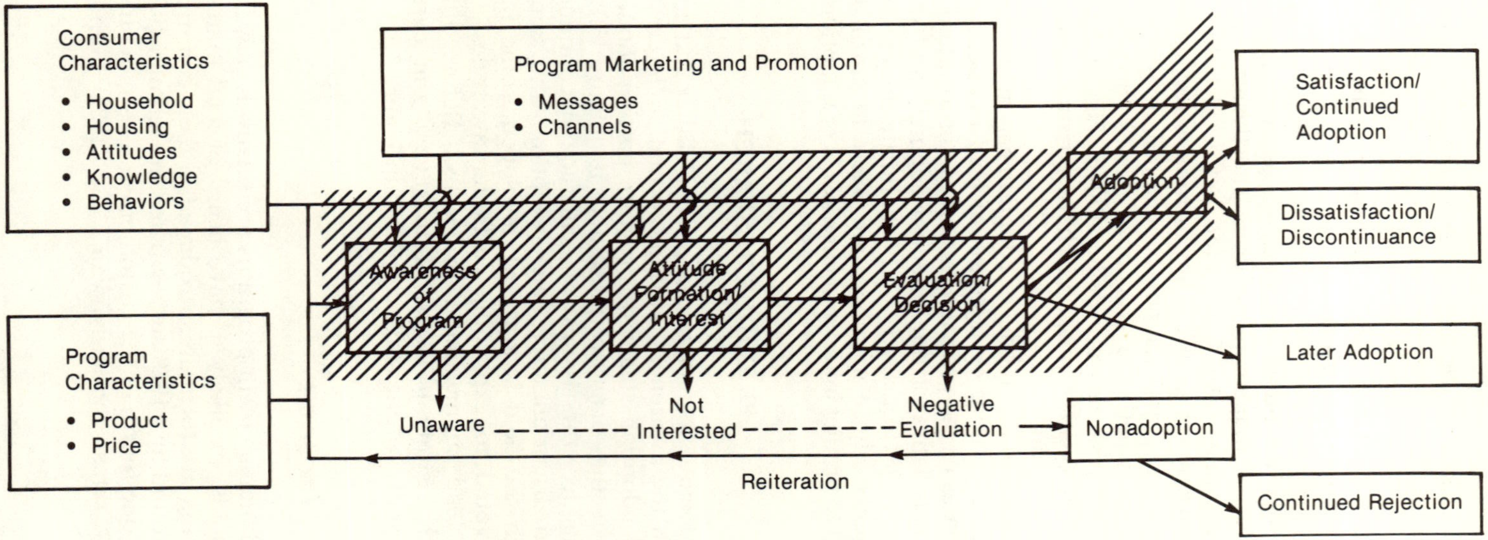

Figure 5.1 Program Adoption Model

Tennessee communities about 80 percent of the people queried did not know very much about electrical load management, implying that 20 percent did. Others suggest that consumers have only a limited understanding of utility rates and peaking problems (Task Force Report No. 10 1977, 7; Hellman 1980, 22). Males and Uhler (1982, 38) found the level of consumer knowledge about electric utility concepts to be moderate, but they also found that consumers had a general understanding of peaking problems. Even so, they reported that consumers have a number of misconceptions about load management programs. These findings from various surveys indicate a general level of awareness of load management programs among a small group of consumers and the need for further information about such programs among the larger population.

Attitude Formation/Interest

Previous studies have reported conflicting findings about consumer attitudes toward load management. Colin et al. (1976), for instance, found widespread support for load management programs that would improve the pricing of electricity. A national survey conducted in 1976 by Elrick and Lavidge, Inc., found, however, that when given a choice among voluntary reduction of peak power usage, time-of-day rates, and direct load control, a majority of electric utility customers preferred voluntary reduction. One-quarter chose time-of-day pricing, and only 10 percent indicated they would choose direct load control (Elrick and Lavidge 1977). A recent survey of consumer attitudes toward a variety of load management options conducted by Van Liere et al. (1981) in Athens and Bristol, Tennessee, found that direct load control and time-of-day rates were the least favored of nine options people were asked to assess. In both cities, more than 75 percent of the respondents were opposed to direct load control. Strongly favored programs included energy conservation, converting coal to oil and natural gas, solar energy, and strict energy standards for cars and buildings.

In contrast to the findings of Elrick and Lavidge and Van Liere et al. Heberlein (1981) has summarized the results of a number of utility-sponsored surveys that indicate more positive attitudes toward load management:

- Three surveys sponsored by the Wisconsin Electric Power Company found from 54 percent to 79 percent of customers had favorable attitudes toward water heater control programs and 60 percent had favorable attitudes toward air conditioner control.
- Corn Belt Power found that approximately three-fourths of its customers would adopt water heater and air conditioner load control programs.
- Eastern Iowa Electric Co-op found that over two-thirds of its cus-

tomers would participate in space heating, water heater, and air conditioner programs.

- Wisconsin Public Service Corporation found that more than two-thirds of its customers would allow the installation of water heater and air conditioner controls.

With the exception of the Wisconsin Public Service corporation sample, each of those surveys also found that a majority of the utility customers queried were willing to participate in load management with no monetary incentive.

In general, the attitude surveys conducted to date show that most people are not inherently opposed to direct load control or time-of-day programs. At the same time, it can be said that customer attitudes are not very well developed or particularly stable (Heberlein 1981, 2-2). Most utility customers have been found to have little prior knowledge of load management programs, which they tend to view as a wholly new concept. As a result, attitudes toward load management programs could change markedly depending on what kinds of programs electric utilities develop and how they are promoted.

Evaluation/Decision

Fewer studies have been conducted concerning the evaluation/decision stage of the adoption process. Many of the studies reviewed above found economic considerations to be important in the decision to adopt load management programs. Van Liere et al. (1982, 25), however, found that in an area where programs had not yet been introduced, few respondents could comment on issues that would need to be resolved at the decision stage of the adoption process. Twenty percent or fewer of the households interviewed in Athens and Bristol, Tennessee, could cite advantages or disadvantages of load management programs in response to open-ended questions.

Consumer Participation Rates

Electric utilities' experience with consumer participation in load control and time-of-day rate programs was reviewed in Chapter 2. The only study to examine factors influencing variation in participation rates was conducted by Heberlein (1981) for the Electric Power Research Institute. As noted in Chapter 2, he concluded that program marketing was the key factor in explaining why some utilities had achieved high rates of participation while others had failed to achieve much customer support of load management. With regard to other variables affecting customer participation, Heberlein concluded:

- Direct financial incentives to customers are helpful in inducing participation, but the size of the incentive has little effect on participation rates. A more important aspect of incentives may be the manner in which they are offered to consumers, whether as lump sum payments, monthly credits on utility bills, or rolled into the regular kWh charge.
- Possibly because utilities have not pushed the length of appliance off cycles far enough, the nature of the control appears to have little effect on participation.
- In the case of market area characteristics, utilities serving fewer customers, particularly rural cooperatives, have had higher rates of adoption. Large utilities, which have many customers and large service areas, "... have to scramble much harder to achieve substantial rates of adoption." (1981)

In comparing marketing techniques, Heberlein (1981) found that direct personal contact with customers (either face-to-face or by telephone) that is designed to answer customer questions and counteract misinformation about the effects of load control has been most effective. Single-shot direct mail appeals have been least effective.

Besides considering marketing techniques, one must remember that the effectiveness of marketing information may vary according to the personality and attitudes of the consumer (Havelock 1971, 10–37; Shoemaker 1981, 188–189), and information needs vary across the stages of the adoption process (Havelock 1971, 10–37; Shoemaker 1981; Williams 1982, 272). Williams and Shoemaker, for instance, maintain that mass-media messages are most effective at the awareness stage; Shoemaker says interpersonal channels are more important at the attitude formation stage (see also Midgely 1977, 112; Robertson 1971). Information messages and channels, therefore, must be tailored to specific marketing objectives.

STRATEGY OF ANALYSIS

The household survey data collected for this research (see Chapter 1) were used in two different ways to investigate consumer decisions to participate in load control and time-of-day programs. First, consumer decisions were examined for each utility's load management program. These utility-specific analyses respond to Hellman's (1980) warning that data aggregated across utilities are likely to mask important idiosyncracies and situational constraints that may affect consumer participation decisions for specific utilities. Second, to detect differences in participation attributable to characteristics of a utility's program and marketing methods, we conducted aggregate analyses that pooled consumer data from all the utilities studied.

TABLE 5.1

ADOPTION DECISION PROCESS:
WATER HEATER LOAD CONTROL

Stage of Adoption Process (8/82)	Percent of Eligible Customers					
	Duke	CP&L	VEPCO	Tarboro	Lumbee River	Four County
Date of Program Introduction	2/81	6/80	6/80	1/80	12/76	11/77
1. Unaware	7	6	15	7	12	1
2. Not Interested	3	5	2	1	3	2
3. Interested - No Decision Yet	36	32	25	17	18	3
4. Negative Decision	28	39	35	10	13	6
5. Adoption	26	18	19	65	54	88

In the first part of the analyses that follow, we estimate what proportion of each utility's customers was at each of the various stages in the load management adoption process and discuss reasons they participated or rejected the program. After this discussion, we analyze program participation decisions for each utility and isolate key differences among consumers who chose to participate in different types of load management programs (water heater control, air conditioner control, time-of-day rates). Finally to investigate the role of program characteristics and utility marketing efforts, we pooled data across all six utilities and estimated a logit regression model.

THE ADOPTION PROCESS

In contrast to previous research, which found that only a minority of electric utility customers were aware of load management programs, we found that substantial proportions of the eligible customers served by each of the six utilities studied were aware of the programs offered. Estimates of the percentages of customers at different stages of the adoption process are presented in Tables 5.1 to 5.3 for water heater load control, air conditioner load control, and time-of-day programs, respectively.[1] The stages are unaware, aware but not interested, interested but undecided about participation, decided not to participate, and already enrolled in a program.

Among all the utilities, 15 percent or fewer of the eligible households

TABLE 5.2

ADOPTION DECISION PROCESS:
AIR CONDITIONER LOAD CONTROL

Stage of Adoption Process (8/82)	Percent of Eligible Customers			
	Duke	Tarboro	Lumbee River	Four County
Date of Program Introduction	2/81	1/80	12/76	11/77
1. Unaware	7	5	11	3
2. Not Interested	3	1	3	6
3. Interested - No Decision Yet	35	12	17	20
4. Negative Decision	28	7	12	22
5. Adoption	27	75	57	59

in areas where programs had been introduced remained unaware of the programs one to five years afterward. Consumers' awareness of Duke Power's time-of-day program and the water heater control programs offered by VEPCO and Lumbee River utilities was lower than consumer awareness of the other utility programs studied. Consumer awareness was slightly higher than average for Four County customers. Only 1 percent of the Four County customers were unaware of water heater control programs, and only 3 percent were unaware of air conditioner control programs.

Of those customers who were aware of load management programs, most were interested in the programs (that is, few were "not interested"), but substantial proportions of interested customers had not yet decided about participation. These percentages of interested, no-decision customers reached a maximum of 50 percent for time-of-day programs and were fully one-fourth to one-third of customers of the investor-owned utilities. Fewer customers had rejected any of the utilities' load management programs, ranging from one-third of the customers of the investor-owned utilities to one-fourth or fewer of the customers of the municipal and EMC utilities. Finally, levels of adoption ranged from 3 percent (Duke's time-of-day programs) to 88 percent (Four County's water heater load control program). The level of adoption appeared to vary by the time since introduction of the programs but was also much higher for municipal and EMC utilities than for investor-owned utilities. The type and intensity of the marketing program may of course also be an important factor.

TABLE 5.3

ADOPTION DECISION PROCESS:
TIME-OF-DAY PROGRAMS

Stage of Adoption Process (8/82)	Percent of Those Eligible Duke
Date of Program Introduction	2/81
1. Unaware	14
2. Not Interested	5
3. Interested - No Decision Yet	50
4. Negative Decision	28
5. Adoption	3

Reasons for Participation

We found that consumers were motivated to participate in any of the six utilities' load management programs largely for economic reasons, which agrees with previous research. As shown in Table 5.4, 84 percent to 97 percent of program participants among all the programs and utilities said they joined to save money on their electric bills, and 60 percent to 85 percent said they joined to benefit from the savings their utilities would incur from such cost-cutting measures. Mentioned third most often (25 percent to 68 percent of respondents) was that someone from their utility suggested the program—a reflection of the active personal selling efforts of many utilities. Environmental benefits from having to build fewer power plants were cited less often, but it was important to 25 percent to 41 percent of respondents. Few mentioned recommendations from friends as a reason for participation. Thus, economic motivations predominated, followed by the effects of utility personal selling efforts and environmental concerns.

There were several exceptions to this general pattern. Participants from the three investor-owned utilities (Duke, CP&L, and VEPCO) and the municipal utility (Tarboro) were more likely than participants from the electric membership corporations (Lumbee River and Four County) to cite saving money as their primary motivation. As mentioned in previous chapters, the EMCs offered the lowest monetary incentive for participation. The municipal utility and CP&L participants were more likely than others to cite the importance of cutting costs for the utility,

TABLE 5.4

REASONS FOR PROGRAM PARTICIPATION, BY UTILITY AND PROGRAM
(percent of program participants)

	Percent Cited as a Reason for Program Participation				
Utility and Program	Save Money on Electric Bill	We All Save If Utility Cuts Costs	Less Damage to Environment	Suggestion by Utility	Recommended by a Friend
Duke Power					
Water heater control	90	59	36	66	7
Air conditioner control	97	65	34	68	5
Both loads controlled	91	69	36	64	8
Time-of-day rates	95	69	38	68	7
Carolina Power and Light					
Water heater control	91	76	41	25	7
VEPCO					
Water heater control	94	83	40	55	8
Tarboro					
Water heater control	95	74	37	42	7
Air conditioner control	98	78	32	49	10
Both loads controlled	95	79	25	45	11
Lumbee River EMC					
Water heater control	84	60	26	47	5
Air conditioner control	91	85	53	56	16
Both loads controlled	84	71	39	37	4
Four County EMC					
Water heater control	85	63	37	56	0
Both loads controlled	84	70	30	60	12

while CP&L participants were less likely than others to indicate that someone from the utility suggested their participation. These differences among customers of the various utilities may reflect the civic-mindedness of some utilities and customers (in the case of the electric membership corporations, customers who were less concerned about saving money on their electric bills). They also may reflect the different approaches various utilities use to market load management (as with the lower percentage of CP&L customers who gave direct contact from the utility as a reason for taking part).

Reasons for Nonparticipation

Nonparticipants were asked about the reasons they were not taking part in a load management program. As noted above, some households had not reached the evaluation stage in the adoption process and were not taking part because they were unaware a program existed, were not interested, or were interested, but had yet to make up their minds. Of particular concern here, however, are households who reached the evaluation stage and came to a negative decision. Why did they choose to reject participation?

Households' reasons for not taking part in load control programs are summarized in Table 5.5. For those who had reached the evaluation stage, the two predominant reasons for rejecting load control programs were not wanting to give up control of the use of electricity and not seeing sufficient monetary incentives to take part. Very few households mentioned as a reason the loss of comfort if their water heaters or air conditioners were shut off. Households served by the Four County EMC were most concerned about the loss of control of their water heaters and air conditioners. Four County was the only utility studied that had a major problem with its load control system. Once it accidentally switched off controlled appliances over an entire weekend. Although Four County had achieved high participation rates since then, the data in Table 5.5 clearly illustrate the negative consumer evaluation that can result from such accidents. One other notable difference among utilities was the relatively higher proportion of nonparticipants served by Duke Power who said they were not taking part in load control because there was an installation charge. Duke was the only utility to levy an installation charge, and that practice clearly has led some customers to reject the load control program.

Households not taking part in Duke Power's time-of-day program also were asked why they had not enrolled. As suggested in Table 5.3 above, most households were either unaware of the program or undecided about participation. Thus, consumers seem to need more information to make a decision about time-of-day rates than they do for load control programs. Relatively few households were not interested in the time-of-day program (3 percent) or had reached a negative decision

TABLE 5.5

REASONS GIVEN FOR NOT PARTICIPATING IN LOAD CONTROL
(percent of nonparticipants)

Reason for Nonparticipation	Duke Power	CP&L	VEPCO	Tarboro	Lumbee River	Four County
Unaware						
Haven't heard about it before	15	10	14	22	27	10
Not available here	16	7	2	6	2	1
Not Interested/Eligible						
We are not eligible	2	7	4	7	2	1
Just not interested	9	12	10	8	5	27
Interested but Undecided						
No one ever asked	32	15	15	25	20	14
Need more information	29	29	27	24	25	17
Negative Evaluation						
We want to control our use of electricity	15	31	27	18	18	41
We would be too uncomfortable	5	4	5	2	0	6
We couldn't save enough on our electric bill	12	11	19	10	11	10
There is an installation charge	24	4	1	2	0	4
Just not worth the effort to call and have it installed	3	7	1	3	11	3
We were on it and didn't like it	0	0	0	1	0	1

(28 percent). Those who consciously decided against participation were most concerned that they would not be able to change the times they used electricity and therefore would not save much by taking part. Far fewer households were concerned about the installation charge for Duke's time-of-day program (only 3 percent) than for its load control programs.

Other aspects of nonparticipation in load control and time-of-day programs are examined in Chapter 6, along with information about how to market load management programs to promote later adoption.

CONSUMER CHARACTERISTICS AND PROGRAM PARTICIPATION

According to the program adoption model presented in Figure 5.1, major influences on the adoption process are consumer characteristics (household, housing, attitudes, knowledge, and behavior); program characteristics (product and price); and program marketing and promotion (messages and media). This section examines the role of consumer characteristics by investigating the demographic, attitudinal, and behavioral profiles of participants in the various programs offered by each of the six utilities.

The consumer characteristics investigated by this study reflect factors that previous research has identified as important determinants of either the adoption of innovations or involvement in energy conservation activities. Program innovators, for instance, have generally been described as younger, more highly educated, and better informed than their counterparts. Energy conservers, on the other hand, are frequently living in homes they own, are more highly educated and better informed, and are predisposed to the need to save energy. Since participation in load management programs may represent innovative behavior or may be closely related to involvement in other conservation activities, those characteristics are meaningful. Furthermore, those characteristics define market segments toward which marketing efforts might be directed at the various stages of program development.

In examining the relation between consumer characteristics and participation in load management programs, it is important to remember that the six utilities studied were at different stages of program diffusion. The municipal and EMC utilities introduced their programs earlier and had achieved much higher rates of program participation than the investor-owned utilities had. In the analyses that follow, then, consumers who were participating in load management programs of investor-owned utilities (Duke, CP&L, and VEPCO) may more closely approximate the image of early program adopters or innovators than the participants served by the municipal and EMC utilities. Participants in load management programs in the municipal and EMC utilities were likely to be drawn from a broader base of the consumer population and therefore would be less likely to be as affluent and well educated as the earlier adopters. The differences between these utilities have important implications for the effective marketing of load management programs at different stages of market maturity.

Duke Power

Program participants in the Duke Power area were significantly different from nonparticipants on a number of characteristics, as seen in Table 5.6. Although specific differences between program options were not tested, water heater participants were less well educated and had lower incomes than the other groups, and there were more nonwhites, more single-person households, renters, and more people who had difficulty paying their electric bill. Water heater program participants also tended to live in older homes and in smaller homes than the others and were more likely to engage in some conservation behavior, such as caulking. Nonparticipants, on the other hand, were less likely than program participants to have engaged in energy conservation by adding water heater insulation or retrofitting their homes, for example. Nonparticipants and water heater program participants were more likely than others to feel uninformed about energy matters. No significant differences were seen between nonparticipants' and participants' attitudes toward the utility or toward conservation, and few differences were seen between the groups' knowledge about load management.

Time-of-day participants were particularly well educated and were more affluent and more conservation-minded than others.

If the images of the early program adopter reflected reality, program participants would be significantly more affluent, better informed, and more conservation-minded than nonparticipants. Those tendencies were characteristic of time-of-day participants and, to a degree, of participants in air conditioner and in both air and water heater programs, but they were not characteristic of water heater program participants. In fact, households with only the water heater controlled were even less affluent and less knowledgeable than those who were not participating in any program. While time-of-day participants approximated the prototypical innovator, the water heater participant clearly did not. Although this difference from expectations could be explained by the greater attractiveness of water heater programs for less affluent consumers, it also could be because the less affluent customers are not eligible for other programs. Fewer than 10 percent of the Duke Power water heater program participants, for example, had central air conditioning. An additional explanation may be that the character of marketing differed for the various types of programs; for instance, Duke Power's active door-to-door marketing program might have produced a different water heater participant population.

TABLE 5.6

ASSOCIATION OF CONSUMER CHARACTERISTICS WITH PARTICIPATION DECISIONS FOR DUKE POWER LOAD MANAGEMENT PROGRAMS (percent of households)

	Program Options				
		Load Control Programs			
Consumer Characteristics	Nonparticipation	Water Heater	Air	Water & Air	Time-of-Day Rates
Demographic Characteristics					
Education					
High school or less	37*	72	28	45	26
Some college	20	14	25	23	26
College graduate	26	6	27	18	25
Post graduate	17	7	21	14	23
Income					
Under $10,000	6*	41	8	8	2
$10,000-$24,999	68	53	53	58	53
$25,000 or more	25	5	39	34	44
Race					
White	93*	89	95	95	98
Nonwhite	7	11	5	5	2
Household Type					
One person	11*	28	17	16	2
Couple	27	32	36	45	42
With children	50	26	41	34	50
Other	11	14	6	6	6
Housing Characteristics					
Tenure					
Own	92*	75	93	98	96
Rent	8	25	7	2	4
Housing Type					
Single family	87*	89	90	97	97
Other	13	11	10	3	3
Year Built					
Before 1960	15*	83	38	47	28
1960-1969	6	12	21	24	35
1970-1974	6	2	12	10	17
1975 or later	73	2	29	19	20

TABLE 5.6 continued

Consumer Characteristics	Program Options				
		Load Control Programs			
	Nonparticipation	Water Heater	Air	Water & Air	Time-of-Day Rates
Size of Dwelling					
800-1,499 sq. ft.	43*	70	29	30	18
1,500-1,999 sq. ft.	24	14	32	38	34
2,000 or more sq. ft	33	16	39	32	49
Reports Difficulty Paying Electric Bill					
Yes	38*	53	31	30	34
No	62	47	69	70	66
Attitudes Toward Utility					
Household feels utility is doing all it can to hold down costs	25	22	20	27	24
Household feels it pays too much for electricity	62	76	64	60	68
Conservation Attitudes					
Extremely important to conserve	66	78	68	71	64
Don't mind personal discomfort to conserve	49	61	48	52	59
Conservation Behavior					
Turn off air conditioner	77*	96	86	83	92
Turn down heat	61*	88	65	60	72
Retrofitting Actions					
Insulation	22*	32	35	42	38
Storm windows	22*	54	46	47	50
Caulking and weather-stripping	23*	47	34	38	42
Water heater insulation	9*	18	16	23	29

TABLE 5.6 continued

Consumer Characteristics	Program Options: Nonparticipation	Load Control Programs: Water Heater	Air	Water & Air	Time-of-Day Rates
Water heater timer	10*	15	5	13	55
Retrofitting index (added two or more of 9 items)[a]	41*	65	63	66	78
<u>Energy Conservation and Load Management Knowledge</u>					
Household feels well informed about how to conserve	73*	77	91	92	95
Energy conservation opinion leader	21	21	19	20	29
Household knows utility costs are higher during peak periods	62	64	62	62	61
Household knows load management levels peaks	73	74	85	88	91
Household knows peak periods are not from 10 a.m. to 4 p.m.	65	39	59	45	48

*Chi-square significant at .05 or less.

[a]Retrofitting behaviors include having added storm windows, storm doors, insulation, water heater insulation, pipe insulation, caulking/weather stripping, attic fan, water heater timer, or wood burning stove.

Carolina Power and Light

Participants in CP&L's water heater load control program were significantly more likely than nonparticipants to own their home, to live in a single-family house, to live in a larger home, to engage in retrofitting and other conservation behavior, and to be knowledgeable about load management (see first panel of Table 5.7). They were also less likely than nonparticipants to believe they paid too much for electricity. There are no differences, however, between program participants and nonparticipants in education level, income, race, household type, age of house, difficulty paying electric bills, and most measures of attitudes toward the utility and toward conservation.

Given the lack of significant associations between program participation and education, income, and conservation attitudes, it appears that participants in CP&L's water heater load control program do not fit the model of a new product innovator either. Most of the observed differences between program participants and nonparticipants reflect CP&L's marketing tactics as much as they reflect factors motivating consumer behavior. By requiring written permission for participation from the owner or building manager, for example, CP&L made it more difficult for renters and households living in multifamily dwellings to participate in its load control programs. Thus, it is not surprising that, when compared with nonparticipants, those taking part in the program were significantly more likely to be homeowners, to live in single-family detached dwellings, to live in larger dwellings, and to have taken various steps to retrofit their homes for greater energy efficiency. Other utilities, however, have found that renters and households in multifamily housing will readily join load management programs (see Tables 5.6 and 5.8). Assuming that a high enough proportion of these households has electric water heaters with capacities large enough to justify load control, utilities that have created barriers to participation by renters and multifamily housing dwellers can boost market penetration rates by taking steps to remove those barriers. Thus, if CP&L wanted a broader base of participation in its load control programs, it could market its programs more effectively to renters and to households living in multifamily units.

Virginia Electric and Power

Participants in VEPCO's water heater load control program are significantly more likely than nonparticipants to own their homes, to be involved in retrofitting such as adding insulation, and to be more knowledgeable about load management issues (see second panel of Table 5.7). Nonparticipants, on the other hand, are more likely to believe they are paying too much for electricity. No differences between program participants and nonparticipants were seen for educational level,

TABLE 5.7

ASSOCIATION OF CONSUMER CHARACTERISTICS WITH PARTICIPATION DECISIONS FOR CP&L AND VEPCO WATER HEATER LOAD CONTROL PROGRAMS
(percent of households)

Consumer Characteristics	CP&L Nonparticipation	CP&L Water Heater Load Control	VEPCO Nonparticipation	VEPCO Water Heater Load Control
Demographic Characteristics				
Education				
High school or less	16	20	42	43
Some college	22	17	34	20
College graduate	30	26	17	22
Post graduate	32	36	8	15
Income				
Under $10,000	5	6	19	22
$10,000-$24,999	48	37	64	44
$25,000 or more	47	57	17	33
Race				
White	94	96	95	98
Black	6	4	5	2
Household Type				
One person	16	11	12	14
Couple	25	30	35	46
With children	40	45	34	31
Other	19	14	19	8
Housing Characteristics				
Tenure				
Own	61*	97	82*	96
Rent	39	3	18	4
Housing Type				
Single family	60*	94	91	96
Other	40	6	9	4
Year Built				
Before 1960	24	29	53	62
1960-1969	29	28	19	12
1970-1974	23	13	14	7
1975 or later	24	30	14	19

TABLE 5.7 continued

Consumer Characteristics	CP&L Nonparticipation	CP&L Water Heater Load Control	VEPCO Nonparticipation	VEPCO Water Heater Load Control
Size				
800–1,499 sq. ft.	53	26	61	54
1,500–1,999 sq. ft.	15	33	18	16
2,000 sq. ft. or more	32	40	21	29
Reports Difficulty Paying Electric Bill				
Yes	44	33	53	43
No	56	67	47	57
Attitudes Toward Utility				
Household feels utility is doing all it can to hold down costs	8	17	12	19
Household feels it pays too much for electricity	76*	62	82*	63
Conservation Attitudes				
Extremely important to conserve	56	59	68	69
Don't mind personal discomfort to conserve	61	59	54	56
Conservation Behavior				
Turn off air conditioner	88	84	97	92
Turn down heat	97	93	81	72
Retrofitting				
Insulation	19*	31	30*	45
Storm windows	36	45	48	52
Caulking and weather-stripping	30	38	45	45
Water heater insulation	20*	34	19	30

TABLE 5.7 continued

Consumer Characteristics	CP&L Nonparticipation	CP&L Water Heater Load Control	VEPCO Nonparticipation	VEPCO Water Heater Load Control
Water heater timer	9*	40	9*	56
Retrofitting Index (add 2 or more of 9 items)[a]	48*	74	58	76
Energy Conservation and Load Management Knowledge				
Household feels well informed how to conserve	83*	94	74*	93
Energy conservation opinion leader	12*	24	17*	33
Household knows utility costs are higher during peak periods	66*	77	66	69
Household knows load management levels peaks	78*	94	66*	80

*Chi-square significant at .05 or less.

[a]See Table 5.6.

income, race, household type, housing type, age of house, size of house, difficulty paying the electric bill, and conservation attitudes and behavior.

Thus, comparisons of VEPCO program participants and nonparticipants provide little information about household characteristics that could be used to target promotional efforts in other communities where VEPCO might introduce the program. The differences that do exist between VEPCO program participants and nonparticipants appear to stem from whether households own or rent their homes. As with the CP&L program, these data may have greater implications for efforts to increase market penetration than for introducing programs in new areas. That is, VEPCO could probably increase participation by allowing rental households to take part in the program.

Tarboro

Participants in the air conditioner and in both water heater and air conditioner programs in the Tarboro municipal utility area were more likely than others to have attended school more years, to have higher incomes, to be married couples with children, to live in newer and larger homes, and to answer correctly some questions about load management. Air conditioner program participants were more likely than others to own their homes, to live in single family homes, and to say they had difficulty paying their electric bills. All participants were more likely than nonparticipants to have engaged in retrofitting and to feel informed about energy issues (see Table 5.8). We found no differences between program participants and nonparticipants as to race or attitudes toward the utility or toward conservation.

Program participants in Tarboro, particularly participants in air conditioner and in both water heater and air conditioner programs, fit expectations about program participants as innovators. (Water heater participants are somewhat less affluent than other participants, probably because they are not likely to have central air conditioners.)

Lumbee River EMC

In the area served by the Lumbee River EMC, participants with both water heaters and air conditioners controlled and those with only their air conditioners controlled were better educated, more likely to be couples, and less likely to believe that it is important to conserve, compared with program nonparticipants and water heater-only participants. Air conditioner-only participants were more likely than others to have higher incomes and to have engaged in retrofitting for conservation. Water heater program participants were more frequently nonwhite than others were. No significant differences between program participants and nonparticipants were found for ownership, housing structure

TABLE 5.8

ASSOCIATION OF CONSUMER CHARACTERISTICS WITH PARTICIPATION DECISIONS RELATED TO TARBORO LOAD CONTROL PROGRAMS
(percent of households)

Consumer Characteristic	Nonparticipation	Load Control Programs: Water Heater	Air Conditioner	Water and Air Conditioner
Demographic Characteristics				
Education				
High school or less	66*	61	41	42
Some college	17	19	21	19
College graduate	11	12	21	28
Post graduate	5	8	16	10
Income				
Under $10,000	24*	31	6	6
$10,000-$24,999	56	51	43	48
$25,000 or more	20	18	51	46
Race				
White	81	72	94	92
Nonwhite	19	28	6	8
Household Type				
One person	17*	32	14	20
Couple	29	17	29	19
With children	38	31	50	50
Other	16	20	7	11
Housing Characteristics				
Tenure				
Own	73*	68	97	75
Rent	27	32	3	25
Housing Type				
Single family	80*	77	98	74
Other	20	23	2	26
Year Built				
Before 1960	58*	67	32	32
1960-1969	16	20	36	11
1970	8	12	19	26
1975 or later	18	1	13	31

TABLE 5.8 continued

Consumer Characteristic	Nonparticipation	Load Control Programs: Water Heater	Air Conditioner	Water and Air Conditioner
Size				
800-1,500 sq. ft.	62	55	33	45
1,500-1,999 sq. ft.	21	26	27	25
2,000 or more sq. ft.	17	19	40	30
Reports Difficulty Paying Electric Bill				
Yes	61*	58	37	45
No	39	42	63	55
Attitudes Toward Utility				
Household feels utility is doing all it can to hold down cost	17	16	12	14
Household feels it pays too much for electricity	90	86	82	80
Conservation Attitude				
Extremely important to conserve	70	78	68	71
Don't mind personal discomfort to conserve	56	62	57	56
Conservation Behavior				
Turn off air conditioner	97	96	94	87
Turn down heat	98	98	98	94
Retrofitting				
Insulation	26	33	34	24
Storm windows	36	51	46	42
Caulking and weather-stripping	30	38	44	35
Water heater insulation	15	21	16	15

TABLE 5.8 continued

Consumer Characteristic	Nonparticipation	Load Control Programs: Water Heater	Air Conditioner	Water and Air Conditioner
Retrofitting index (added 2 or more items)[a]	47*	72	68	58
Energy Conservation and Load Management Knowledge				
Household feels well informed about how to conserve	63*	71	85	87
Energy conservation opinion leader	17	17	17	26
Know utility costs are high during peak period	69	74	72	68
Knows load management levels peaks	60*	66	81	79

*Chi-square significant at .05 level.

[a]See Table 5.6.

type, age or size of house, reported difficulty paying the electric bill, attitudes toward the utility, several measures of retrofitting, and knowledge of load management issues (see first panel of Table 5.9).

Although program participants and nonparticipants did not differ on a number of characteristics, participants fit the model of a new product innovator. With the exception of water heater-only participants, they tended to be more affluent and more likely to engage in some retrofitting. However, because marketing was at a late stage, we found fewer differences between program participants and nonparticipants for this utility than for the investor-owned utilities. To encourage adoption among nonparticipants, the utility should direct marketing efforts toward a less well educated and less affluent population, toward nonwhite renters, and toward those who live in older and smaller homes.

Four County

Water heater program participants served by the Four County EMC were distinguished from program nonparticipants and participants in the utility's joint water heater/air conditioner program in that they were less well-educated, had lower incomes, were more likely to be nonwhite, were more likely to live in older and smaller homes, and were more supportive of the utility. Water heater/air conditioner program participants were more likely to have engaged in some retrofitting, while nonparticipants were more likely to believe they paid too much for electricity. We found no differences among program participants and nonparticipants as to household type, ownership status, housing type, reported difficulty paying the electric bill, and conservation attitudes and behavior (see second panel of Table 5.9).

Although the characteristics we found for participants in the water heater/air conditioner control program fit those of the model program innovator, those of water heater participants do not. They are less affluent and live in older and smaller homes than nonparticipants. This utility, however, has gone far beyond the stage of market introduction at which such comparisons are meaningful. Efforts to isolate early program participants by asking households to specify the month and year they enrolled failed; most households could not remember that information. Thus, the Four County case provides an interesting description of participants in a mature program, but is not much help in isolating the characteristics of program innovators.

CONSUMER CHARACTERISTICS, PROGRAM CHARACTERISTICS, AND PROGRAM MARKETING

According to the model of program adoption guiding this study and presented in Figure 5.1, three sets of factors are important in determin-

TABLE 5.9

ASSOCIATION OF CONSUMER CHARACTERISTICS WITH PARTICIPATION DECISIONS FOR LUMBEE RIVER EMC AND FOUR COUNTY EMC LOAD CONTROL PROGRAMS
(percent of households)

Consumer Characteristics	Lumbee River EMC				Four County EMC		
		Load Control Programs				Load Control Programs	
	Nonparticipation	Water Heater	Air Conditioner	Water and Air	Nonparticipation	Water Heater	Water and Air
Demographic Characteristics							
Education							
High school or less	66*	61	41	42	67*	87	58
Some college	17	19	21	19	19	11	29
College graduate	11	12	21	28	6	2	12
Post graduate	5	8	16	10	8	0	2
Income							
Under $10,000	18*	20	3	10	21*	58	11
$10,000-$24,999	82	57	66	71	67	42	71
$25,000 or more	0	23	31	19	12	0	18
Race							
White	44*	60	84	79	80*	65	87
Nonwhite	56	40	16	21	20	35	14
Household Type							
One person	3*	15	3	3	9	18	10
Couple	12	17	23	23	38	34	19
With children	58	63	60	61	42	36	62
Other	27	6	13	13	11	11	10
Tenure							
Own	86	92	97	95	91	93	100
Rent	14	8	3	5	9	7	0
Housing Type							
Single family	91	98	98	98	97	98	100
Other	9	2	2	2	3	2	0
Year Built							
Before 1960	25	18	8	8	47*	63	19
1960-1969	25	31	23	23	11	12	21
1970-1974	12	20	15	16	15	10	24
1975 or later	38	31	53	52	27	15	36

TABLE 5.9 continued

Consumer Characteristics	Lumbee River EMC: Nonparticipation	Lumbee River EMC Load Control Programs: Water Heater	Lumbee River EMC Load Control Programs: Air Conditioner	Lumbee River EMC Load Control Programs: Water and Air	Four County EMC: Nonparticipation	Four County EMC Load Control Programs: Water Heater	Four County EMC Load Control Programs: Water and Air
Size							
800-1,499 sq. ft.	67	51	49	50	65	73	37
1,500-1,999 sq. ft.	17	30	32	38	22	13	41
2,000 or more sq. ft.	17	19	18	12	12	13	22
Reports Difficulty Paying Electric Bill							
Yes	76	64	60	59	70	76	60
No	24	36	40	41	30	24	40
Attitudes Toward Utility							
Household feels utility is doing all it can to hold down costs	15	19	17	23	15*	35	26
Household feels it pays too much for electricity	83	83	86	89	87*	84	73
Conservation Attitudes							
Extremely important to conserve	86*	83	67	66	76	87	74
Don't mind personal discomfort to conserve	66	61	61	66	46	56	60
Conservation Behavior							
Turn off air conditioner	89	94	93	95	96	92	85
Turn down heat	93	98	93	89	94	97	92
Retrofitting							
Insulation	23	33	25	19	35	33	20
Storm windows	37	48	45	38	42	37	39
Caulking and weatherstripping	43	30	23	30	42	26	32

TABLE 5.9 continued

Consumer Characteristics	Lumbee River EMC Nonparticipation	Lumbee River EMC Load Control Programs: Water Heater	Air Conditioner	Water and Air	Four County EMC Nonparticipation	Four County EMC Load Control Programs: Water Heater	Water and Air
Water heater insulation	23	11	17	13	15	20	8
Retrofitting index (add 2 or more of items)[a]	60*	68	70	56	63	61	66
<u>Energy Conservation and Load Management Knowledge</u>							
Household feels well informed about how to conserve	66*	87	88	85	82	80	93
Energy conservation opinion leader	20	21	26	34	14	11	23
Household knows utility costs are high during peak periods	71	77	80	76	63	56	67
Household knows load management levels peaks	43	58	90	82	66	54*	82

*Chi-square significant at .05 level.

[a]See Table 5.6.

ing program participation: consumer characteristics; program characteristics, particularly monetary incentives; and program marketing, including the degree of marketing effort. We investigated the relative influence of these sets of factors by means of a logistic regression model[2] of program participation with data drawn from a combined sample of program participants and nonparticipants from the six utilities. Besides the three sets of factors, the length of time a utility's program had been in effect was included in the regressions; as will be noted below, this variable was found to be highly significant (as expected). Since Lumbee River already had achieved its targeted level of participation before the consumer survey and had not promoted the program since the target was achieved, the time period we selected for Lumbee program duration was the time between the month the program was initiated and the month program promotion ceased. Complete information on the construction of variables used in the logistic regression and the results of a stepwise logistic regression is presented in the appendix to this chapter. The substantive findings from this complex set of analyses are discussed here.

The analyses considered the effect of nine consumer characteristics on program participation: home ownership, length of residence, size of the housing unit, use of electricity, household income, size of the monthly electricity bill, level of education, and race. We considered two monetary incentive variables: the size of the water heater program incentive and the ratio of the size of the incentive to the consumer's electricity bill. Four marketing effort variables were considered: how much advertising was used, degree of personal contact used, ease of enrolling, and size of the incentive for enrolling in the program. The length of time the program had been marketed was included as a final explanatory variable.

Of all the factors considered, the most important variable explaining the level of program participation was the length of time the program had been marketed. Program duration is also related to degree of personal contact, ease in joining, and size of monetary incentives.

The size of the monetary incentives also was a significant predictor of program participation, particularly for higher-income households. This finding suggests that utilities could boost program participation by increasing the size of the monetary incentive, and the gains are likely to be greater for higher-income households (who are also likely to use more electricity).

Program participation was influenced by home ownership and the presence of electrically-powered space air conditioning units. Having electrically-powered central air conditioning and electric ranges and owning the home made people more likely to participate in the program.

These analyses illustrate that consumer characteristics, program characteristics, and program marketing are all important considerations in meeting utility objectives for the level of participation in load management programs. Consumers respond to economic incentives to participate, but homeowners and users of more electricity are particularly likely to respond. The analyses also indicate that program marketing must be geared to where a given load management program is in the process of introduction and marketing. The type of consumer who is attracted to load management programs at the initial stage of program introduction is typically more affluent and better educated than the consumer who decides to participate at later stages. Marketing strategies need to be adaptable to those differences over time.

SUMMARY AND CONCLUSIONS

Analyses presented in this chapter indicate that consumer characteristics, program characteristics, and program marketing are associated with consumer participation in load management programs. Analyses of consumer characteristics indicated that household income, homeownership, size of the housing unit, living in a single-family house, and energy conservation-mindedness were positively correlated with program participation. Not associated were education, race, age of the structure, and size of the electric bill. These results were substantiated in analyses that looked not only at consumer characteristics but also program characteristics and program marketing. Consumer characteristics such as homeownership, size of the housing unit, and income were significant predictors of participation. In addition, program characteristics such as size of the incentive and marketing factors such as program duration, which was associated with the type of marketing among the utilities studied, were found to be important.

Although these factors are significant predictors of program participants among all the utilities and types of programs studied, analyses for specific utilities indicated that each utility should design program plans that reflect the characteristics of eligible populations and address specific stages of the marketing effort as the program matures. In addition, different utilities may have different market penetration objectives and, therefore, may have different needs.

The variations in program duration and penetration rates observed among the six utilities suggest that different consumer populations are attracted to various load management programs, at various stages of market maturity. Early program participants may closely approximate the image of the innovator as seen in studies of the investor-owned utilities. As programs gain more and more participants, they attract a broader base of participants, as seen in studies of the electric membership corporations. These findings have important implications for targeting marketing efforts at various stages of market maturity. As programs are introduced, marketing should be directed toward the more affluent homeowners. As programs mature, more intensive efforts directed toward broader segments of the population are required to continue progress toward utility goals for market penetration.

NOTES

1. The percentages aware and interested are the obverses of the percentages of the sample who indicated they had not heard of load control or time-of-day and of those who were not interested in either. Due to the nature of the construction of these measures, they must be interpreted with caution.

2. A dichotomous response variable (Y), such as program participation, poses practical and theoretical problems for the analyst. Both theoretical and empirical considerations suggest that when the dependent variable is dichotomous, the shape of the response functions is often curvilinear. Logistic regression addresses this problem by estimating the effect of a constant change in the independent variables under the assumption that they produce a constant relative change in the probability. This is done by making log y depend linearly on X. The ratio (y/(1−y) is called the odds ratio and its log is called log odds or Logit. The relation is estimable by the use of maximum likelihood (MLE) techniques.

The LOGIST procedure in SAS was used to estimate the parameters of the Logit model. This procedure fits the logistic multiple regression model to a single binary (0 or 1) dependent variable. The procedure can fit one model, or use a backward elimination procedure or a stepwise technique based on a strategy which requires very few calculations, to determine the "best" variable to be added to the model in any given step. The LOGIST procedure, developed by Frank Harrell, is described in detail in *SAS Supplementary Library Users' Guide.* 1980 Edition. SAS Institute Incorporated: Cary, North Carolina, pp. 83–102.

APPENDIX

This appendix describes the construction of variables and analyses conducted for the examination of the relative influence of consumer characteristics, program characteristics, and program marketing on participation in load management programs.

Construction of Variables

The explanatory variables used in the Logit analysis of participation were developed from the survey responses and load management program data. Nine customer characteristic variables were developed. Two monetary incentive variables were constructed from the survey responses and from the customer bill discounts offered for load management program participation. Four marketing effort variables were constructed from data on load management program characteristics. The program time duration variable introduced earlier was defined as the number of months from program initiation to either the end of program promotion (Lumbee River) or the date of the survey (all other utilities).

The *customer characteristics* variables that were created included the following:

1. A dichotomous (0,1) variable labeled "OWN" that denotes whether the customer rents or owns his residence.

2. A continuous variable labeled "MOVE" that denotes the year the customer began to occupy his residence.
3. A continuous variable labeled "FEET" that denotes the number of square feet of floor space in the residence.
4. A dichotomous (0,1) variable labeled "CENTRAL" that denotes whether the customer has a central air conditioning system or a heat pump.
5. A dichotomous (0,1) variable labeled "STOVE" that denotes whether the customer has an electric stove.
6. A multichotomous variable (with seven possible values) labeled "INCOME" that denotes the midpoints of the income ranges listed on the questionnaire (see Appendix A).
7. A multichotomous variable (with three possible values) labeled "JUNE BILL" that denotes the midpoints of the ranges for the customer's June (1982) bill that were listed on the questionnaire. This variable did not attain statistical significance and was dropped from the analysis.
8. A multichotomous (with 18 possible values) variable labeled "YOUED" which measures the highest grade completed by head of household. This variable was not statistically significant and was not included in the analysis.
9. A dichotomous (0,1) variable labeled "FURNACE" that denotes whether the customer has an electric furnace. This variable was not statistically significant and was not included in the analysis.

The *monetary incentive* variables created include the following:

1. A multichotomous (with six possible values) variable labeled "WH-INC" that denotes the amount of water heater program incentive (monthly bill discount) offered by the utility that was effective immediately prior to the survey.*
2. A ratio variable labeled "WH-INC/JUNE BILL" that denotes the ratio of the water heater program incentive to the customer's June bill range midpoint. This variable did not attain statistical significance and was dropped from the analysis.

The monetary incentive (monthly bill discount) for participation in water heater load control programs is summarized in Table 5A.1.

---

* A problem arises in interpreting the effect that financial incentives paid to customers had on participation and nonparticipation in water heater programs. For each utility these values had changed during the time the program had been in effect. Although the survey attempted to determine the month respondents enrolled, few could remember this information. Nevertheless, the monetary incentive changes were not great, amounting to increases between $1 and $2 per month, but they may have caused us to assign an incorrect coefficient to the variable WH-INC. As the incentive actually has been overstated in the model, the resulting coefficient is too low and represents a conservative estimate. Therefore, one would expect a more accurate coefficient to actually be both higher and more significant.

The *marketing effort* variables that were created include the following:

1. A multichotomous variable (with three possible values) labeled "MEDIA" that denotes the degree to which advertising was relied on to generate water heater program awareness.
2. A multichotomous variable (with three possible values) labeled "CONTACT" that denotes the extent of customer contact involved in trying to enroll customers in the water heater program.
3. A multichotomous variable (with three possible values) labeled "EASE" that denotes the degree of difficulty inherent in enrollment procedures and contract terms and conditions (in terms of the time investment a customer must make before enrolling in the program and the minimum length of time he must stay in the program without penalty).
4. A multichotomous variable (with three possible values) labeled "PAYMENTS" that denotes the "upfront" incentive (i.e., VEPCO's payment of $27, the annual sum of monthly bill discounts, at the beginning of each year of participation) or disincentive (i.e., Duke's installation charge of $25) associated with program participation, where customers of those utilities without such an incentive or disincentive were assigned a code of of zero for this variable.

A zero-order correlation matrix was estimated to identify variables that are highly correlated and that could cause statistical problems if employed as regressors in the same regression. Several important findings emerged from a review of this matrix. Most notably, several of the marketing variables were highly correlated, suggesting that their effects cannot be estimated separately with a high degree of confidence within the same regression. The PAYMENTS variable was highly correlated with EASE and DURATION, indicating that more liberal "upfront" incentives are associated with greater customer ease of getting on and off the program and with programs that have been promoted for a longer period of time. The CONTACT variable was highly correlated with EASE and DURATION, indicating heavier customer contact by the utilities is associated with those programs that are easier for customers to get on and off and those that have been promoted for a longer period of time. CONTACT was also highly correlated with WH-INC, indicating heavier customer contact is associated with those offering higher monthly bill discounts for participation in the water heater control program. EASE and DURATION are particularly highly correlated, indicating those programs that are easiest to sign up for are those that have been in existence the longest. Additionally, several of the marketing variables show a statistically significant relationship to each other but not necessarily a positive correlation. For example, the association between MEDIA and PAYMENTS is statistically significant but not positive. Therefore, programs with heavy advertising emphasis are not

TABLE 5A.1

KEY FEATURES OF UTILITY RATES FOR LOAD CONTROL

Utility	Install Charge	Monthly Customer Charge	Monthly[a] Bill Discount	Minimum Contract Requirement	Penalty for Early Cancellation	Eligibility Criteria
Duke Power						
Water heater	35[b]	$5.40[c]	$ 2.00[d]	2 years[e]	$25.00	Available to residential service customers including those on special energy conservation time-of-day rates.
Air conditioner	35	5.40	3.25 (for 4 mos.)	2 years	25.00	Water heater is an automatic insulated type of not less than 30 gallon capacity (15 gallon capacity for residential service customers).
Water heater & air conditioner	50	5.40	5.25			
CP&L						Residential service customer.
Water heater	0	6.75	2.00	NA	NA	Insulated storage type water heater not less than 40 gallons with a wattage rating less than 5,500 watts.
VEPCO						Residential service customer.
Water heater	0	6.64/mo	$28 advanced credit[f]	NA	NA	Type, design, size, and method of operation of water heater is subject to company approval.
Tarboro						Residential service customers.
Water heater	0	6.64/mo	5.00	NA	NA	
Air conditioner	0	6.64/mo.	5.00 (for 4 mos.)			
Water heater & air conditioner	0	6.64/mo	10.00	NA	NA	

Utility	Install Charge	Monthly Customer Charge	Monthly[a] Bill Discount	Minimum Contract Requirement	Penalty for Early Cancel-lation	Eligibility Criteria
Four County						Residential service customers.
Water heater	0	4.75	$ 2.00			
Water heater & air conditioner	0	4.75	5.75 (over 4 mos.)	NA	NA	
Lumbee River						Residential service customers.
Water heater	0	6.50	1.25	NA	NA	
Air conditioner	0	6.50	1.25	NA	NA	
Water heater & air conditioner	0	6.50	2.50	NA	NA	

[a]The figures in this column indicate the monthly bill discounts at the time of the survey. These have changed over time for all utilities.

[b]If no additional wiring is needed, there is no charge.

[c]Accept time-of-day customers whose customer charge is $14.40 per month.

[d]Minimum bill is at least the customer charge and the credit cannot exceed 35% of monthly bill or customer charge.

[e]Customer may terminate service after 1-year without a charge.

[f]If a water heater insulation wrapper is installed, the advanced credit is $10. After the first year regular billing credits of $2.34 per month are made.

associated with programs offering large up-front payments. Similarly, programs that used personal contacts in marketing tended not to use advertising or large up-front payments. Advertising was negatively associated with program duration. The newer load management programs were those that were promoted heavily through the mass media. The statistically significant and frequently large correlations between these variables resulted in their not being employed together, either as a group or two at a time, in the Logit model.

Key Results

Several model specifications were formulated in terms of alternative combinations of variables. These models typically involved one or more variables from each of the three categories of variables described in the previous section, while avoiding the use of highly correlated variables in the same model specification.

The next step was to estimate the Logit model using a stepwise procedure. The procedure introduces variables into the model in an ordered sequence; the order is such that the independent variable that explains the largest amount of variation in the dependent variable is introduced first, the one that explains the largest amount of variation in the dependent variable given that the first independent variable has already been introduced is entered next, and so forth. The procedure terminates when the incremental contribution (in terms of explaining variance in the dependent variable) of the next independent variable is not statistically significant at the 5 percent level. This procedure yields the model specification that provides the best fit to the data and includes only those variables that contribute to this fit in a statistically significant manner.

A major problem arose in attempts to include the variable INCOME in any of the specifications. Inclusion of this variable had the effect of reducing the sample size, because of higher nonresponse to this question than to others in the survey questionnaire. The regression procedure removed the entire customer record when this response was missing; no attempt was made to impute values for INCOME in these cases so as to retain the customer record and thus increase the number of observations used to estimate model parameters and goodness of fit. To circumvent the problem with INCOME, the survey data were stratified by income classes as follows: (1) Lower income = less than $1,000 per month; (2) Moderate income = between $1,100 and $1,900 per month; and (3) Higher income = more than $1,900 per month. This stratification was based on the seven response categories listed on the survey questionnaire, grouped so that each stratum has about one-third of the respondents.

Stepwise logistic regression was performed for each stratification and for all customers in the sample with usable data for the regressions

TABLE 5A.2

RESULTS FROM STEPWISE LOGISTIC REGRESSION

Variable	Income Group			Overall
	Higher Income	Moderate Income	Lower Income	
INTERCEPT	-6.067[a] (24.09)[b]	-0.557[a] (0.26)[b]	-3.145[a] (24.03)[b]	-6.215[a] (144.55)[b]
DURATION (months since program introduction)	0.068 (27.93)	0.057 (33.98)	0.057 (18.59)	0.067 (159.81)
WH_INC ($ incentive for participation)	0.409 (12.21)			0.355 (53.81)
STOVE (electric stove)	1.77 (5.05)			0.620 (7.83)
FEET (size of dwelling)	0.530 (4.26)			0.245 (4.83)
CENTRAL (air conditioning)		1.054 (9.92)	0.383 (5.49)	1.043 (40.97)
MOVE (year moved to current residence)		-0.034 (5.38)		
OWN (homeownership)				1.040
Observations in regression	209	232	142	1,105

[a]Regression coefficient estimating direction and magnitude of the variable on participation and nonparticipation in water heater load control programs.

[b]The chi-square statistic. The model was created specifying a variable must be significant at a 0.05 level to be included in the model. Therefore, all variables above are significant at a 5 percent level. The greater the value of the chi-square statistic the higher statistical significance of the estimate above it.

with the requirement that any variable added to the model must be statistically significant at the 5 percent level. The results are summarized in Table 5A.2. The last column of the table indicates the independent variables that were included by the STEPWISE procedure to explain participation and nonparticipation in load management programs for the entire set of usable observations. The first three columns indicate which of these variables were significant by income group stratifications. The last column is for all pooled income groups with usable data.

Each cell in this table has two entries. The first entry is the estimate of the direction and magnitude of effect of the regressor on participation and nonparticipation. The second entry (in parentheses) is the χ^2 statistic associated with the estimate immediately above it. All parameter estimates in the table are significant at the 5 percent level and all of the regressions indicate reasonable goodness of fit. They were formulated requiring significance at the 5 percent level.

These results indicate that for all income groups pooled, all the regressors listed, except MOVE, contribute positively to participation in water heater load control programs. The negative association between the year households moved to their current residence and participation is not unexpected since these occupants have had less time to enroll in a program and frequent movers are less likely to participate in programs of this type.

The single most important explanatory variable in the table is program duration, a result that holds across all income groups. However, DURATION was highly associated with the variables CONTACT, EASE, and PAYMENTS, so that the regression coefficient estimated for DURATION also includes the effect on participation of marketing strategies such as amount of personal contact, ease of enrolling in the program, and payment made to the consumer at the outset of his decision to participate.

The influence of a monetary incentive (the WH-INC variable) on participation was also consistently significant in these regressions, despite its relatively small overall range of variation. This incentive was estimated as having a positive effect on the decision to participate in a water heater program. When the regressions were run on data partitions by income group, the only income group for which the monetary incentive was statistically significant was the high-income group; this may indicate that high-income customers are more responsive to incentives, or simply that there was too little variation in this incentive and too few observations prevailed in the usable data to detect such an effect for lower-income customers. Had the monetary incentives been larger, they may have shown up as being even more important.

The question "How large would your monthly credit have to be to make it worth your while to take part in the water heater control program?" was asked in the survey of all nonparticipants in load control and time-of-day programs. The responses of all nonparticipants (both exposed and unexposed) were examined. They indicated that 46 percent would be enticed to participate if up to $5.00 were offered, and an additional 21 percent would be enticed to participate if $10 monthly payments were offered. Fifteen percent indicated they would need no monthly dollar incentive to participate in the program and an additional 5 percent indicated they would participate if up to $2 per month were offered. Only 14 percent indicated no amount would be enough to induce them to participate. Table 5A.3 summarizes the cumulative percentages necessary to encourage these nonparticipants to participate in load management programs.

These results are even more pronounced across income groups. For the lower income groups, there were large increases in willingness to participate at the $5 and the $10 levels of monthly incentive. These

TABLE 5A.3

MONETARY INCENTIVES NEEDED TO ENCOURAGE NONPARTICIPANTS TO PARTICIPATE

Dollar Incentive to Participate	Cumulative Percent
$0	15
1	18
2	20
3	25
5	46
10	86
"No amount would be enough"	100

Note: Data are based on responses of nonparticipants in any local control or time-of-day program across all utilities.

increases became less pronounced as monthly household income increased. For example, 23 percent of respondents in the lowest income category indicated that $3 per month would be a sufficient incentive to participate, 48 percent would participate if the monthly incentive was $5, and 90 percent indicated willingness to participate at $10 a month. Of the group of respondents earning $729 a month, however, 40 percent indicated willingness to participate at a $3 incentive, 65 percent at $5, and 88 percent at $10. For each income group at least 20 percent indicated they would be willing to participate if offered up to $2 per month. The percentage indicating that no amount of money would induce them to take part was also relatively stable across income groups.

Examining the differences in significant variables that explain participation across income groups, it appears from these data that the presence of central air conditioning has a significant effect on participation, particularly for the moderate- and lower-income groups. The central air conditioning effect is probably present for high-income groups as well, but its effect may be rolled into that reported for the FEET variables. Additionally, the variable STOVE is indicated as having a positive effect on the decision to participate in load management programs in the higher income group. This variable in part may also be representing the tendency to participate in a program because of higher electricity use and STOVE and FEET together may be acting as a proxy for CENTRAL. It should also be noted that the correlation analysis that was used to help determine which variables should not be included in the same regression was conducted at the aggregate (pooled) level, and not by specific income group. Thus, problems of specification and interdependence among variables are not likely to be major difficulties in the aggregate (pooled) estimates, but may be difficulties in the estimates for a single income group.

Finally, when examining Table 5A.2, the reader may question the absence of the MEDIA variable. This variable was included in several early model specifications. Although it often appeared significant in both the overall model and stratified income models, its associated coefficient was always negative. In general the coefficient was about -0.643 with an associated χ^2 of 27.85. Its effect seemed to increase as household income increased, from -0.686 to 1.068 with associated chi-squares of 8.15 and 11.95. This indicated programs with heavy advertising emphasis actually made consumers less interested in participating in load management. Several hypotheses were developed to explain these unusual results.

First, advertising increases program awareness, which is a necessary but not a sufficient condition for program enrollment. Therefore, mass media advertising alone may not stimulate participation; yet when coupled with ease of entry, advanced payments, and program duration, its effect probably would be felt. One utility, Lumbee River, had no mass media advertising program. Since rural electric cooperatives typically have more participation and support when instituting innovative programs, and since many Lumbee customers signed up for the program before any financial incentive was offered, it was thought that the utility's experience might be unduly influencing the analysis results. Subsequent models not including Lumbee did not substantiate that hypothesis, however, and the coefficient remained negative.

Another possible explanation is the relationship between MEDIA and CONTACT. MEDIA is strongly and negatively correlated with CONTACT. The MEDIA regressor was dropped from the model displayed in Table V-11 and CONTACT added in its place. It was hypothesized that CONTACT would be selected by the STEP-WISE regression procedure and that its sign would be positive. CONTACT was found not to be significant, however, in the subsequent regressions.

6

Marketing for Later Adopters

The first households to adopt new programs and products are critical to marketing management. The speed with which these innovating and early adopting consumers enroll in load management programs and their satisfaction with a program once they have joined have significant effects on the subsequent success of the program. But the job of the marketing manager does not stop with program introduction. Promotional efforts must continue over the life of a product or program if consumer participation goals are to be achieved. This chapter provides information that will help in the marketing of mature programs.

The focus is on nonparticipating households–households that have been given an opportunity to enroll in load management but are not taking part. As shown in Figure 6.1, this pool of nonparticipants includes households at various stages of the adoption process. Some are not taking part simply because they are unaware–they have not yet heard that the load management program exists. A second group is aware of the program, but the households decided they were not interested and did not seek additional information about program benefits and costs. A third group consists of households that are in the process of making a decision but have not made up their minds; a fourth group has reached a negative evaluation, concluding that program costs outweigh potential benefits. Households in all of these groups are candidates for future program participation.

Three aspects of program marketing are examined in this chapter. The chapter begins by comparing the characteristics of nonparticipants in six utility load management programs. Findings are reported separately for each utility but are grouped according to whether the utilities are investor-owned or municipal/electric membership corporations. The former had similar, relatively low rates of participation and appeared to be at the stage of market introduction. In the latter, participation rates exceeded 50 percent of those eligible to take part. This initial discussion highlights variation in the pool of nonparticipating households across utilities and market areas, and it reinforces the often-noted need to adapt promotional efforts to the characteristics of each geographic area served and each target market segment.

Besides tailoring marketing strategies to the stage of product diffusion, utilities must tailor their marketing strategies to the different

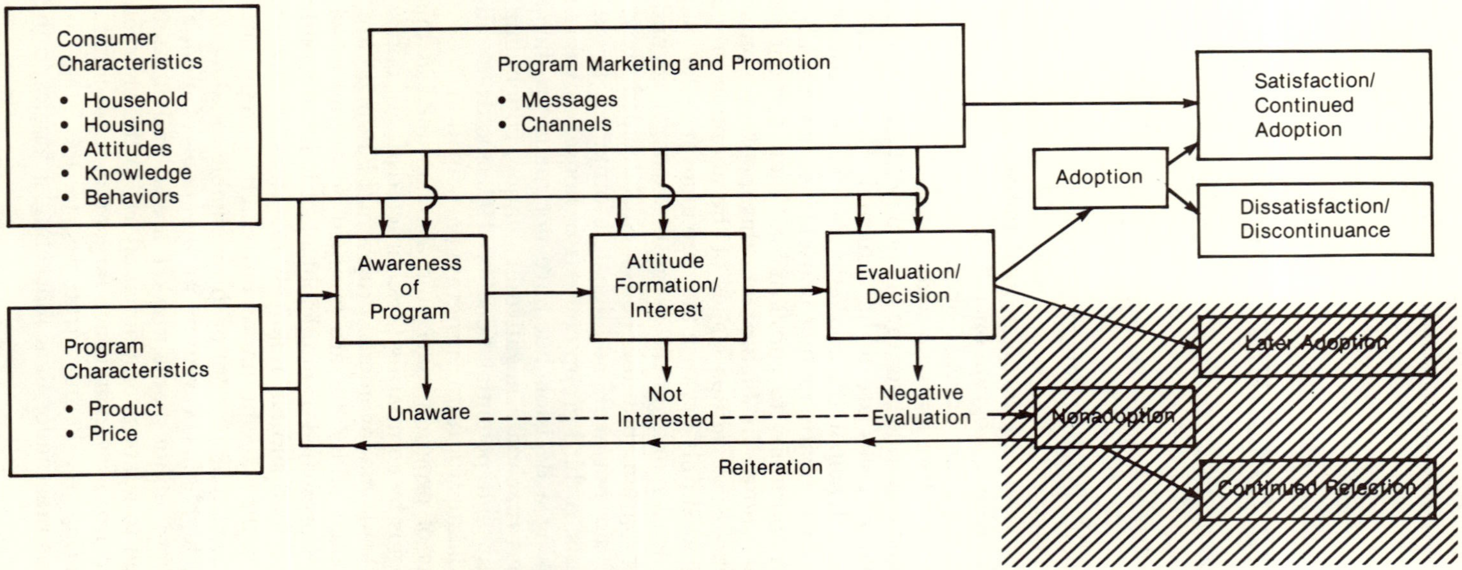

Figure 6.1 Program Adoption Model: Nonparticipating Households and Later Adoption

consumer populations that exist across market areas. Analyses presented in this chapter add to those presented in Chapter 5 to further help identify factors that are associated with program adoption. In this case, however, the focus is on later program adoption by initial nonparticipants. Analyses of nonparticipants' knowledge of program options and the channels of information they use to learn about load control, as well as a profile of "unaware" households, suggests targets for future awareness-building campaigns. Since marketing will be more effective if it is targeted at households with a higher-than-average propensity to take part, such households are identified in the third part of this chapter. In addition, motives for participation are identified and linked to specific household characteristics so that appeals can be formulated and directed to those households most likely to respond positively. The bottom line, of course, is a marketing program's success in converting households into active program participants. Analyses presented here will provide information to speed this process.

NONPARTICIPATING HOUSEHOLDS

Load control and time-of-day programs are not offered systemwide at one point in time. Typically, programs are introduced substation by substation as the necessary load management equipment is installed. This characteristic of program introduction complicates the task of program marketing. Rather than one systemwide diffusion process, marketing management must contend with a large number of diffusion processes, which may vary by the community in which a program has been introduced. If a typical nonparticipating household can be identified for different stages of the diffusion process, however, this information can be used by marketing management in each community at the same stage of program diffusion, thus simplifying the development and application of promotional material.

Previous consumer research (Robertson 1971; Rogers and Shoemaker 1971; Midgely 1977) suggests that as program diffusion advances in a market area, the pool of nonparticipants will be composed increasingly of older, less educated, and lower-income households who are less venturesome and, in the case of load management, less and less interested in and concerned about energy costs and energy conservation. The characteristics of nonparticipating households living in the six utility service areas studied provide a basis for testing whether these characteristics are constant across communities at the same stage of program diffusion. As reported in Chapter 3, the group of three investor-owned utilities had all achieved low to moderate rates of water heater load control program participation, so that between 74 percent and 82 percent of the target population had yet to enroll. The group of three municipal/electric membership corporation utilities, on the other hand, had achieved higher rates of participation, and the pool of nonparticipating households was a smaller proportion of the original target population, ranging from 12 percent to 46 percent. If the concept of a typical nonparticipant is to be a useful construct for marketing management, the characteristics of nonparticipating households in each group should be similar, but the groups should differ from each other, reflecting their positions at earlier and later stages of program diffusion.

The data summarized in Table 6.1 show clearly that nonparticipant characteristics in the six utility market areas do *not* meet the test for the construction of an ideal type or model nonparticipant. Differences in nonparticipant characteristics among utilities that were at a similar stage of program diffusion, such as CP&L and VEPCO, were as great as those between utilities at very different stages of diffusion, such as VEPCO and Tarboro Municipal. The message for utility marketing management is clear. Marketing programs must be founded on consumer data specific to each community or other area in which program diffusion is taking place rather than information obtained from other utilities or through aggregated systemwide consumer surveys.

PROGRAM AWARENESS AND KNOWLEDGE

By the time a load management program has been in place a year or so, most households are aware of its existence. Among the six electric utilities studied, the proportion of nonparticipating households that had not reached the awareness stage of the adoption process was rather low, ranging from 6 percent for the CP&L water heater load control program to 26 percent for the Lumbee River EMC water and air conditioning load control programs (see Figure 6.2). Although lack of awareness is obviously not the most important reason for nonparticipation, knowledge of a program's existence is a critical first step toward adoption.

Who should be the targets for an awareness building campaign? Since unaware households differ systematically from the aware but nonparticipating population, statistical tests can be used to construct a profile of target households. Tests were performed for two groups of nonparticipating utility customers: those served by investor-owned utilities and those served by municipal or electric membership corporation utilities. Where the same characteristics differentiate aware and unaware households in each group, there is strong evidence that these characteristics might be applicable in other similar market areas.

Five sets of factors were examined in relation to consumer awareness: household characteristics; housing characteristics; information sources used by households; households' use and conservation of electricity; and attitudes toward their electric utility and energy conservation in general. The results of statistical tests relating these factors to program awareness are summarized in Table 6.2, which also provides profiles of those groups that were most and least likely to be aware of utility load control programs.

TABLE 6.1

SELECTED CHARACTERISTICS OF NONPARTICIPATING HOUSEHOLDS
(percent of nonparticipating households)

Characteristic	Investor-owned Utilities			Municipal/EMC Utilities		
	Duke Power	CP&L	VEPCO	Tar-boro	Lumbee River	Four County
Nonparticipants as a Percent of Population	74	82	81	35	46	12
Household Characteristics						
Type of Household						
Single	11	16	11	16	2	9
Married couple	32	26	39	26	12	35
Married couple with children	49	37	35	42	53	46
Single head of household with children	7	6	8	12	16	6
Other	1	15	7	4	17	4
Age of Oldest Adult						
Under 35	32	34	10	26	31	28
35–64	57	56	65	53	55	52
65 or older	12	11	25	21	14	20
Education						
High school or less	33	15	47	65	50	73
Some college	21	20	30	18	34	17
College or more	46	65	23	17	16	13
Income						
Under $10,000	7	8	22	29	22	25
$10,000–24,999	62	49	59	52	78	67
$25,000 or more	31	43	19	18	0	9
Race						
White	90	91	94	78	40	82
Nonwhite	10	9	6	22	60	18
Persons at Home In Daytime						
No one	42	49	43	44	36	39
One or more	58	51	57	56	64	61

TABLE 6.1 continued

Characteristic	Investor-owned Utilities			Municipal/EMC Utilities		
	Duke Power	CP&L	VEPCO	Tarboro	Lumbee River	Four County
Housing Characteristics						
Type of Dwelling						
One-family	90	69	93	84	92	98
Multi-family	7	28	4	12	7	1
Mobile home	3	3	4	4	1	1
Tenure						
Own	94	67	85	71	80	90
Rent	6	33	15	29	20	10
Size						
Less than 1500 sq. ft.	39	45	65	61	69	67
1500–1999 sq. ft.	28	19	16	21	17	22
2000 or more sq. ft.	33	36	19	18	14	11
Energy Efficiency						
Low	27	57	42	55	65	42
Moderate	52	31	43	32	33	41
High	22	12	15	13	2	17
Electric Appliances						
Water heater	92	76	93	67	75	99
Central air	89	70	18	35	46	43
All electric[b]	34	29	18	13	27	30
Use of Electricity						
June 1982 Electric Bill						
Less than $50	30	40	28	34	24	24
$50–$99	57	46	62	47	61	48
$100 or more	13	14	10	19	14	28
Reports Difficulty Paying Electric Bill						
Yes	40	41	55	62	71	70
No	60	59	45	38	29	30
Feels Electric Utility is Doing Everything Possible to Hold Down Costs						
Yes	22	10	12	21	16	20
No	42	58	57	36	39	42
Not sure	36	32	31	43	45	38

TABLE 6.1 continued

	Investor-owned Utilities			Municipal/EMC Utilities		
Characteristic	Duke Power	CP&L	VEPCO	Tar-boro	Lumbee River	Four County
Conservation Actions/Attitudes						
Behavioral Index [c]						
Low	17	13	6	11	20	8
Moderate	61	70	67	68	50	54
High	22	17	27	20	30	38
Retrofitting Index [d]						
Low	40	38	19	42	31	21
Moderate-low	29	27	34	28	31	37
Moderate-high	21	20	19	26	15	15
High	10	15	10	13	7	7
Retrofitting Intentions Next Year						
Yes	34	27	27	20	40	31
No	66	73	73	80	60	59
Conservation Attitudes						
Conservation is extremely important	67	61	75	71	76	81
Everyone should conserve	66	60	72	63	64	68
Don't mind discomfort to reduce use of electricity	84	59	56	56	54	54

[a]Use of low, 0-5, moderate, 6-7, or high, 8-9, number of the following energy conservation measures: attic/ceiling fan; caulking or weather stripping; insulation attic, walls or floor; insulation around water heater; insulation around heating ducts or hot water pipes; storm windows, Thermopane glass, plastic sheeting; storm doors; water heater timer; wood stove.

[b]All electric includes households with electric water heater, electric furnace, electric central air conditioning and electric stove.

[c]Low, moderate, or high performance of following: use less water in baths and showers; turn off air conditioner to save money; turn off lights; turn down heat at night.

[d]Added low, moderate or high number of energy conservation measures listed in footnote "a" above to dwelling unit.

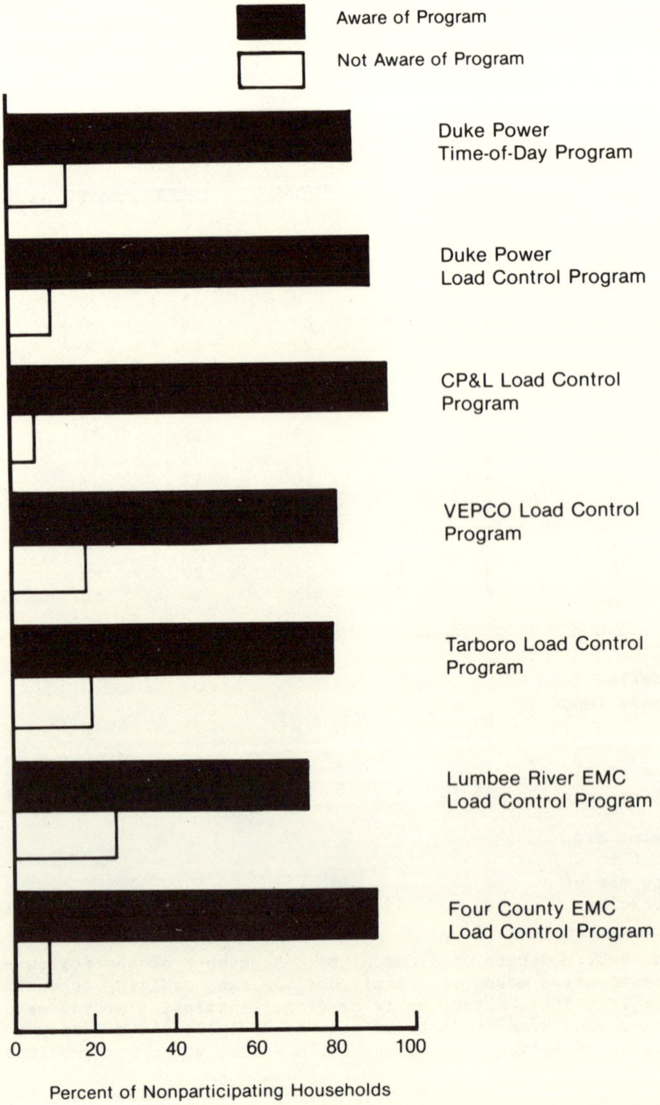

Figure 6.2 Program Awareness Among Nonparticipating Households

Not unexpectedly, the unaware population included households with low incomes (under $10,000 per year), low levels of educational attainment (less than high school), minorities, and households who were hesitant to try new products. They were more likely than the aware group to be renters and to live in energy-inefficient dwellings. In keeping with their economic status, they used a lower-than-average amount of elec-

TABLE 6.2

CORRELATES OF PROGRAM AWARENESS AMONG NONPARTICIPATING HOUSEHOLDS

	Gamma: Measure of Association[a]		Profile of Groups Most Likely to Be:	
Variable	IOU[b]	M/EMC[c]	Aware	Unaware
Household Characteristics				
1. Type of household	.10	.11	Married/w children	Single with children
2. Size of household	NS	.12	2-4	1.5 or more
3. Education	.19	.23	College grad	Less than high school
4. Income	.29	.58	$25,000+	Less than $10,000
5. Employment	.19	NS	Full-time	Seasonal employee
6. Race	.55	.71	White	Black/Indian
7. Age	NS	NS	--	--
8. Venturesomeness	.29	.21	High	Low
9. Conservation knowledge	.59	.53	Well informed	Not well informed
10. Consumer opinion leadership	NS	NS	--	--
Housing Characteristics				
1. Type of dwelling	NS	NS	--	--
2. Tenure	.38	.49	Own	Rent
3. Size of dwelling	.13	.35	2-3,000 sq. ft.	3,000 sq. ft.+
4. Energy efficiency	.16	.43	Very high	Low
5. Electric appliances:				
a. Furnace	NS	.31	Yes	No
b. Water heater	NS	NS	--	--
c. Central air	NS	.24	Yes	No
d. All electric	NS	NS	--	--
Information Sources Used				
1. Watch television	.30	.54	Yes	No
2. Listen to radio	NS	NS	--	--
3. Read newspaper	.55	.41	Yes	No
4. Read bill stuffers	.32	.26	Frequently	Never
Use/Conservation of Electricity				
1. Amount June electric bill	.24	.31	$100+	Less than $50
2. Reported difficulty paying bill	NS	.23	No	Not sure/Yes
3. Conservation behavior index[d]	NS	NS	--	--
4. Home retrofit index[e]	.28	NS	High	Low
5. Retrofit plans next year	NS	NS	--	--

TABLE 6.2 continued

Variable	Gamma: Measure of Association[a] IOU[b]	M/EMC[c]	Profile of Groups Most Likely to Be: Aware	Unaware
Attitudes				
1. Toward utility:				
a. Utility is trying to hold down prices charged for electricity	NS	NS	--	--
b. We pay too much for electricity	NS	NS	--	--
2. Toward conservation:				
a. Importance of conservation	NS	.39	Important	Not important
b. Ethic - Conserve even if can afford not to	NS	.17	Moderate	Low
c. Don't mind discomfort if can save on electricity costs	NS	NS	--	--

NS = Gamma less than .10 and/or chi-square significance level less than .10.

[a]Gamma is a nonparametric statistical measure of correlation between two variables, varying from -1(+1) indicating perfect negative (positive) monotonic association between two variables and zero, indicating the lack of any association.

[b]IOU = measures of association in this column were calculated for households served by investor-owned utilities (Duke, CP&L, VEPCO).

[c]M/EMC = measures of association in this column were calculated for households served by municipal or electric membership utilities (Tarboro, Lumbee River EMC, Four County EMC).

[d]See Table 6.1, footnote c for measures used to calculate index.

[e]See Table 6.1, footnote d for measures used to calculate index.

tricity but they did not feel well informed about how to conserve energy. This suggests that messages designed to inform households about load management programs could be included in more broadly framed efforts designed to enable this group to use energy more efficiently. In fact, given unaware households' low use of electricity and the lower payoff to utilities from controlling their appliances, this might be the only way in which an awareness building campaign could be justified as cost-effective after initial program introduction.

Since unaware households have less education, reaching them will require less complex messages conveyed with more personalized communication approaches than are used earlier when programs are first being introduced. Table 6.3 shows the proportions of aware nonparticipating households that learned about load control through various means. For five of the six utilities studied, information included in bill

TABLE 6.3

CHANNELS OF INFORMATION ABOUT LOAD CONTROL PROGRAMS: NONPARTICIPATING HOUSEHOLDS (percent of nonparticipating households)

Channel Household Learned About Load Control	Investor-owned Utilities			Municipal/EMC Utilities		
	Duke Power	CP&L	VEPCO	Tarboro	Lumbee River	Four County
Utility						
1. People at electric utility	50	21	43	35	35	58
2. Information with electric bill	51	71	62	29	53	61
Interpersonal Communication						
1. Friends or relative	24	25	21	25	20	34
2. People at work	15	13	17	18	10	14
Media						
1. Television	34	41	29	33	27	26
2. Radio	6	20	13	16	14	10
3. Newspaper	17	23	28	31	16	15

QUESTION: Have you read or heard about load control of water heaters and air conditioners from any of the following?

stuffers was the most frequently cited channel of information.[1] Other mass marketing channels, such as television and newspapers, also ranked among the most frequently cited sources. The information summarized in Table 6.2 suggests, however, that these channels are not likely to be effective in program marketing. After program introduction, the unaware households consist of those who are most likely not to watch television, not to read the newspaper, and to throw away bill stuffers before reading them. Therefore, personal selling may be required.

One goal of awareness building is to increase households' understanding of the peak load problem and the reasons utilities are asking people to enroll in load management programs. The assumption—which is given some limited support later in this chapter—is that households who know why a program is being offered and how it works will be more likely to take part. Previous studies have found that the public has limited knowledge of energy conservation measures in general (Beck et al. 1980) and at best only a superficial understanding of electric rates and utility problems (Task Force 10 1977; Hellman 1980; Van

Liere et al. 1982). Studies by Elrick & Lavidge (1977b) indicate, however, that when these matters are explained to utility customers, they are able to grasp the basic concepts involved in peak load conditions and load management.

The six utilities included in this study had attempted to inform their customers about load management fundamentals: when peak power use occurs, that it costs utilities more to generate electricity during peak than during off-peak periods, and that load management programs are designed to level out the peaks and valleys in the use of electricity. Their success in this regard is indicated by the proportions of nonparticipating households who knew this fundamental information:

	Electrical use is not highest betwen 10 am and 4 pm	Costs to generate electricity are higher during peak periods	Load management seeks to level peaks and valleys in electricity use
Duke Power	59%	62%	78%
CP&L	48	62	76
VEPCO	27	70	66
Tarboro Municipal	37	69	58
Lumbee River EMC	25	63	40
Four County EMC	39	66	67

Since those questions were worded as true-false items (50 percent of the utility customers could have answered correctly by flipping a coin), these data show that considerable misinformation still existed, particularly with regard to when peak household use of electricity occurs. Differences among utilities reflect differences in population characteristics and the extent of recent load management program advertising. In the case of the Lumbee River EMC, for example, the program had not been aggressively promoted for several months before this question was asked, which may explain why Lumbee River customer knowledge trailed that of other utilities' customers.

Even though many customers are still ignorant of load management fundamentals, utility efforts to increase customers' knowledge have had some success. This is illustrated by data from a recent survey of a similar population in Athens and Bristol, Tennessee, where load management programs had not yet been offered: fewer than half of the Tennessee households surveyed knew that utility costs were higher during peak periods or the purpose of load management (Van Liere et al. 1982, 25).

WILLINGNESS TO PARTICIPATE

If relatively few households did not take part because they hadn't heard of load management programs, what accounts for the rather sizable

TABLE 6.4

STAGE OF ADOPTION PROCESS: NONPARTICIPATING HOUSEHOLDS
(percent of households)

	Investor-Owned Utilities				Municipal/EMC Utilities		
	Time-of Day Program	Direct Load Control Programs					
Stage	Duke Power	Duke Power	CP&L	VEPCO	Tarboro	Lumbee River	Four County
Not aware of program	14	10	7	19	20	26	9
Aware but not interested in program	5	4	6	3	4	7	14
Interested but have not decided yet about participation	52	48	39	35	47	39	24
Decided not to participate	29	28	48	43	29	28	53

rates of nonparticipation, particularly among customers served by investor-owned utilities? In some cases, the programs simply did not arouse customers' interest. As shown in Table 6.4, however, this is unlikely to be a major cause of nonparticipation.[2] Most nonparticipating households had advanced through the adoption process to a point at which they were interested in a program, but were still making up their minds whether or not to participate. Less often, households had made a conscious decision not to take part. Reasons for negative evaluations principally included households' concern about the loss of control of their electric appliances. (See Chapter 5, Table 5.5.) Other and less important reasons were dissatisfaction with the size of the monthly credit utilities were offering, worry about potential discomfort, and the cost of having switching equipment installed. In the case of time-of-day rate programs, reasons for negative evaluation centered on households' perceptions that they could not save enough on their electricity bills to make participation worthwhile or could not change the times they used electricity.

Households who have consciously decided not to take part are poor prospects for later program adoption. When asked whether they would take part later, most reported they would continue to reject the load control program offered by their electric utility. On the other hand, households in earlier stages of the adoption process—those previously unaware of the programs, uninterested, or still making up their minds—were for the most part still willing to consider program participation.

TABLE 6.5

NONPARTICIPANTS'S WILLINGNESS TO TAKE PART IN LOAD MANAGEMENT PROGRAMS
(percent of nonparticipating households)

Indicator	Investor-Owned Utilities			Municipal/EMC Utilities		
	Duke Power	CP&L	VEPCO	Tarboro	Lumbee River	Four County
"Would you take part in a load control or time-of-day program in the future?"						
Yes - Load Control	43[a]	32[a]	28[a]	29[a]	32[a]	12[a]
Yes - Time of Day	37	42	31	29	26	19
Don't Know	39	42	52	53	52	55
No, Neither One	6	8	8	6	4	25

[a]Percentages add to more than 100 percent because some households are willing to participate in both load control and time-of-day programs.

This pool of potential program participants can be divided into two groups: those who had made a decision (they were predisposed to take part in or reject a load control or time-of-day program) and those who didn't know and needed more information to make up their minds. As shown in Table 6.5, the proportion of households in each group varied somewhat from one utility to another. In general, however, it appears that of every ten nonparticipating households, about four to five didn't know whether they would participate, three to four were predisposed to take part, and fewer than one in ten was predisposed to reject participation.[3] Thus, in each utility a large proportion of nonparticipants might be converted to active participants if an aggressive marketing effort was begun.

The most appropriate marketing strategy, discussed in greater detail in Chapter 9, will vary for households who have made up their minds about taking part and those who are still undecided (the "don't know" group). For those who are undecided about future participation, the program marketing task is to provide information about program benefits that is sufficiently compelling to move households toward adoption. Information about program benefits will be most effective if it is founded on the motives nonparticipants themselves cite as likely reasons they might take part in a load control or time-of-day rate program. Those motives for participation are examined in the next section of this chapter.

Different marketing strategies are needed for households who have already formed predispositions toward program participation. Those with negative predispositions constitute a small proportion of the nonparticipating population and, as discussed above, are not likely to change their minds. The best marketing strategy probably is to ignore this group. On the other hand, households who are willing to take part are prime targets. Marketing's task here is to reach the appropriate households and sign them up. Personal selling is probably most appropriate for this group. The profiles of nonparticipating households who were most likely to be positively predisposed to program participation, provided in the concluding section of this chapter, will help utilities focus personal sales campaigns on those households where the potential for success is greatest.

MOTIVATING UNDECIDED HOUSEHOLDS

Nonparticipating households were asked which potential program benefits would induce them to take part in a load control or time-of-day rate program in the future. Their responses, which are summarized in Figure 6.3, are similar to those discussed in the preceding chapter as motivations of current program participants. Saving money on the electric bill ranks first, followed by general savings accruing to all customers when the utility can cut its costs, reduced damage to the environment when fewer power plants have to be built, and suggestions from utility representatives and personal acquaintances.

Compared with the program participants examined in the preceding chapter, nonparticipants were much less likely to indicate they would take part for the general good of the utility and its customers ("we all save if our utility can cut costs"). This suggests that altruism is less likely to be a useful appeal in marketing mature programs than in promoting introduction, even though a sizable portion of the target population will still respond to appeals based on the general good.

Targeting Promotional Appeals

Promotional appeals based on motivations for participation will be more effective if they are targeted toward the households who are most likely to be swayed by each motive. For example, appeals based on saving money on the electric bill will have the greatest effect on the households who are most eager to save money, which tend to be those with children living at home, those living in multifamily housing, and those who do not feel well informed about how to cut electricity costs in the home. The less well-informed households may find load control a particularly attractive way of cutting their utility bills, since it does not require them to learn complex energy conservation techniques. (See Table 6.6 for a summary of suggestions for targeting specific appeals

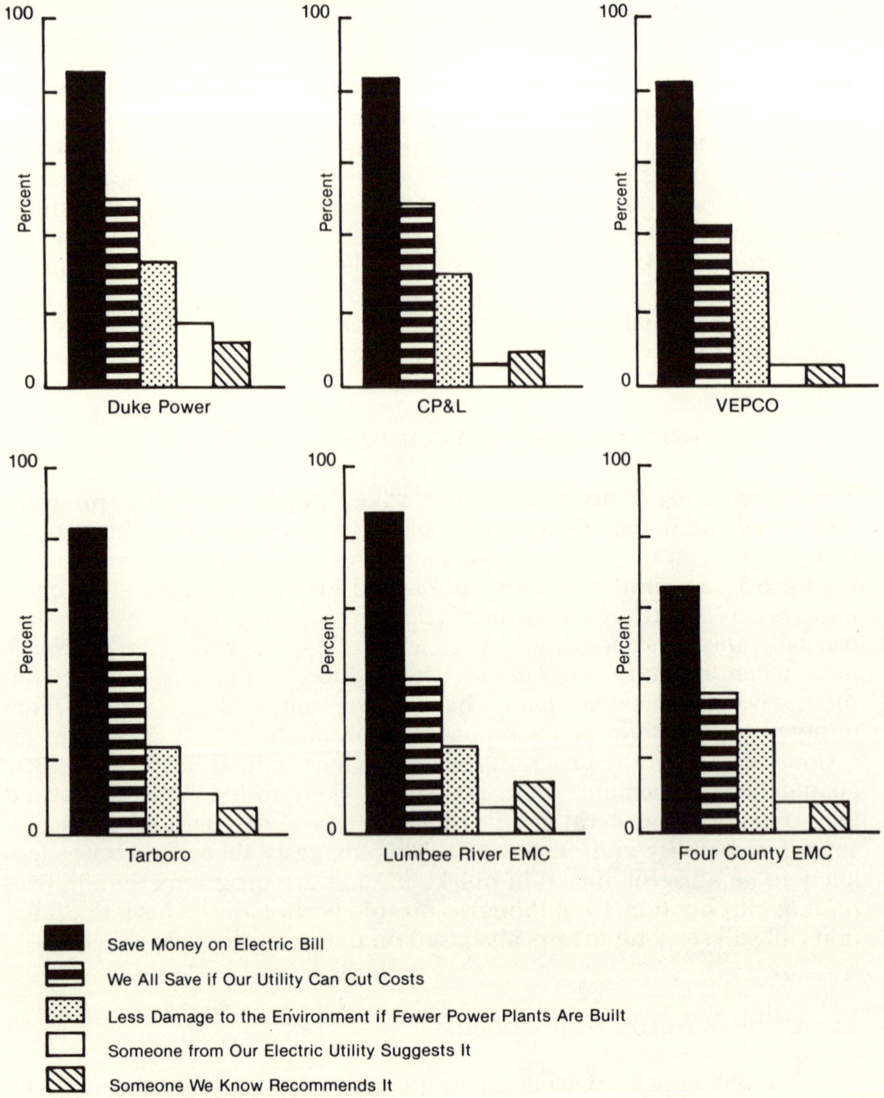

Figure 6.3 Potential Motives for Participation Cited by Nonparticipating Households

based on statistical correlations between household characteristics and households' indications of reasons they would take part.)

Indirect economic incentives based on savings accruing to utility customers as a whole are most likely to appeal to younger households, single-person households, and those living in multifamily housing.

Those households are likely to have lower incomes than the overall target population of nonparticipating households. They tend to be energy conservation opinion leaders—others come to them for advice about saving energy—and to be more knowledgeable about load management fundamentals than other utility customers are.

Appeals based on environmental benefits will be most effective if directed toward better-educated households, younger households, households living in multifamily housing, and those with lower to middle incomes. These households also tend to be energy conservers, both in attitude and in their personal behavior.

Personal recommendations from utility personal are most likely to affect the decisions of households who do not feel well informed about how to reduce their electricity bills. In addition, those most receptive to utility recommendations are more likely to be black, to have children living at home, to live in multifamily housing, and to rent.

Appeals based on savings to utility customers as a whole and authoritative recommendations from utility personnel can all be implemented without reference to program design characteristics—load control cycling strategies and the amount of the credit that can be offered for taking part. Appeals based on personal savings on electricity costs, on the other hand, have to be carefully coordinated with the actual level of savings that consumers want in order to take part and that the utility can afford, based on calculations of program net benefits.

How much did nonparticipating households want in order to take part? They wanted much more than utilities were offering. As noted in Chapter 3, incentives for participation in water heater load control programs averaged about $2 per month in North Carolina. When asked how large a monthly credit they would need to make it worth their while to take part in a water heater load control program, fewer than 20 percent of the households not participating in load management indicated $2 per month. About one-quarter said they would take part for $3 or $5 per month, while more than 40 percent wanted $10 per month. For about one in six, no amount of money would be enough to induce them to take part (or so they reported).

If the incentive schedules offered represent the net benefits utilities can achieve from water heater load control, i.e., incentives cannot be raised without imposing costs on nonparticipating customers or stockholders, then marketing appeals based on personal savings may have limited effectiveness in marketing mature programs, since households who do not initially enroll in load management programs may want higher payoffs than utilities can offer.[4] For example, only 20 percent or fewer of the nonparticipants were likely to respond to a promotional campaign featuring a $2 monthly credit on water heater bills. While personal savings was mentioned most often as a potential motive for participation, it probably should not be the sole, or even the dominant, theme of promotional campaigns aimed at later adopters unless utilities can increase the level of the incentives.

TABLE 6.6

TARGETING APPEALS FOR PARTICIPATION: PROFILES OF NONPARTICIPATING HOUSEHOLDS MOST RECEPTIVE TO DIFFERENT APPEALS

Appeal		Nonparticipating Households Most Receptive to Appeal[a]
Personal Savings on Electric Bill:	0	With children living at home
	0	Larger households
	0	More formal education
	0	Employed full time (one or more adults)
	0	Live in multifamily housing
	0	Listen to radio while traveling to work and on weekends
	0	Watch television
	0	Do not feel well informed about how to cut electricity costs in the home
	0	More knowledgeable about load management fundamentals
	0	Learned about program from television, not from utility personnel or bill stuffers
Savings Accruing to Utility Customers As A Whole:	0	Single persons/households composed of unrelated adults
	0	Younger (under age 35)
	0	Lower income
	0	White
	0	Energy conservation opinion leader
	0	Live in multifamily housing
	0	More knowledgeable about load management fundamentals
	0	Don't mind discomfort to save on electricity costs
	0	Listen to radio during evening hours and on weekends
	0	Do not read newspaper
	0	Learned about program from friends

Consumers who indicated they would take part at lower incentive levels tended to have lower electric bills than those who said they would require larger payoffs from participation. They also had stronger orientations toward energy conservation—they viewed conservation as important and something people should do regardless of their ability to pay for energy—and tended to believe the electric utilities were doing everything they could to hold down costs. Other types of households most likely to accept lower incentive levels included those with higher educational levels, blacks, energy conservation opinion leaders, younger households, households living in multifamily housing, and those who were renting.

TABLE 6.6 continued

Appeal		Nonparticipating Households Most Receptive to Appeal[a]
Environmental Protection:	0	Younger (under age 35)
	0	More formal education (college +)
	0	Lower or middle income (under $25,000)
	0	White
	0	Live in multifamily dwelling
	0	Live in all-electric dwelling
	0	Live in smaller dwelling
	0	Energy conserver--personal behavior and attitudes
	0	Reads newspaper
	0	Learned about program through mass media (television, radio)
Utility Recommendations:	0	With children living at home
	0	Younger (under age 35)
	0	Employed less than full time (part-time seasonal) or unemployed
	0	Black
	0	Live in multifamily dwelling
	0	Rent dwelling
	0	Newer dwelling
	0	Do not feel well informed about how to cut electricity costs in home
	0	Unaware of program
	0	Listen to radio at home in the evening

[a]Profiles are based on results of nonparametric statistical tests of associa-association between profile variables (see Table 6.1 and reasons households indicated would induce them to participate in a load control or time-of-day program. Criterion for inclusion are chi-square level of .10 or less and Gamma of .10 or more.

Using Appropriate Communication Channels

Utility customers with different motives for participation also differed in their attention to the various communication channels that might be employed in a promotional campaign. For example, households who seem most receptive to recommendations from the utility are those least likely to attend to newspapers and other mass media. If they are to be persuaded to take part in a load management program, personal selling will be required. Households who may be motivated by appeals based on personal savings on electricity bills are more likely than average to have learned about load management from television and less likely than average to have learned about these programs from bill stuffers or from utility personnel. Thus messages emphasizing personal savings might be most effective if delivered through the media.

The households who were most receptive to appeals based on generalized savings from more efficient utility operations tended to be energy conservation opinion leaders. In keeping with this trait, they were more likely than average to have learned about their utility's load management program from friends. Since opinion leaders are often highly sociable and tend to engage in interpersonal communication more than other households (Shoemaker 1981), appeals based on indirect savings (the good of the whole) will be most effective if used in advertising that simulates interpersonal communication. For example, personalized direct mailing might be employed to attract this group. In addition, direct appeals for participation through discussion groups, civic club talks, town meetings, and the like are also likely to be effective in reaching this group.

Finally, households who mentioned environmental protection as a motive were more likely than others to have learned about load management from television and radio. They were also somewhat more likely than average to read one or more daily newspapers, suggesting that appeals based on environmental benefits might be delivered effectively through the various mass media.

CONSUMERS LEANING TOWARD PARTICIPATION

While informing and persuading undecided households of the advantages of load management, program marketing must also capitalize on the fact that some households do not have to be persuaded. They already believe that participation is to their advantage and merely have to overcome inertia to join the rolls of program participants. As noted above and explained in greater detail in Chapter 9, personal selling is probably the most effective means of communicating with this group. Although personal selling is expensive, it may be cost-effective if households leaning toward adoption can be identified as targets for sales personnel. Table 6.7 summarizes the results of a series of statistical tests designed to pinpoint those nonparticipating households most likely to take part in load control programs.

In comparison with households who were predisposed to reject program participation, those who said they would take part in the future—both customers of investor-owned utilities and those served by municipal and electric membership corporation systems—tended to be working full time and to have graduated from college. They had a higher conservation ethic, believing that everyone should conserve regardless of his ability to pay for energy, and were less likely to mind personal

TABLE 6.7

TARGETING APPEALS FOR PARTICIPATION: PROFILES OF NONPARTICIPATING HOUSEHOLDS MOST AND LEAST LIKELY TO PARTICIPATE IN THE FUTURE

Variable	Gamma: Measure of Association[a] IOU[b]	M/EMC[c]	Profile of Groups Most Likely to Be:[d] Adopt	Reject
Household Characteristics				
1. Type of household	NS	NS	--	--
2. Number of persons at home during daytime	-.27	-.28	None	One or more
3. Education	.26	.28	College +[e]	Less than HS
4. Income	NS	NS	--	--
5. Employment	NS	.36	Full-time	Retired
6. Race	NS	NS	--	--
7. Age	NS	.25	Under age 65	Age 65 +
8. Venturesomeness	NS	.39	High	Low
9. Conservation knowledge	NS	NS	--	--
10. Conservation opinion leadership	.58	NS	Yes	No
Housing Characteristics				
1. Type of dwelling	NS	NS	--	--
2. Tenure	NS	NS	--	--
3. Size of dwelling	NS	NS	--	--
4. Energy efficiency	.30	NS	High	Low
5. Electric appliances:				
a. Furnace	NS	NS	--	--
b. Water heater	NS	NS	--	--
c. Central air	NS	NS	--	--
d. All electric	NS	NS	--	--
Information sources used				
1. Watch television	NS	NS	--	--
2. Listen to radio	.55	NS	Yes	No
3. Read newspaper	.60	NS	Yes	No
4. Read bill stuffers	NS	NS	--	--
Use/Conservation of Electricity				
1. Amount of June electric bill	NS	NS	--	--
2. Reported difficulty paying bill	NS	NS	--	--
3. Conservation behavior index[f]	.27	NS	High	Low
4. Home retrofit index[g]	NS	NS	--	--
5. Retrofit plans next year	NS	NS	--	--
Attitude				
1. Toward utility				
a. Utility is trying to hold down prices	NS	NS	--	--
b. We pay too much for electricity	.24	.23	Disagree	Agree/not sure

TABLE 6.7 continued

Variable	Gamma: Measure of Association[a] IOU[b]	M/EMC[c]	Profile of Groups Most Likely to Be:[d] Adopt	Reject
2. Toward Conservation:				
a. Importance of conservation	NS	NS	--	--
b. Ethic conserve even if can afford not to	.25	.29	High	Low
c. Don't mind discomfort if can save on electricity costs	.23	.36	Yes	No
Program Knowledge/Attitude				
1. Household knows peak period	NS	NS	--	--
2. Household knows costs higher during peak period	NS	NS	--	--
3. Household knows load management levels peaks	.30	.24	Yes	No
4. Channels of information about program:				
a. People at utility	NS	NS	--	--
b. Information on bill	NS	-.35	No	Yes
c. Friends	NS	NS	--	--
d. People at work	NS	NS	--	--
e. Television	.34	NS	Yes	No
f. Radio	NS	NS	--	--
g. Newspaper	NS	.35	Yes	No

discomfort if they could save on energy costs. Lists of people requesting energy audits and lists of those purchasing various conservation supplies and equipment might be used to target these energy conservation households for personal selling. This is particularly true among the investor-owned utilities, where those consumers more willing to take part in load control were also those who were likely to be living in energy-efficient homes and trying to conserve in their day-to-day activities.

In some cases the characteristics of customers leaning toward participation differ between investor-owned utilities and municipal and electric membership systems. These differences may reflect the fact that each group of utilities was at a different point in program diffusion or other unknown factors. Regardless of the reason, greater caution

TABLE 6.7 continued

Variable	Gamma: Measure of Association[a] IOU[b]	M/EMC[c]	Profile of Groups Most Likely to Be:[d] Adopt	Reject
5. Motives for participation:				
a. Personal conservation on electric bill	.77	.81	Yes	No
b. Indirect savings when utility cuts costs	.48	.42	Yes	No
c. Environmental protection	.36	NS	Yes	No
d. Utility recommendation	.50	.51	Yes	No
6. Size of Incentive desired	.37	.37	Lower	Higher, $10 or no amount enough

NS = Gamma less than .10 and/or chi-square significance level less than .10.
[a] Same as Table 6.2.
[b] Same as Table 6.2.
[c] Same as Table 6.2.
[d] Groups in the "deciding" stage of the adoption process only; excludes undecided households.
[e] M/EMC households = some college or more.
[f] See Table 6.1 footnote a.
[g] See Table 6.1 footnote d.

should be observed in using the following information than is needed when relationships transcend type of utility and stage of program diffusion.

Likely program participants among the investor-owned utilities, but not among the municipal and electric membership utilities, were households who already had taken various conservation actions. Not surprisingly, they tended to be energy conservation opinion leaders as well. Among households served by the municipal and electric membership corporation utilities, but not necessarily the investor-owned systems, nonparticipating customers who were willing to take part in load control tended not to be retired or over age 65 and tended to be more venturesome in trying new products. In this latter regard, lists of people who adopt new consumer products, such as personal computers or home video games, might indicate likely prospects for participation in a load control program.

SUMMARY

After the initial flurry of promotional activities that accompany program introduction, marketing management must devise a carefully thought-out strategy to maintain momentum and convert lagging households into program participants. Three marketing tasks are essential at this stage. First, the marketing program must continue to build program awareness. Second, undecided households must be convinced that program participation is in their self-interest. Third, households who are predisposed to take part in load management must be signed up. Each task required a different set of marketing measures that must be targeted at a different group of customers.

Accompanying program introduction with advertising was successful in alerting a large portion of the target populations that load control programs were available in the six utilities studied. Thus, lack of awareness is not a major reason for nonparticipation. Even so, some effort may be justified in reaching the uninformed, since awareness is a basic precondition for participation. After program introduction, the unaware population is weighted toward households with lower income and educational attainment, minorities, and people who are generally not well informed about ways of reducing household energy costs. They are likely to be most receptive to personalized communication approaches and messages that are less complex than those used earlier in advertising program introduction.

The main reasons for nonparticipation are that households are not yet convinced that program benefits outweigh potential costs and that they are bound by simple inertia. Very few households—usually fewer than 10 percent—will have consciously rejected participation. Those rejecting participation are unlikely to be willing to take part in the future and are best ignored.

Households who are undecided about participation constitute about 40 percent of the nonparticipating population, although the proportion varies somewhat from one utility to another. When asked to choose among various reasons that might lead them to participate in a load control or time-of-day program, they chose saving money on their electric bills by a large margin over other possible motives for participation. General savings that customers can realize when the utility can cut costs, less damage to the environment, suggestions from utility personnel, and recommendations from friends were also cited, in the order given, as potential reasons for participating in the future.

When asked how much money they would have to be able to save in order to take part in a water heater load control program, four out of five nonparticipating households reported monthly savings levels that exceeded the credits utilities typically offer as inducements. If personal savings is to be an effective appeal in marketing after program introduction, monetary incentive levels will need to be increased or steps taken to make the incentives seem larger, possibly by emphasizing annual rather than monthly savings.

Promotional messages will be most effective if they are formulated and delivered in a way most likely to appeal to households who will be motivated by the particular reason for participation. Analyses of consumer characteristics and participation motivations discussed in this chapter suggest a number of ways of framing messages for maximum impact. For example, since households motivated by personal savings are less likely than average to feel well informed about how to conserve on electricity costs, load control participation may be marketed as an easy way to conserve. Households most likely to be moved by savings to all utility customers from more efficient operations or environmental benefits tend to be more knowledgeable about load management fundamentals, to have more formal education, and to be energy conservation opinion leaders. They may be receptive to more complex messages than those used to promote personal savings and by messages that tie load management to, rather than separate it from, other energy conservation measures.

Links also were found between the benefits consumers mentioned as potential motives for participation and the communication channels they used, suggesting that certain appeals are most appropriate for certain channels of communication. For example, households likely to be moved by appeals based on personal savings were more likely than average to have learned about load management from television and less likely than average to have learned about the programs from bill stuffers and utility personnel. Thus, mass media advertising probably will work best for those motivated by financial savings. On the other hand, households most likely to be moved by appeals based on indirect savings from more efficient operations tend to be tied to interpersonal networks, so advertising that simulates interpersonal communication, such as personalized letters, might be the best approach to selling them on the merits of program participation. Finally, households most likely to be moved by recommendations from utility personnel were those least likely to attend to the mass media. Personalized approaches are also best for them.

In the case of customers who are already leaning toward taking part, the marketing task is to convert predispositions into participation. Personal selling is probably the most effective means of bringing this group into the fold. Although expensive, personal selling may be the best alternative if target households can be identified. In the concluding section of this chapter, consumers leaning toward participation in load control and time-of-day programs were identified to help pinpoint likely prospects.

NOTES

1. Other utilities have reported similar levels of program awareness and channels for learning about load management programs. For example, after introducing a comprehensive energy conservation program, Seattle City Light found that 92 percent of its customers were aware of the program. Most had learned about the program from bill stuffers; newspapers and radio public service announcements also were important channels of information (Booz, Allen and Hamilton 1980).

2. Nonparticipating households were assigned to different stages of the adoption decision process on the basis of their responses to a question that asked why they were not taking part. Those who reported they had not heard of the programs before were classified as unaware. Those who checked "just not interested" were classified aware but not interested. Those who checked various negative evaluations, such as "we couldn't control our use of electricity," "we couldn't save enough," etc., were classified as having reached the evaluation stage and made a conscious decision not to take part. All other households were assumed to be aware, but still making up their minds.

3. The much higher-than-average negative predisposition of nonparticipating households served by the Four County Electric Membership Corporation may be a function of the program's advanced state of market penetration, with almost 90 percent of eligible households taking part. At this stage of the diffusion process the program has absorbed most of the households who are undecided and positively predisposed to participate, so that the remaining households are increasingly likely to consist of those who have considered participation and decided not to take part.

4. In Chapter 9 several methods of overcoming this problem are discussed. For example, while not raising the costs of incentives to utilities, the perceived size of the incentive might be increased by offering lump sum rather than monthly payments and by combining monetary incentives with other types of bonuses for participation, such as energy conservation prizes (water heater wraps, flow restrictors, and other relatively low-cost measures for cutting electricity use).

7

Consumer Satisfaction with Load Control and Time-of-Day Programs

Consumers' satisfaction with load management programs is important for three reasons. First, satisfied customers are likely to continue to participate in the future. Since most utilities do not recover the full costs of load control switches and time-of-day meters until after a customer has been enrolled for some time (Gorzelnik 1982), it is critical to minimize the number of people who drop out of the programs. Second, after program introduction, word-of-mouth is vital for rapid diffusion. Early participants will not recommend adoption to their friends and neighbors, however, if they do not believe that a program provides good value or if they find it entails unreasonable discomfort or changes in household routines. Third, consumers' satisfaction with load management is likely to affect their general attitudes toward a utility. Thus, load management programs can improve or detract from the positive images utilities wish to project to the communities they serve.

Discontinuance—subsequent rejection of an innovation after initial adoption—is common enough that a number of authors recommend regular follow-ups to reinforce participation and forestall program termination by dissatisfied customers (e.g., see Havelock 1971; Midgely 1977; Leonard-Barton 1981). This chapter explores the likely need for such procedures in load management marketing by examining consumer satisfaction and intentions to continue to participate in load management (see Figure 7.1). It reviews utilities' experience with experimental load control and time-of-day rate programs nationally and examines in depth customers' satisfaction with the six programs studied in North Carolina. Besides determining absolute levels of satisfaction, we isolate factors contributing to positive and negative customer evaluations to help in designing follow-up marketing strategies. Four types of load management programs are considered: water heater load control, air conditioner load control, combined water heater and air conditioner load control, and time-of-day rates. To begin, however, it is useful to see firsthand why customer satisfaction is an important concern in program marketing.

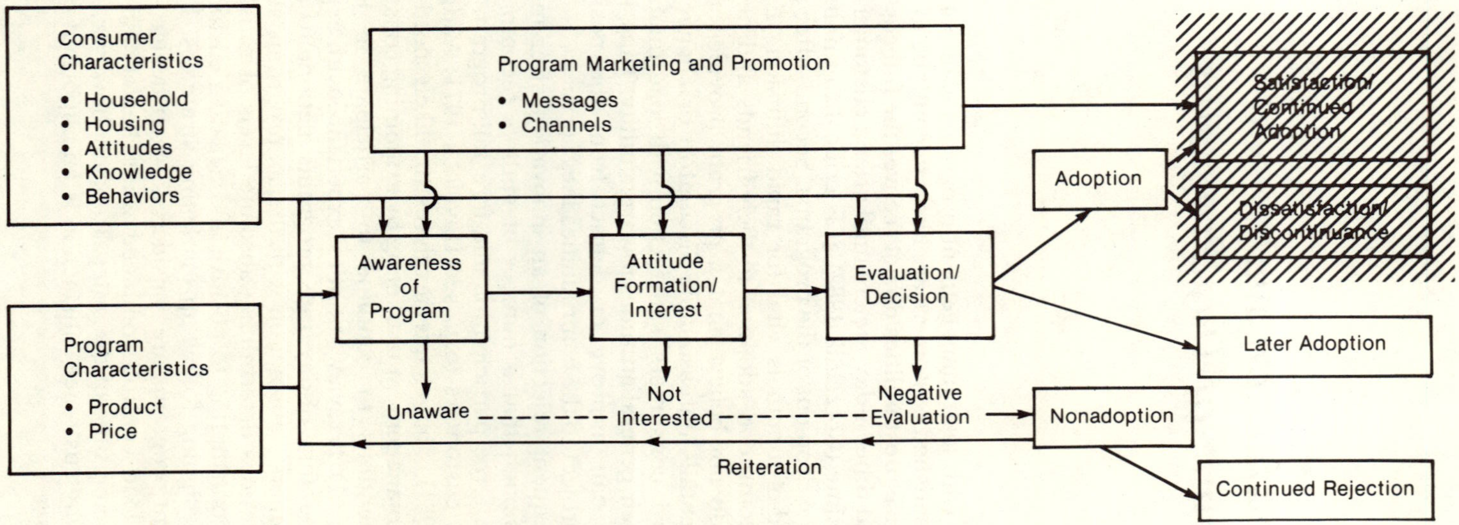

Figure 7.1 Program Adoption Model: Consumer Satisfaction and Program Continuation

POTENTIAL PAYOFFS FROM SATISFIED CUSTOMERS

Three payoffs from high levels of customer satisfaction were listed above: decreased likelihood of discontinuance, increased likelihood of recommending program adoption to other households, and a positive image of the electric utility. The data summarized in Table 7.1 show that these benefits occur in fact as well as in theory. With each of the four programs examined, the more satisfied program participants were, the more likely they were to intend to continue in their load management program, to encourage others to participate, and to believe that their electric utility was making an effort to contain price increases.

Consumers' satisfaction had the least effect on their intentions to continue with direct load control programs. A high proportion of customers, including a surprisingly high percent of those who were dissatisfied, intended to continue in these programs. The six utilities involved had a similar experience, with very low—less than 1 percent—rates of actual customer discontinuance. In large part this may be because load shedding and cycling strategies had yet to be pushed to the point at which many customers had experienced discomfort from the lack of air conditioning or hot water. As will be shown later in this chapter, however, consumer satisfaction is directly tied to the degree of load control exercised. Thus, there may be a threshold level of control that, when reached, produces higher levels of discomfort or inconvenience, more intense consumer dissatisfaction, and higher levels of program discontinuance. (For example, see Groome and Levy 1977 for a report of higher dropout rates with longer cycling periods on the Pacific Gas & Electric Co. air conditioner load control experiments.)

The overall rate of intended continuation among participants in Duke Power's time-of-day rate program, 73 percent, falls within the range of program continuation rates reported for earlier experimental time-of-day rate programs (see Table 7.2). However, intentions to continue on the program, while very high (100 percent) for those who reported themselves very satisfied, dropped off sharply as dissatisfaction occurred. Only 18 percent of the households who were dissatisfied intended to continue to take part. Obviously, to the extent that utilities can counteract the causes of dissatisfaction, costly program dropouts might be reduced or avoided. Factors accounting for program dissatisfaction are noted later in this chapter and provide several leads about how to minimize discontent among customers on time-of-day rates.

A majority of the households who were very satisfied with their direct load control or time-of-day program reported that they had encouraged several other people to participate. This type of word-of-mouth advertising can be a very important factor in the diffusion of load management programs. Since few households have had prior experience with any of the programs discussed in this book, all but the most venturesome are likely to ask about others' experiences before making up their minds about taking part. Although not the deciding factor in

TABLE 7.1

THREE PAYOFFS FROM SATISFIED CONSUMERS:
PROGRAM CONTINUATION, WORD OF MOUTH ADVERTISING, AND UTILITY IMAGE
(percent of program participants)

Program and Satisfaction Level	Household Will Continue to Participate[a]	Household Encouraged others to Participate[b]	Household Has Positive Image of Utility[c]
Water Heater Load Control Participants			
Consumer satisfaction level:			
Very satisfied	97	69	16
Somewhat satisfied	92	43	5
Dissatisfied	56	17	3
Air Conditioner Load Control Participants			
Consumer satisfaction level:			
Very satisfied	99	53	11
Somewhat satisfied	96	41	8
Dissatisfied	43	29	5
Water Heater and Air Conditioner Load Control Participants			
Consumer satisfaction level:			
Very satisfied	98	67	18
Somewhat satisfied	91	43	7
Dissatisfied	64	13	4
Time-of-Day Rate Participants			
Consumer satisfaction level:			
Very satisfied	100	82	33
Somewhat satisfied	72	25	12
Dissatisfied	18	18	7

[a]Positive responses to question, "Will you continue to take part in the future?"

[b]Agreement with statement, "After we signed up for this program, we encouraged several other people to participate."

[c]Average of percent agreeing with statement, "Our electric utility is doing everything it can to hold down the prices it charges for electricity," and disagreeing with statement, "We pay too much for electricity."

the final adoption decision (as was shown in the preceding two chapters), personal recommendations undoubtedly condition households' attitudes toward these programs and the speed with which they enroll.

Marketing management must view with some concern the sharp declines in program endorsements that occurred as soon as households were no longer extremely satisfied. In the case of Duke Power's time-of-day program, for example, the proportion of households who had encouraged others to take part dropped from 82 percent of the very satisfied program participants to only 25 percent of those who were "somewhat satisfied." Similar, although less drastic, declines in reported endorsements also characterized the load control programs when customer satisfaction declined.

During the past ten years, electric utilities increasingly have been subject to criticism from consumers because of rapidly rising prices for electricity. Because load management programs are designed to hold down escalating prices, they have the potential for improving customers' image of their utilities. In fact, comparisons of customer attitudes between areas where programs are offered and areas where they have yet to be introduced consistently indicate more positive consumer attitudes toward the electric utility where load control and time-of-day rates are already in place. Even so, most consumers still believe that they pay too much for electricity and that the electric utilities are doing little to hold down price increases. Table 7.1 reveals that positive attitudes were relatively infrequent, even among load management program participants, but that the improvements in image these programs have fostered can be lost if customers are not very satisfied after they have enrolled in load management.

In summary, electric utilities appear to have much to gain from marketing efforts to ensure customer satisfaction with load control and time-of-day rate programs. Satisfied customers are not likely to drop out of the programs; they encourage others to take part; and they are more likely to believe the utilities are trying to do something to contain rapid rises in prices. Given these benefits, how can customer satisfaction be maximized?

SATISFACTION WITH LOAD CONTROL AND TIME-OF-DAY RATE PROGRAMS

A number of the time-of-day rate experiments sponsored by the U.S. Department of Energy and individual utility experiments with time-of-day and load controls have included follow-up surveys designed to gauge customer reactions. In summarizing this experience, Males and Uhler (1982) concluded, "Both voluntary and mandatory load management programs actually experienced were well accepted and overall the new rate or load control was preferred to the previous system."

TABLE 7.2

CONSUMER SATISFACTION INDICATORS REPORTED IN THE LITERATURE

Study	Consumer Satisfaction Indicators
Load Control Programs	
Arkansas Power & Light Air Conditioner Load Control Experiment (Task Force No. 10 1977)	- General attitude of participants was positive - 57% would not mind if controls were left on their air conditioners
Nevada Power Co. Air Conditioner Load Control Experiment (Correy et al. 1981)	- 16% reported some discomfort
Pacific Gas & Electric Air Conditioner Load Control Experiment (Groome and Levy 1979; Seeto 1979)	- Overall satisfaction high - 86% willing to participate a second year - Discomfort and inconvenience primary reasons for dissatisfaction
Potomac Electric Power Load Control Experiment (Dyer 1981)	- Nearly 90% very probable to continue to participate in the future - Lowest satisfaction with combined water heater and air conditioner controls - Satisfaction levels not associated with discomfort or inconvenience attributed to program
Summary: Above Programs Plus Pioneer Rural Electric Cooperative and Cobb Electric Membership Corporation (Dyer 1981)	- Generally positive attitudes toward programs - Low levels of awareness of controls, discomfort, inconvenience - High intentions to take part in future

TABLE 7.2 continued

Study	Consumer Satisfaction Indicators
Time-of-Day Programs	
CP&L Time-of-Day Rate Experiment (Miedema et al. 1980)	- "Over half had favorable reaction to the experimental rates used by the utility" - "About one-third chose to continue on the rates at the conclusion of the study"
Connecticut Light and Power Time-of-Day Experiment (Heberlein 1981)	- 81% of volunteer time-of-day rate participants would continue for another year
Dayton Power and Light Co. Time-of-Day Rate Experiment (Hellman 1980)	- 92% said they would continue
Georgia Power Time-of-Day Rate Experiments (Smith 1978)	- Customer satisfaction with rates varied from 37% to 79% satisfied, depending on type of rate - 49% to 90% would continue on rates - Most popular rates were on- and off-peak rate differential with no demand charge
Green Mountain Power Corporation Time-of-Day Rate Experiments (Hellman 1980)	- As a whole, the majority of demand charge rate customers were not satisfied
Los Angeles Department of Water and Power Time-of-Day and Seasonal Rate Experiment (Hellman 1980)	- Over three quarters consider their plan good or very good for them
Wisconsin Time-of-Day Rate Experiment (Heberlein 1981)	- 52% of customers over nine rate designs were satisfied with program - 64% wanted to continue on rates - 70% felt savings were worth the effort required to shift use of electricity to off-peak

Nevertheless, as indicated by the studies summarized in Table VII-2, these good feelings were far from universal, particularly in the case of the time-of-day rate programs. Following the Green Mountain Power Corporation's time-of-day experiment, for example, a majority of the participants indicated they were dissatisfied with the new rates, which included a demand charge. Although it was reported that more than half the participants in CP&L's time-of-day rate experiment, which did not include a demand charge, had favorable attitudes, only about one-third chose to continue on the rates after the experimental period ended. Thus, based on past experience it is clear that consumer satisfaction cannot be taken for granted. In addition, the findings reported from the experimental program follow-ups have to be viewed with some caution. There is the strong possibility that participants' attitudes were colored by a "Hawthorne effect," in which attitudes are shaped not only by the objective characteristics of the experimental program but also by the fact that participants know that they are taking part in an experiment.

The load control programs and the one time-of-day rate program examined for this book provided an opportunity to gauge customer satisfaction in nonexperimental settings and to compare responses to two different approaches to load management—load control and time-of-day rates. Three measures of customer satisfaction were used: (1) an indicator of satisfaction with the value received ("the savings we have received have been worth it"); (2) an indicator of the costs of the program in terms of personal discomfort ("this program has caused discomfort for my household"); and (3) an overall indicator of satisfaction ("How satisfied are you with your load control or time-of-day program? "). Results are reviewed for each of the programs examined.

Satisfaction with Load Control Programs

Water heater program participants believed the savings they received from taking part were worth the effort involved in signing up for a program and the risk of some discomfort or inconvenience. Although these beliefs were not strongly held in most cases, as shown in Table 7.3, very few customers regarded participation in water heater control as a bad deal. Positive reactions to the value received stem in part from the fact that few customers had experienced any discomfort, even those served by utilities such as the Lumbee River and Four County Electric Membership Corporations where water heaters were regularly cycled off. The fact that most customers did not feel strongly about the value received from participation may stem from the low amount, about $2 per month, most utilities offered as an incentive for taking part. As reported in Chapters 5 and 6, many households view $5 or $10 per month as the appropriate compensation for allowing their water heaters to be controlled. General content with the value received, even

TABLE 7.3

CONSUMER SATISFACTION WITH WATER HEATER LOAD CONTROL PROGRAMS
(percent of program participants)

	Investor-Owned Utilities			Municipal/EMC Utilities		
Indicator	Duke Power	CP&L	VEPCO	Tarboro	Lumbee River	Four County
"The savings we have received have been worth it"						
Agree strongly	19	32	35	31	5	17
Agree	66	47	53	45	49	41
Not sure	8	17	9	16	33	32
Disagree	5	4	3	6	13	0
Disagree strongly	1	1	1	1	0	3
"This program has caused discomfort for my household"						
Agree strongly	3	0	1	0	0	0
Agree	4	2	2	1	11	7
Not sure	6	1	4	5	3	11
Disagree	65	57	56	56	78	59
Disagree strongly	22	40	38	38	8	22
"How satisfied are you with your load control or time-of-day program?"						
Very satisfied	66	84	86	74	42	48
Somewhat satisfied	29	16	14	25	50	48
Somewhat dissatisfied	4	0	0	0	8	0
Very dissatisfied	1	0	0	1	0	4

though not strongly felt, and the lack of discomfort have combined to produce very high consumer satisfaction with water heater load control programs, as shown in the bottom panels of Table 7.3.

Tables 7.4 and 7.5 summarize similar measures obtained from households with air conditioners controlled and with both water heaters and air conditioners controlled. Comparison of the two tables reveals that, for the most part, consumer responses are similar. Comparison with the responses of households with only the water heater controlled (Table 7.3) indicates that a higher proportion of those in the air conditioner programs believed strongly that the value received from participation was worthwhile. This difference may be attributed to the higher financial incentives, ranging from $1.25 to $5.00 per month, utilities offered for participation in an air conditioner control program. Also, utilities did not cycle air conditioners off for long periods, so participants were no more likely to experience discomfort than those with only the water heater controlled. As a result, they, too, tended to be highly satisfied. As with the water heater programs, fewer than 10 percent of those with air conditioners controlled or with both water heaters and air conditioners controlled indicated they were dissatisfied.

Even though satisfaction levels are exceptionally high, utilities will find it beneficial to periodically reinforce participation. One reinforcement–personal savings on the electric bill–is built into program design. The key here is to be certain that bills are formatted so that load control credits can be seen easily. In Chapter 5 a number of other motives for participation were noted. For example, some households take part because of their commitment to energy conservation, while others are attracted by the possibility of minimizing the environmental damage caused by new generating facilities. These households need to be told from time to time that the programs are achieving these desired ends.

Although most reinforcements will be directed to all program participants, there is some merit in paying particular attention to those who are most likely to be dissatisfied and, as shown above, to subsequently drop out or cease endorsing programs to their friends and acquaintances. Because very few households make the effort to formally express their dissatisfaction to utility officials, other means have to be used to identify likely candidates for special mailings and similar efforts utilities might employ to keep them interested in continuing to take part in load management. One approach, illustrated in Table 7.6, is to use consumer survey data to develop a profile of less satisfied customers. Special attention would then be given to those households who match the profile characteristics.

Several profile characteristics summarized in Table 7.6 should be readily accessible to marketing management. For example, less satisfied program participants tended to have higher electric bills—more than $100 per month during June 1982–and to have been living in multifamily housing and renting. Less satisfied households also were more likely than average to have had lower incomes and to have been unemployed, black, and younger. Using census and other data, areas of a community where households with these characteristics concentrate can be identified and used to target promotional efforts designed to increase satisfaction.

The attitudinal data summarized in Table 7.6 suggest some themes that might be employed in reinforcing participation. For example, less satisfied households tend to believe their utilities are not making efforts to hold down the prices charged for electricity. They may feel it is

TABLE 7.4

CONSUMER SATISFACTION WITH AIR CONDITIONER LOAD CONTROL PROGRAMS
(percent of program participants)

Indicator	Investor-Owned Utilities			Municipal/EMC Utilities		
	Duke Power	CP&L	VEPCO	Tarboro	Lumbee River	Four County
"The savings we have received have been worth it"						
Agree strongly	33	NA	NA	26	22	NA
Agree	47	NA	NA	51	61	NA
Not sure	17	NA	NA	19	14	NA
Disagree	21	NA	NA	4	4	NA
Disagree strongly	1	NA	NA	0	0	NA
"This program has caused discomfort for my household"						
Agree strongly	0	NA	NA	0	0	NA
Agree	2	NA	NA	5	6	NA
Not sure	10	NA	NA	6	4	NA
Disagree	60	NA	NA	63	57	NA
Disagree strongly	28	NA	NA	27	33	NA
"How satisfied are you with your load control or time-of-day program?"						
Very satisfied	78	NA	NA	77	72	NA
Somewhat satisfied	17	NA	NA	22	20	NA
Somewhat dissatisfied	3	NA	NA	1	4	NA
Very dissatisfied	2	NA	NA	0	4	NA

NA = Not applicable.

TABLE 7.5

CONSUMER SATISFACTION WITH WATER HEATER-AIR CONDITIONER (BOTH LOADS CONTROLLED) PROGRAMS (percent of program participants

Indicator	Investor-Owned Utilities			Municipal/EMC Utilities		
	Duke Power	CP&L	VEPCO	Tarboro	Lumbee River	Four County
"The savings we have received have been worth it"						
Agree strongly	33	NA	NA	43	21	15
Agree	50	NA	NA	44	40	49
Not sure	12	NA	NA	9	29	28
Disagree	1	NA	NA	3	8	8
Disagree strongly	4	NA	NA	0	2	0
"This program has caused discomfort for my household"						
Agree strongly	1	NA	NA	0	2	0
Agree	1	NA	NA	2	4	8
Not sure	1	NA	NA	4	10	13
Disagree	66	NA	NA	52	53	66
Disagree strongly	31	NA	NA	42	31	13
"How satisfied are you with your load control or time-of-day program?"						
Very satisfied	78	NA	NA	75	63	48
Somewhat satisfied	17	NA	NA	22	37	44
Somewhat dissatisfied	1	NA	NA	3	0	8
Very dissatisfied	4	NA	NA	0	0	0

NA = Not applicable.

wrong for consumers to receive lower-quality service, represented by load control, while utilities are not making a similar sacrifice. By counteracting these attitudes with information about utility cost-containment efforts, satisfaction with load controls, as well as a utility's general image, may be enhanced.

For the most part, motives for participation are not associated with program satisfaction. One exception to that, however, may be useful in program marketing, particularly if tied to efforts to show consumers that load management is part of a general strategy to operate efficiently and keep costs low. As shown in Table 7.6, households who were participating because of the indirect savings achieved when utilities can cut their operating costs tended to be those most satisfied with their load control program. If the proportion of households who enroll in the future for this altruistic reason increases, then subsequent satisfaction levels may also be higher.

Satisfaction with Time-of-Day Rates

Follow-up surveys conducted in conjunction with earlier experimental load control and time-of-day programs generally found lower acceptance of time-of-day rates (see Table 7.2). That also tended to be true of Duke Power's time-of-day program, when compared with the load control programs offered in the same market area by Duke and in other areas by CP&L, VEPCO, Tarboro Municipal, and the electric membership corporations. (Compare Table 7.7 with Tables 7.3, 7.4, and 7.5.) For example, only 56 percent of the time-of-day participants believed the savings they had received had been worth the effort. In contrast, 80 percent or more of Duke's customers who were enrolled in various load control options thought the savings they received were worthwhile. Since Duke did not regularly cycle off the water heaters and air conditioners of load control participants, this comparison can be misleading. If loads were actually controlled by Duke, then one would expect greater discontent among participants. In fact, when people who were taking part in Duke's time-of-day rate program are compared to load control participants where loads were regularly cycled, such as those who were taking part in the Lumbee River and Four County programs, differences in the proportions of customers who thought they were receiving a good value narrow considerably, although the gap is not closed completely.

Very few load control participants reported that the programs had caused discomfort for their households. In contrast, 39 percent of the Duke Power time-of-day rate participants reported discomfort, and another 10 percent said they were not sure. The highest rates of reported discomfort among the load control programs examined were the 8 percent of Four County Electric Membership Corporation customers who reported discomfort from combined water heater and air

TABLE 7.6

CORRELATES OF CONSUMER SATISFACTION WITH LOAD CONTROL PROGRAMS

	Gamma: Measure of Association[a]			
Variable	Water Heater Program	Air Conditioner Program	Water and Air Program	Profile of Less Satisfied Consumers
Household Characteristics				
1. Type of household	NS	NS	NS	--
2. Size of household	NS	NS	.18	Five or more persons
3. Education	NS	NS	NS	--
4. Income	NS	-.10	NS	Lower
5. Employment	.21	NS	NS	Unemployed
6. Race	-.41	NS	-.29	Black
7. Age of oldest adult	-.19	NS	-.28	Younger
8. Venturesomeness	NS	NS	NS	--
9. Conservation knowledge	.53	NS	.34	Lower
10. Conservation opinion leadership	NS	NS	NS	--
Housing Characteristics				
1. Type of dwelling	.39	NS	NS	Multifamily
2. Tenure	.47	.71	NS	Rent
3. Size of dwelling	NS	NS	NS	--
4. All electric	NS	.25	.25	Yes
Use/Conservation of Electricity				
1. Amount of June electric bill	.25	NS	.28	Higher - $100 or more
2. Reported difficulty paying bill	.24	.24	.55	Yes
3. Conservation behavior index[b]	NS	NS	NS	--
4. Home retrofit index[c]	NS	NS	.25	Lower
Attitudes				
1. Toward Utility				
a. Utility is trying to hold down prices charged for electricity	.36	NS	.31	Disagree
b. We pay too much for electricity	.38	NS	.35	Agree

TABLE 7.6 continued

	Gamma: Measure of Association[a]			
Variable	Water Heater Program	Air Conditioner Program	Water and Air Program	Profile of Less Satisfied Consumers
2. Toward conservation:				
a. Importance	NS	.26	NS	Extremely
b. Ethic - conserve Even if can afford not to	NS	NS	NS	--
c. Don't mind discomfort if we can save on electricity costs	NS	NS	NS	--
Motives for Participation				
1. Personal savings on electric bill	NS	NS	-.44	Not a reason for participation
2. Indirect savings when utility cuts costs	-.29	NS	-.51	Not a reason for participation
3. Environmental protection	NS	NS	NS	--
4. Utility recommendation	NS	NS	NS	--
5. Personal recommendation	NS	NS	NS	--
Length of Time in Program	NS	NS	NS	--

NS = Gamma less than .10 and/or chi-square significance level of .10 or less.

[a]Gamma is a nonparametric statistical measure of correlation between two variables, varying from -1(+1) indicating a perfect negative (positive) monotonic association between two variables and zero, indicating the lack of any association.

[b]Low, moderate, or high performance of the following: use less water in baths, and showers, turn off air conditioner to save money, turn off lights, turn down heat at night.

[c]Added low, 0-5, moderate, 6-7, or high, 8-9, number of the following energy conservation measures: attic/ceiling fan; caulking or weather stripping; insulation of attic, walls or floor; insulation around water heater; insulation around heating ducts or hot water pipes; storm windows, thermopane glass, plastic sheeting; storm doors, water heater timers; and wood stove.

TABLE 7.7

CONSUMER SATISFACTION WITH DUKE POWER
TIME-OF-DAY RATE PROGRAM
(percent of program participants)

Indicator	Percent
"The savings we have received have been worth it"	
Agree strongly	24
Agree	32
Not sure	32
Disagree	7
Disagree strongly	5
"This program has caused discomfort for my household"	
Agree strongly	4
Agree	35
Not sure	10
Disagree	45
Disagree strongly	7
"How satisfied are you with your load control or time-of-day program?"	
Very satisfied	30
Somewhat satisfied	55
Somewhat dissatisfied	9
Very dissatisfied	6

conditioner load control and the 11 percent who were unsure whether they had experienced any discomfort.

High uncertainty about whether the savings received were worth the effort involved and higher rates of actual discomfort from program participation produced lower levels of program satisfaction. In the case of the program options offered by Duke Power, the proportion of very satisfied time-of-day rate customers was less than half that for Duke's various load control options. The proportion of time-of-day customers who were dissatisfied—15 percent—was three times as high as program dissatisfaction among any other utility's load control customers.

The data summarized in Table 7.8 provide some clues about factors that lead to dissatisfaction with time-of-day programs. The profile of less satisfied customers includes households with two or more people in the home during the daytime. These households probably find it more difficult than others to postpone using electricity during peak periods, particularly when peaks occur during daylight hours. Less satisfied customers also tended to have higher-than-average electric bills—more than $100 during June 1982—and were more likely than average to report difficulty in paying for electricity. In many cases, these households may have found that their electric bills rose rather than declined after they switched to time-of-day rates, which easily could occur if a household has problems switching the use of electricity from peak to off peak periods.

In fact, the profile of less satisfied households includes those who reported that they found it difficult to change the times they performed various activities, as shown in Table 7.8. The magnitude of the gamma measures of association between difficulty shifting an activity and satisfaction levels provides an indication of those activities that, if they cannot be shifted, are likely to result in dissatisfied customers. Heading the list is clothes drying, followed by water heating, clothes washing, air conditioning, cooking the evening meal, and electric heating. These profile characteristics can be used by utilities in counseling households who are interested in switching to time-of-day rates. By discouraging those who believe they would have difficulty shifting activities such as washing and drying clothes, water heating, and air conditioning to off-peak times, later customer dissatisfaction and program discontinuance may be avoided.

As shown in Table 7.9, shifting some of these activities from on- to off-peak periods has not been difficult for most households. Two-thirds or more of the time-of-day program participants queried reported no difficulty in shifting dishwashing, water heating, clothes washing and drying, and personal care to off-peak times. On the other hand, cooking the evening meal and space heating and cooling posed some problems for many households. Since difficulty shifting each of these latter three activities led to program dissatisfaction, they might receive particular attention when counseling prospective time-of-day program participants. In addition, utilities should consider counseling households after they have enrolled in time-of-day programs to show them how to avoid discomfort and inconvenience in shifting activities to off-peak times. For example, households could be shown how to keep their homes cool during peak hours without running the air conditioner, such as by adding insulation, keeping drapes drawn on south-facing windows, using natural air circulation, and other appropriate means. By careful screening in the beginning and customer education after households have enrolled, utilities may go far in eliminating program dissatisfaction caused by problems in shifting activities from on- to off-peak periods.

Like customers dissatisfied with load control programs, dissatisfied time-of-day rate participants tended to believe their utilities were not trying to keep down electricity prices and that they themselves were

TABLE 7.8

CORRELATES OF CONSUMER SATISFACTION WITH DUKE POWER'S TIME-OF-DAY RATE PROGRAM

Variable	Gamma: Measure of Association[a]	Profile of Less Satisfied Participants
Household Characteristics		
1. Type of household	NS	--
2. Size of household	.22	Two or More
3. Education	NS	--
4. Income	NS	--
5. Employment	.45	Not Working Full Time
6. Race	NS	--
7. Age of oldest adult	NS	--
8. Venturesomeness	NS	--
9. Conservation knowledge	NS	--
10. Conservation opinion leadership	NS	--
Housing Characteristics		
1. Type of dwelling	NS	--
2. Tenure	NS	--
3. Size of dwelling	NS	--
4. All electric	NS	--
Use/Conservation of Electricity		
1. Amount of June electric bill	.61	Higher ($100+)
2. Reported difficulty paying bill	.11	Yes
3. Conservation behavior index[b]	-.15	Lower
4. Reported difficulty shifting Activities from on-peak to off-peak hours:		
Drying clothes	-.47	Very Difficult
Water heating	-.45	Very Difficult
Washing clothes	-.43	Very Difficult
Air conditioning	-.18	Very Difficult
Cooking evening meal	-.16	Very Difficult
Electric heating	-.11	Very Difficult
Bathing/showering	NS	--
Personal care	NS	--
5. House retrofit index	NS	--

TABLE 7.8 continued

Variable	Gamma: Measure of Association[a]	Profile of Less Satisfied Participants
Attitude		
1. Toward utility:		
a. Utility is trying to hold down prices charged for electricity	.50	Disagree
b. We pay too much for electricity	.33	Agree
2. Toward Conservation:		
a. Importance	.23	Lower
b. Ethic-conserve even if we can afford not to	NS	--
c. Don't mind discomfort if we can save on electricity costs	.17	Disagree
Reasons for Participation		
1. Personal savings on electric bill	NS	--
2. Indirect savings when utility cuts cost	.71	Not a Reason
3. Environmental protection	.46	Not a Reason
4. Utility recommendation	.32	Not a Reason
5. Suggestion from acquaintance	.25	Not a Reason
Length of Time in Program	NS	--

NS = Gamma less than .10.

[a]See footnote a, Table 7.7.

[b]See footnote b, Table 7.7.

[c]See footnote c, Table 7.7.

TABLE 7.9

DIFFICULTY SHIFTING USE OF ELECTRICITY
FROM ON- TO OFF-PEAK PERIODS:
TIME-OF-DAY PROGRAM PARTICIPANTS
(percent of program participants)

	Difficulty Shifting			
Activity[a]	Not at All Difficult	Somewhat Difficult	Very Difficult	Do Not Try
1. Dishwashing	83	11	2	4
2. Electric Water Heating	77	17	3	3
3. Clothes Washing	74	19	3	3
4. Baths/Showers	69	24	2	5
5. Clothes Drying	69	24	2	5
6. Personal Care	66	25	7	2
7. Electric Space Heating	45	35	11	6
8. Cooking the Evening Meal	24	38	30	8
9. Air Conditioning	17	52	18	13

[a]QUESTION: Please indicate how hard it has been for your household to shift each of these from on-peak to off-peak periods.

paying too much. Also, dissatisfied customers were less likely than average to have enrolled in time-of-day rates for altruistic reasons such as greater efficiency of utility operations and environmental protection. Having joined solely to cut their own electricity costs and finding that the savings were not as great as anticipated, these households tended to become dissatisfied with the time-of-day program and with their utility in general. This problem can be counteracted if utilities try to build participation based on a broad spectrum of motives, paying particular attention to the societal benefits of load management. In addition, by showing customers how utilities are working to contain escalating prices customer satisfaction with load management programs should be enhanced, as was noted earlier in the discussion of satisfaction with load control programs.

SUMMARY

Electric utilities cannot afford dissatisfied participants in load management programs. Enrolling customers in these programs is expensive. Initial costs typically are not recovered until households have taken part for some time. As shown in this chapter, however, dissatisfied customers are much more likely than average to say they intend to discontinue participation. They are also much less likely to recommend participation to others (thus dampening program diffusion rates) and to believe their utilities are not making honest efforts to hold down escalating electricity prices. Thus, the task of load management marketing does not stop after households have been signed up to participate. Marketing management must devise a carefully thought-out strategy for building and sustaining customer satisfaction.

At present most customers taking part in load control programs—both water heater and air conditioner control—are highly satisfied with these programs. Few have experienced discomfort, and most think the value received has been highly worthwhile, particularly in the case of the air conditioner control programs, where financial rewards from participation are highest. General satisfaction levels were highest for those programs with the most infrequent load shedding and cycling schedules. As programs become fully operational and loads are regularly cycled on and off, dissatisfaction can be expected to mount.

In general, households most likely to become dissatisfied are those with higher electric bills, lower incomes, and those living in multifamily housing and renting. Also, black and younger households were less satisfied than others. These characteristics form a profile that might be used to target reinforcements designed to build and sustain satisfaction. In reinforcing participation in load control programs, utilities should emphasize the savings accruing to each household, for example, by formatting the electric bill to highlight the load control credit. In addition, households need to be shown that the programs are producing general societal or community benefits. Utilities should tell customers how the programs are cutting peak demands and how this translates into savings to utility customers as a group and in a cleaner, healthier environment.

Customer satisfaction with time-of-day rates tended to be much lower than with load control. Almost four of every ten time-of-day program participants reported that the program had caused their households discomfort. The proportion of dissatisfied consumers in the time-of-day program was three times that of any of the load control programs examined. As a result, a relatively high proportion—27 percent—were uncertain about future participation in the program or expected to drop out. As with the load control programs, less satisfied time-of-day participants tended to have higher-than-average electric bills. In addition, they tended to find it difficult to shift times at which they engaged in various electricity-using activities. Most likely they found that after switching to time-of-day rates, they could not switch enough electricity use to off-peak periods to produce a significant reduction in their bills, hence their dissatisfaction.

Utilities can reduce dissatisfaction and dropouts among time-of-day program participants by screening customers to discourage from joining in the first place those who think they are unlikely to switch activities such as washing and drying clothes and air conditioning to off-peak periods. Customers who had difficulty switching the times they performed these activities tended to become dissatisfied. Activities that households had the most difficulty postponing were air conditioning, cooking the evening meal, and space heating. An effort should be mounted to help households avoid the discomfort and inconvenience that may occur when activities are postponed to off-peak periods. By carefully screening households before enrolling them in time-of-day programs, and by showing them how to live comfortably with the program after they have joined, utilities can go a long way toward maintaining high levels of satisfaction and reducing program dropout rates.

8

Forecasting Market Penetration

Systematic forecasting enables utility management to remove the guesswork from estimating the market and sales of load management programs. This chapter discusses the design, specification, and evaluation of the forecasting process. We focus our attention on forecasting the penetration of direct load control programs, using for an example data drawn from one of the six utilities studied in this research. First we examine the definition and purpose of forecasting. Factors that affect a utility's choice of forecasting techniques are discussed briefly and the diverse methods available are illustrated. Finally, we evaluate the efficiency of the information system developed to support a utility's market forecast. A major emphasis throughout the chapter is the need to combine statistical analysis with management judgment to arrive at useful predictions of future program adoption (sales) rates.

DEFINITION AND PURPOSE OF FORECASTING

A forecast of the future is a prerequisite to planning the functions of any organization. The forecasting process is not, however, an isolated activity. A common misconception about sales forecasts, for example, is that the forecast provides an independent estimate of sales. The flaw in that assumption is that forecasts cannot be developed independently of other organizational functions. The definition of a sales forecast presented here stresses its dependence on the planned marketing activities of the utility. The sales forecast is defined as "the expected level of sales for an expected level of a firm's marketing effort and the given environment" (Kotler 1972).

An effective forecasting system is continuous and systematic. The forecast should be viewed as a means to integrate utility objectives with operating plans rather than an end in itself (Bolt 1972). The scale of operation, for example, will depend on actual sales. Likewise actual sales will depend on the selected marketing plan. The dynamic relationship between sales and the marketing effort is an important consideration in understanding and using forecasting techniques (Cleary and Levenbach 1982).

The *purpose* of a particular forecast will influence the importance and desired achievement of the forecast. The major purpose of a forecast is to translate the utility's general objectives into operating plans and schedules (Firth 1977). Purchasing, production, finance, marketing, and personnel are the activities that most closely interact with the forecasting function.

Aside from accomplishing its major purpose, the forecasting process also has side effects that will benefit management. Forecasting's close relationship to the utility's objectives forces management to evaluate those objectives regularly. The analyses and research program that are part of the forecasting process will increase the knowledge of the load management program and add to management understanding of it. Thus, forecasting is a learning process (Chambers, Mullick, and Smith 1974).

Example

With these general notions about forecasting in mind, we can use an example to indicate how forecasting can be applied to the marketing of direct load control devices. A useful tool for specifying the system dynamics and components is the flow chart (Chambers, Mullick and Smith 1974; Firth 1977). A hypothetical flow chart for the sales and distribution of direct load control devices is shown in Figure 8.1. The development of the system flow chart gives management a preliminary indication of how well the operation of the system is understood.

The model shown in Figure 8.1 is hypothetical, but is representative of a number of direct load control programs. The flow chart illustrates a utility that keeps in stock the load control devices its customers use. Installations are made by trained utility employees. Customers can sign up for the program by responding on their bills or by visiting the utility office. A program coordinator is responsible for processing requests for the devices. Other interdependent functions in the system are purchasing, finance, and marketing.

Several important relationships in the model can be evaluated. The load control program coordinator must process and schedule the installations according to the availability of the devices in inventory and the manpower to install them. The purchasing agent can buy and stock an optimal number of devices based on the sales forecast and cash flow situation. The manpower requirements for installing the devices can be derived from the same estimate of sales. The marketing effort, however, is the driving force in the system. The timing and intensity of promotion will influence the number of customers who sign up for the program. A given number of sign-ups will require a given number of personnel to process the requests. The interdependencies in the cycle underscore the need to forecast program adoption accurately. And the forecast must be communicated to persons responsible for different aspects of a load

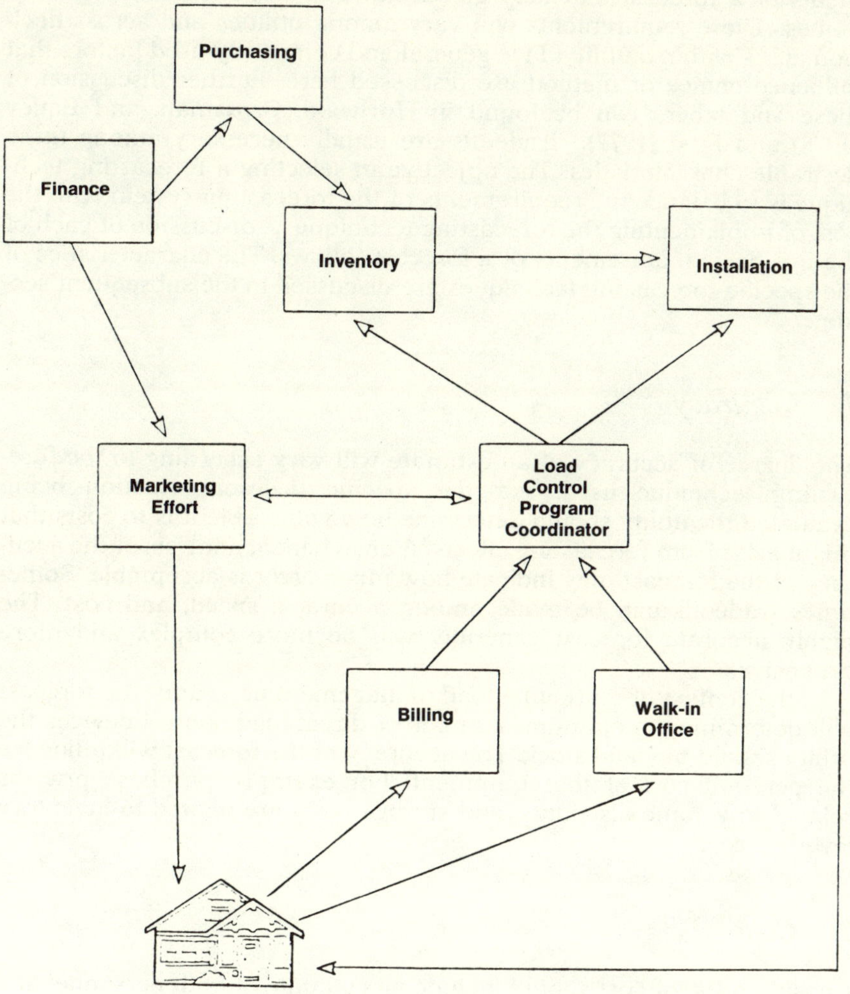

Figure 8.1 Hypothetical Load Control Marketing System

management program to improve coordination and achieve maximum efficiency.

REQUIREMENTS OF THE FORECAST

With the insight gained from the development of a system flow chart, we now consider the factors that affect a utility's choice of forecasting techniques. There are numerous quantitative and qualitative requirements of a forecast that help guide the selection of forecasting techniques. These requirements will vary among utilities and across decision areas within a utility. Five general and commonly used factors that influence choice of method are discussed here. Further discussion of these and others can be found in Hurwood, Grossman, and Bailey (1978) and First (1977). Tradeoffs are usually necessary among these desirable characteristics. The objective in selecting a forecasting technique is to balance the requirements of the forecasting system with the cost of implementing the forecasting technique. A discussion of each of the five basic requirements of a forecast follows. The characteristics of the specific forecasting techniques are discussed in the subsequent section.

1. Accuracy

The degree of accuracy of an estimate will vary according to the forecasting technique used. For the specific decision situation being evaluated the utility should determine how vulnerable it is to costs that might arise from forecasting efforts. A cost/benefit analysis of the accuracy of the forecast may indicate how much error is acceptable. Sometimes tradeoffs can be made among accuracy, speed, and cost. The highly accurate forecast generally will be more complex and more expensive.

In the context of marketing load management programs, the forecast will determine the optimum number of direct load control devices the utility should buy and stock. The accuracy of the forecast will influence the per unit cost of the equipment. For example, purchase price is related to volume discounts, and storage costs are related to inventory level.

2. Cost

Consideration of cost should include an estimate of both personnel and computer resources. The cost of making the forecast will depend heavily on the availability and type of data, the technical expertise required, and the computer calculations necessary (Hurwood, Grossman and Bailey 1978).

Although it may be appropriate for the forecast to be made at the substation level, the utility may have the resources to develop a forecast only at its central office. The utility must weigh the costs of producing substation forecasts in the central office against the costs of having substation management hire outside contractors for the forecast.

Concerning the availability of data, the utility may need to consult secondary sources of information to develop a meaningful forecast. Information about such things as housing and population characteristics of the target market may be available only from secondary sources.

Unless utility personnel are already active in the collection of such data, the incremental costs of obtaining additional information must be considered in the cost of the forecasting technique.

3. *Time Horizon*

The time span over which management decisions will have an effect also is an important factor in the selection of a forecasting technique. Short-, medium-, or long-term forecasting requirements will vary by decision areas. The relevant time span will have significance for the way data are prepared, the technique selected, and the subsequent analysis. The level of aggregation of the data is another relevant factor. Long-term demand forecasts for the utility-wide system concern the construction of power plants. Mid-range forecasting might identify goals for the load management program over a five-year period. The short-term forecast, which defines specific marketing plans to achieve participation goals, will be most useful to operating managers.

The time horizon also affects the size of the error associated with a forecast. Larger errors are usually characteristic of longer-range forecasts (Hurwood, Grossman, and Bailey 1978). That makes intuitive sense, since it is always more difficult to forecast with accuracy further into the future.

4. *Data Requirements*

The availability of information and the level of detail in the data will greatly influence the techniques that can be applied. Most often forecasts have to use existing data and that limits the tools available for the analysis. In areas where load management programs are just being introduced no data on past program performance will be available. As part of the continuous forecasting process, however, the data required for improved forecasting techniques can be built into an information system within the organization.

The type of data to be collected will depend on the purpose for which it is used. To forecast responsiveness to promotional efforts, management would be interested in the timing of each promotional tactic and the length of decision time of the customer. For the purpose of system-wide capacity planning, management would focus on demographic and housing characteristics, which are correlates of participation.

5. *Relevance*

In selecting a forecasting technique one should consider how appropriate a given technique is to the decision situation. Management must understand and accept the technique if the forecast is to aid in decision making. Certain techniques require highly specialized expertise to develop and to implement. The creators of the forecast must interpret the analysis for the users of the forecast within the context of a relevant decision situation. Consider, for example, the level of aggregation of the data. The implementers of the load control program are interested in simple sales and marketing objectives and are not concerned with the complexity of the forecasting technique employed. The manner in which the forecast is disaggregated and presented to the users will influence its effectiveness at the operations level.

The above discussion of the requirements of forecasting techniques underscores a previous point: the interdependency of functional decisions has a crucial impact on the forecasting process.

FORECASTING TECHNIQUES

A wide variety of forecasting techniques is available. They range from subjective estimates by management to complex quantitative methods. Here we briefly review the techniques generally used by utilities and their potential for forecasting market penetration of direct load control.

Manager Intuition

Lack of good data is a widespread problem in predicting sales of direct load control devices (Hurwood, Grossman, and Bailey 1978). In the absence of any previous experience with a given product the utility must rely heavily on professional judgment. If the load control concept is new to a utility, management will not be able to use data from previous product introductions to forecast the adoption of the load control devices. The techniques below, when combined with management's intuition, will increase the likelihood of developing useful forecasts.

Historical Analogy

It may be possible to look at the pattern already set by an existing product in another market (Bolt 1972). For utilities offering direct load control for the first time, the experience of other utilities in various markets will provide insight. The difficulty with using this type of data is that adjustments must be made for differences in the environment from market to market. Allowances can be made for various factors, such as those identified earlier in this book, that affect the rate at which consumers adopt the program.

Market Research

Surveying existing or potential customers is a useful technique. Analysis of the characteristics of present customers may indicate what groups are likely to adopt load management programs, as shown in Chapter 5. The early adopters can provide feedback about their satisfaction with the program. As shown in Chapter 6, analysis of the intentions of potential customers also will indicate what is likely to happen under a given set of conditions. (Also see Kotler 1972 and Bolt 1972.)

Test Market

When a direct test of likely program adoption is needed, a test market can be set up to provide important information. This technique is especially useful when other methods are not feasible because of cost, unavailability of data, or unreliability of data (Kotler 1972). In responding to a questionnaire the potential customer may not be able to totally comprehend the new concept or picture himself using it. This may be true of the person who has no previous knowledge of the direct load control device and may account for the high proportion of nonparticipants (Chapter 6) who were uncertain whether they would participate in the future. In these cases, stated intentions of consumers will not be a reliable indicator of their subsequent purchase behavior. The test market, on the other hand, will indicate actual purchase behavior for a certain environment. When these data are used to forecast in different locations, regional and other differences can be incorporated (Bolt 1972).

Time Series Analysis

Time series analysis is a statistical technique that can be used when several years' data are available. Projections are made from historical data using trends from past performance to predict future penetration levels. The cost of and time required to use this technique will vary greatly depending on what computer resources are available and what form the data are in. There are several methods of time series analysis. The most common are moving average, exponential smoothing, and Box-Jenkins, all of which involve fitting a mathematical model to the data (Cleary and Levenbach 1982). The complexity and comprehensiveness of the model vary across methods. The Box-Jenkins technique is the most comprehensive. It permits intervention analysis, in which the effect of a specific marketing effort (the intervention) can be determined over a series of data points. The technique provides a quantitative estimate of the effect of a specific promotional activity for a given set of conditions.

Diffusion Models

Mathematical models that predict the market penetration of a new product over time are referred to as diffusion models. Included are a variety of models that vary according to the type of data required and the assumptions about the rate of penetration. The parameters of the model are estimated from experience with similar new products, consumer pretests, or early sales returns. The form of the model and the estimation of parameters depend on assumptions about the immediacy of market appeal, the length of time between exposure to and adoption of the product, the effects of word of mouth, the effects of advertising, and other factors.

Multiple Methods of Forecasting

The most practical technique for estimating the rate of adoption of load control programs is to use several of the methods simultaneously. No one estimation technique will provide accurate forecasts under all circumstances. The techniques discussed above are often combined for the best estimate of the likelihood that a product will achieve some intended level of market acceptance (Hurwood, Grossman, and Bailey 1978). The discussion now turns to an application of forecasting techniques with actual data.

THE APPLICATION OF FORECASTING TECHNIQUES TO LOAD MANAGEMENT

The data used in this example were taken from Carolina Power and Light Company's introduction of a residential water heater control program in Raleigh, North Carolina. These data are representative of the type of information that is readily available from utility company records. We discuss the usefulness of these data for forecasting and illustrate techniques that are appropriate. In the next section, "Designing Information Systems," we will discuss the type and form of data required for more complex methods of forecasting.

A description of CP&L's residential water heater control program is presented in Chapter 3. The available data are summarized in Tables 8.1 and 8.2. The actual number of installations and removals, and the net number of installations, that were made each month are reported in Table 8.1. The number of contract cards, or requests for installation received each month, is reported in Table 8.2. It must be remembered,

TABLE 8.1

INSTALLATIONS OF DIRECT LOAD CONTROL DEVICES

Month, Year	Number of Devices			
	Installed	Removed	Net in Place	Cumulative Total
July 1980	114	0	114	114
August 1980	324	0	324	438
September 1980	630	0	630	1,068
October 1980	984	0	984	2,052
November 1980	644	0	644	2,696
December 1980	936	3	933	3,629
January 1981	867	3	864	4,493
February 1981	1,005	9	996	5,489
March 1981	1,215	9	1,206	6,695
April 1981	882	13	869	7,564
May 1981	442	3	439	8,003
June 1981	105	1	104	8,107
July 1981	124	9	115	8,222
August 1981	31	10	21	8,243
September 1981	34	1	33	8,276
October 1981	18	11	7	8,283
November 1981	43	5	38	8,321
December 1981	27	2	25	8,346
January 1982	84	8	76	8,422
February 1982	99	7	92	8,514
March 1982	79	5	74	8,588
April 1982	108	8	100	8,688

TABLE 8.2

CONTRACT CARDS RECEIVED BY MONTH

	Number of Cards	
Month Year	Received By Month[a]	Cumulative Total
June 1980	108	108
July 1980	128	236
August 1980	352	588
September 1980	1,715	2,303
October 1980	1,177	3,480
November 1980	423	3,903
December 1980	540	4,443
January 1981	760	5,203
February 1981	1,070	6,273
March 1981	1,218	7,491
April 1981	663	8,154
May 1981	206	8,360
June 1981	117	8,477
July 1981	53	8,530
August 1981	36	8,566
September 1981	21	8,587
October 1981	31	8,618
November 1981	61	8,679
December 1981	43	8,722
January 1982	84	8,806
February 1982	46	8,852
March 1982	154	9,006
April	1,060	10,006

[a]This figure has been adjusted to show only those contracts where installation can be made.

however, that the installation is not always made during the month in which the contract card is received. One must review the raw data carefully before using it in an analysis to detect any such biases that may produce error in forecasting.

The data on installations in Table 8.1 include information about control devices that were subsequently removed. From the raw data, it cannot be determined in which month a device was installed that later was removed. An important question to ask before the analysis is which of the sets of figures to use, installations by month or net installations.

When compiling the available data for forecasting analysis, it is essential to investigate the need for possible adjustments to raw data. The raw data in Table 8.2 have been adjusted for noninstallation. Not all contract cards received lead to installation. For this example, 8 percent to 12 percent of the requests do not result in installation. Among the reasons for this are that the household is not within range of the signal, is not eligible because its water heater is not big enough, or does not want the wiring or the device installed.

After adjusting the available raw data, the question arises again as to what set of data is relevant to use in the forecasting analysis. Such questioning returns attention to the objectives of the forecasting process. Perhaps management is interested in the predicted sales of the program. In that case, analysis of contract card responses would be appropriate. If management wanted to forecast installations, however, it would use those data instead. In practical terms, two forecasts will be needed since the sales of the program and the installation of the devices are closely interdependent.

The discussion that follows focuses on the contract card data. The aims here are to estimate the impact of marketing efforts and to predict the number of customers who will sign up for the program. The important point, however, is that all the components of the system are interdependent. For instance, the timing of installations will be planned and coordinated based on both the estimated sales of the program and the specified goal (i.e., how much time should elapse between sign-up and installation).

Now we can examine the contract card data more closely. One can look at the data in Table 8.2 and quickly pinpoint opportunities to use the various forecasting techniques. Complex trend analysis (discussed above in "Time Series") is not possible, since that kind of analysis requires at least fifty data points. Although such mathematical analysis is not feasible, some qualitative intervention analysis is still possible. That is, we can evaluate the impact of specific kinds of intervention.

A comparison of Table 8.2 and Figure 8.2 shows that numbers of contract cards received correspond to the timing of the bill inserts and follow-up letters sent to customers. (Figure 8.2 shows mailings and other promotions by month. This information was available only for June 1980 to April 1981.) Management thus can predict the estimated response for promotional activities based on the available data.

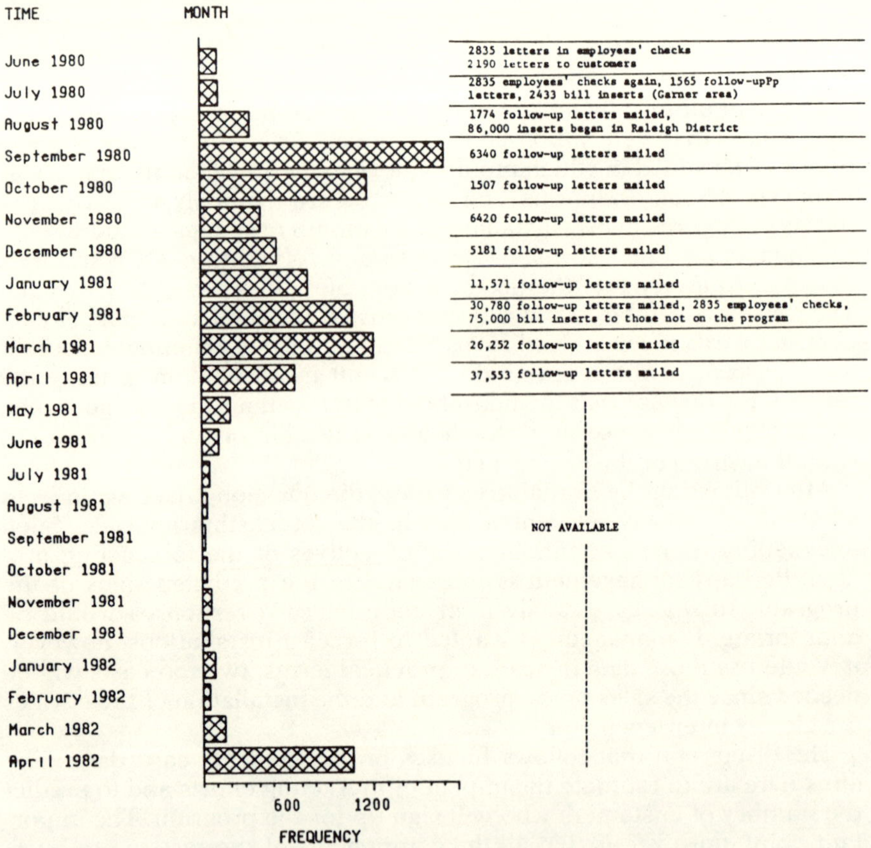

Figure 8.2 Promotional Mailings

When estimating sales in a new market, one should focus on relative penetration rates. The number of potential customers used here for the water heater control program is about 48,000. The participation goal set by the utility may be 50 percent of the potential, or 24,000. Using that figure as the goal for participation, we calculated the actual proportion of potential customers signing up over monthly time intervals; that proportion is shown in Figure 8.3.

The most effective way to use these data is to view them as a test market. For a market of similar characteristics and environment, a marketing effort based on these data should yield comparable results. To determine whether the market of interest is similar to the test market, however, requires market research data. For example, cross-sectional analysis of attitudes toward energy conservation combined with analysis of demographic characteristics will serve as a basis for

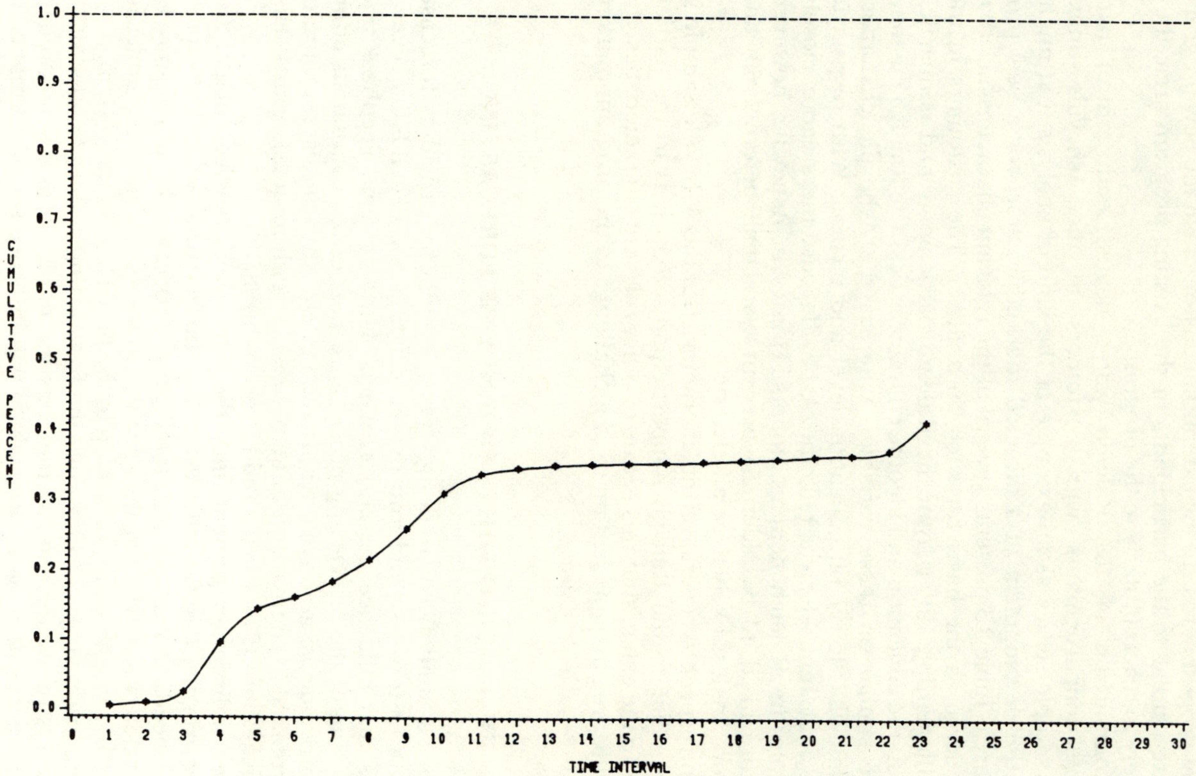

Figure 8.3 Cumulative Percent of Participation Goal

comparison between the test market and the target market. These data should be examined for all participants and nonparticipants in the existing program area. To the extent that customers in the new program area are similar to the participants in the existing program area, they are likely to react similarly to the program.

A comparison of the Raleigh water heater load control participants/nonparticipants with customers in the Asheville unexposed sample serves as an example of the kind of analysis that might guide the development of a targeted marketing effort for a new program area. Table 8.3 presents several of the relevant characteristics that might serve as the basis for such an analysis. The customers in the Asheville sample differ from the Raleigh participants and nonparticipants on the education and income characteristics. The Raleigh customers are similar on these variables, whereas the Asheville customers are somewhat lower on education level and income. With respect to tenure and June electric bill, the Asheville customers more closely resemble the Raleigh nonparticipants. Homes in Asheville, however, are more likely to be older (58 percent were built before 1960) and therefore are less likely to be all-electric.

With respect to several of the characteristics the Asheville sample is more similar to the Raleigh nonparticipants than it is to the participants. To the extent that this is true of other relevant characteristics, the Asheville area may present more of a challenge to the program marketing effort.

EVALUATING THE EFFICIENCY OF FORECASTING

Whether a utility needs to design a new system for providing forecasting data or to revise and improve an existing one depends on several factors that influence the performance of the system. Feedback and monitoring of the forecasting process are part of the continuous effort to improve decision making within the system; the starkest measure of performance is comparison of actual results with forecast results (Hisrich and Peters 1978; Cleary and Levenbach 1982).

When utility management finds the differences between actual and forecast results ("forecasting error") to be in excess of an acceptable level it needs to evaluate the forecasting process. The utility may be able to determine whether the specific causes of the error are under its control by, as a first step, returning to the flow chart of the system.

There are two ways to improve the forecasting system (Kotler 1972). The first is to use the existing methods but to collect more comprehensive and accurate information, which will improve the performance of the forecast while pinpointing strategic opportunities. For example, the utility might reclassify sign-ups according to the source of the request (from billing or through office contact). Contract cards might be modified to ask marketing research information, such as where the cus-

TABLE 8.3

SELECTED CHARACTERISTICS FOR
RALEIGH WATER HEATER LOAD CONTROL PARTICIPANTS AND NONPARTICIPANTS
AND
ASHEVILLE UNEXPOSED SAMPLE

	Raleigh		Asheville
	Participant	Nonparticipant	Unexposed
Education:			
Less than high school	6	6	13
High school	13	.9	16
Some college	17	20	27
College graduate or more	64	66	43
Income:			
Low (≤ $9,900)	6	8	25
Medium ($10,000-24,999)	37	49	50
High ($725,000)	57	43	25
Tenure:			
Own	97	67	75
Rent	3	33	24
June Bill:			
Low (< $50)	22	40	45
Medium ($50-99)	61	46	46
High (> $100)	17	14	9
Age of Structure:			
Before 1960	29	33	58
1960-1969	28	30	18
1970-1974	13	17	8
Since 1974	30	19	16
Appliance:			
Electric water heater	100	76	85
Electric air conditioner	83	70	28
All electric	43	29	19

tomer first heard about the program. The additional information would help indicate the relative effectiveness of the various marketing efforts.

The second way to improve the system is to supplement or replace the present forecasting technique with a more elaborate one. In some cases that may mean hiring outside experts capable of performing a more detailed analysis and forecast. On the other hand, the utility might simply rely on present personnel either to develop a new model or to seek out existing secondary market data. Regardless, the organization must decide *a priori* what the requirements of the forecasting system are.

9

Marketing Load Management—Analysis, Planning, and Control

After utility management establishes formal objectives for its load management programs within a specified time frame, it needs to do three things to market those programs effectively. First, marketing management must select market segments that appear to be promising and worthwhile. Second, a marketing program must be planned for each identifiable market segment within the selected service area. Management should select the staff to market the load management program to each segment and decide what product characteristics, price, promotion, and distribution tactics are likely to achieve the load management program's formal objectives. Third, the load management marketing program must be carefully implemented, and consumer response to it must be monitored. Control of the marketing effort enables management to revise objectives, shift resources, and modify the mix of marketing tactics used as the load management environment and consumer response change over time.

This chapter discusses the load management marketing process. The first section describes several ways to identify marketing opportunities for load management programs. Next, the main variables that affect marketing decisions are reviewed as they apply to planning the load management marketing program. Various ways to market load management are identified and the implications of likely consumer responses to each management decision are discussed, based on findings reported earlier in this book. The next section cites several issues in managing the marketing effort and provides guidelines to manage the marketing effort and maintain its adaptability to the changing marketing environment and program objectives.

ANALYZING LOAD MANAGEMENT MARKETING OPPORTUNITIES

The first step in devising a load management marketing program is to estimate the potential market. As suggested in Chapter 8, this requires market research data. Information is needed to estimate how many water heaters and air conditioners that can be controlled are in the target area and to determine customers' willingness to take part in load management programs. If customers in the target area are similar to those in areas where load management programs already have been introduced, then experience from those areas can be used to estimate market potential. On the other hand, if the new market area is substantially different from the area(s) already served, then consumer surveys should be conducted to provide the needed information. To illustrate the types of data that should be assembled, we surveyed households in five North Carolina market areas where load management programs had not been introduced. The results show that the number of loads that can be controlled and the degree of customer acceptance differ substantially from one area to another.

Appliance Saturation

The saturation of electric water heaters and central air conditioners in the five study areas where load management programs had not yet been introduced is summarized in Figure 9.1. A high proportion of households in each area, ranging from 85 to 98 percent, had electric water heaters. Although water heater capacity varied somewhat from one area to another, so that the potential benefits of controlling water heater loads might differ, it appeared that enough customers owned controllable water heaters to warrant the introduction of water heater load control programs in each area.

In contrast to the rather uniform saturation of electric water heaters, ownership of central air conditioners varied substantially among market areas. Relatively few households in the Asheville area, which has a cool mountain climate, had central air conditioners, while almost three of every four households in Greensboro, located in the hotter Piedmont section of the state, had central air conditioners. In the small towns and rural areas studied, central air conditioner ownership also varied somewhat, ranging from 62 percent of the households in Laurinburg to 45 percent in Plymouth; both towns are located in the hot, humid Coastal Plain.

In sum, these data clearly show that appliance saturation, particularly in the case of central air conditioners, cannot be taken for granted or even assumed to be constant throughout a utility service area. Thus, before the market potential for load management can be determined for an area, the utility must conduct an appliance saturation survey.

Program Awareness and Knowledge

Very high levels of program awareness were reported in Chapters 5 and 6, which examined participating and nonparticipating households in

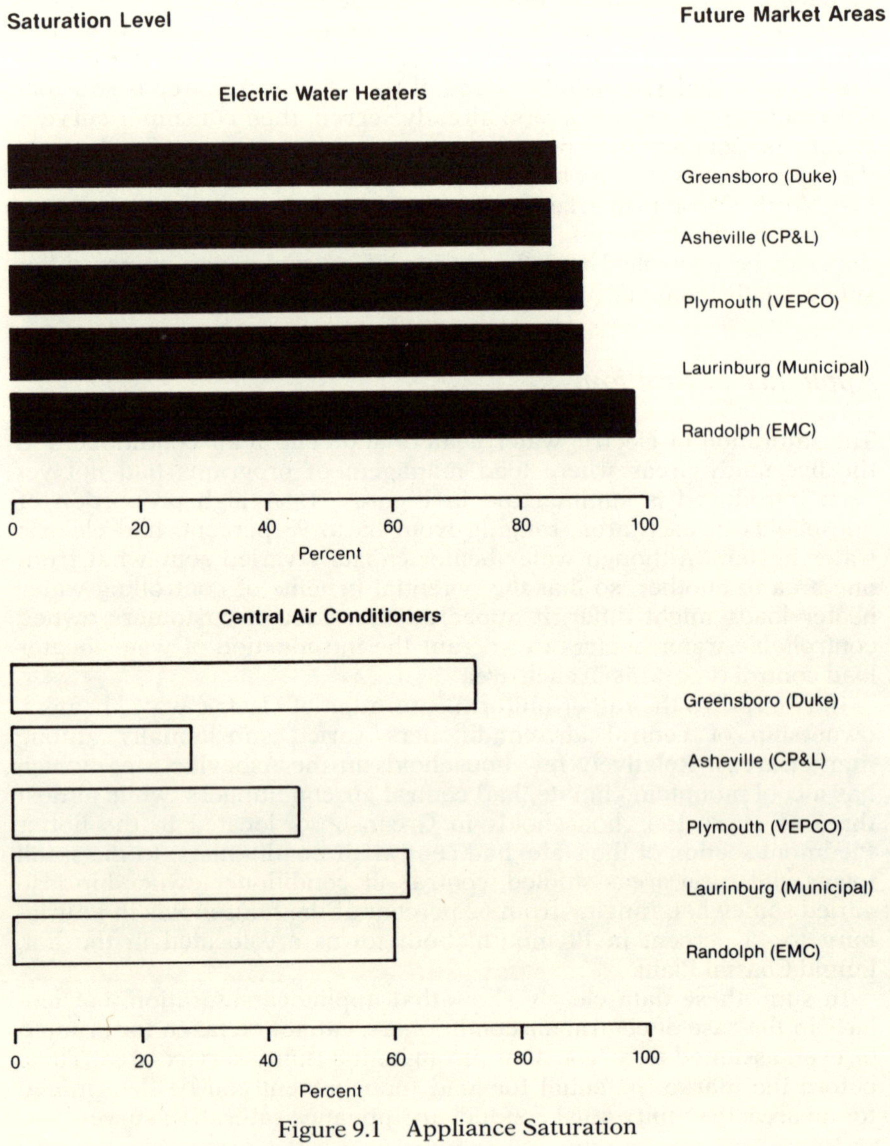

Figure 9.1 Appliance Saturation

areas where load management programs already had been introduced. As shown in Table 9.1, customer awareness levels also tended to be high in areas where programs had yet to be offered. In four of the areas, Greensboro, Asheville, Laurinburg, and the Randolph EMC, more than seven of every ten households queried indicated they had heard about load management. Customer awareness of time-of-day programs was lower, reflecting the more limited availability of time-of-day programs in the state; but even so more than one-third of the households in each area, and more than half of those in the two metropolitan communities, had heard of time-of-day rates.

Households living in these areas reported two major sources of information about load management: television advertising and bill stuffers. Apparently, utility advertising on television stations whose signals reach a wide geographic area was serving to alert customers not only where programs were being actively marketed, but also where programs had yet to be introduced. This spillover of information should ease the introduction of load management as utilities move from limited pilot to systemwide programs. It also suggests that there is ample justification for public or nonprofit agencies to advertise the availability of load management programs. Television advertising is effective in establishing program awareness, but it is also very expensive. Since utilities cannot limit viewers to those living solely in geographic areas they serve, in buying broadcast time they are subsidizing other utilities that serve customers within the television station's viewing areas, or area of dominant influence. As a result, utilities may tend to underinvest in television and radio advertising of load management, since the cost per thousand exposures for a single utility's customers is likely to be relatively high. This problem could be averted if a third party, such as the state utility commission or a nonprofit cooperative organization, assumed responsibility for coordinating media advertising and load management program introductions from one major geographic area to the next.

Consumers' knowledge of load management fundamentals was measured by a true-false test. By choosing answers randomly, 50 percent of the households surveyed would have selected the correct responses. The data summarized in Table 9.1 show that knowledge of load management fundamentals is somewhat better than would be predicted solely by chance, but not by much. About two-thirds (17 percent more than could have answered correctly by chance) knew that it costs utilities more to produce power during peak periods than during off-peak periods. About the same proportion knew that load management programs attempt to level out the peaks and valleys in electrical use.

Analyses reported in Chapters 5 and 6 indicated that households who were more knowledgeable about load management fundamentals were also more likely to have enrolled in a program already or, if not enrolled, to say that they intended to join in the future. The rather mod-

TABLE 9.1

CUSTOMER AWARENESS AND KNOWLEDGE
(percent of households)

	Future Market Areas (Utility)				
Indicator	Greensboro (DUKE)	Asheville (CP&L)	Plymouth (VEPCO)	Town of Laurinburg	Randolph EMC
Awareness					
Aware of load control programs	76%	88%	57%	73%	75%
Aware of time-of-day programs	52	53	34	48	45
Knowledge					
Household knows that it costs more to produce electricity during periods of peak demand	63	72	67	68	65
Household knows that load management programs attempt to level out peaks and valleys in electricial use	77	69	60	67	72

est levels of program knowledge illustrated in Table 9.1 suggest that most utilities should strongly consider using program marketing resources to improve customers' understanding of why load management programs are needed and how load management reduces the costs of producing power. Consumer surveys can be used to indicate what proportion of the population is ill-informed and to gauge progress as education efforts are undertaken.

Consumer Willingness to Participate

The wide variation in levels of market penetration achieved by load management programs in North Carolina indicates that consumer participation in any new program cannot be taken for granted. As described in Chapter 8, one way to gauge likely consumer participation when programs are to be introduced in different communities is to assume that past market penetration rates will be repeated, with some adjustment for differing community characteristics. Another approach, illustrated here, is to ask households whether they would take part if a program were introduced in their communities.

Figure 9.2 summarizes responses to such a question in five North Carolina communities. As illustrated, very few households in any of these communities stated flatly that they would not take part in a load management program. A large proportion, however, ranging from 31 percent to 52 percent, indicated they did not know whether they would take part. Since households were given little information about program characteristics before the question was asked (see questionnaire in Appendix A), a good deal of consumer uncertainty is to be expected. In fact, given the lack of descriptive material in the questionnaire and the absence of promotional efforts in these communities, it is noteworthy that sizable proportions of the households said they would take part in either a time-of-day rate program or a load control program if such were introduced. This readiness to participate and the fact that very few households are disinclined to take part suggest that utilities can expect to achieve modest market penetration of 10 to 20 percent with a very low-key promotional effort.

Consumers' willingness to participate in time-of-day programs stands in stark contrast to the very low market penetration levels achieved by Duke Power. As reported in Chapter 3, only about 1 percent of the households in Salisbury, North Carolina, had elected to take part by the time of our survey, whereas more than 25 percent of the eligible Salisbury households were participating in Duke's direct load control programs. The data reported here suggest that consumers' resistance did not result from dislike of time-of-day programs compared to load control programs. Apparently the Duke time-of-day program, with its high demand charges and customer service charges, and other characteristics of the Salisbury marketing effort were not sufficiently attractive to convert households who liked the time-of-day concept into actual program participants.

Consumer Attitudes Toward Their Electric Utility

In addition to appliance saturation, program awareness and knowledge, and consumer willingness to participate, a final determinant of consumer acceptance and market potential is consumers' attitudes toward their electric utilities. Even though a consumer may like the idea of load management, he may not enroll in a load control or time-of-day program if he does not like the utility that offers the program. The analyses of focus group discussions reported in Chapter 4 indicate that many North Carolina consumers have extremely negative opinions of electric utilities. As shown in Table 9.2, these negative feelings are not limited to any one type of utility—investor-owned, municipal, or electric member-

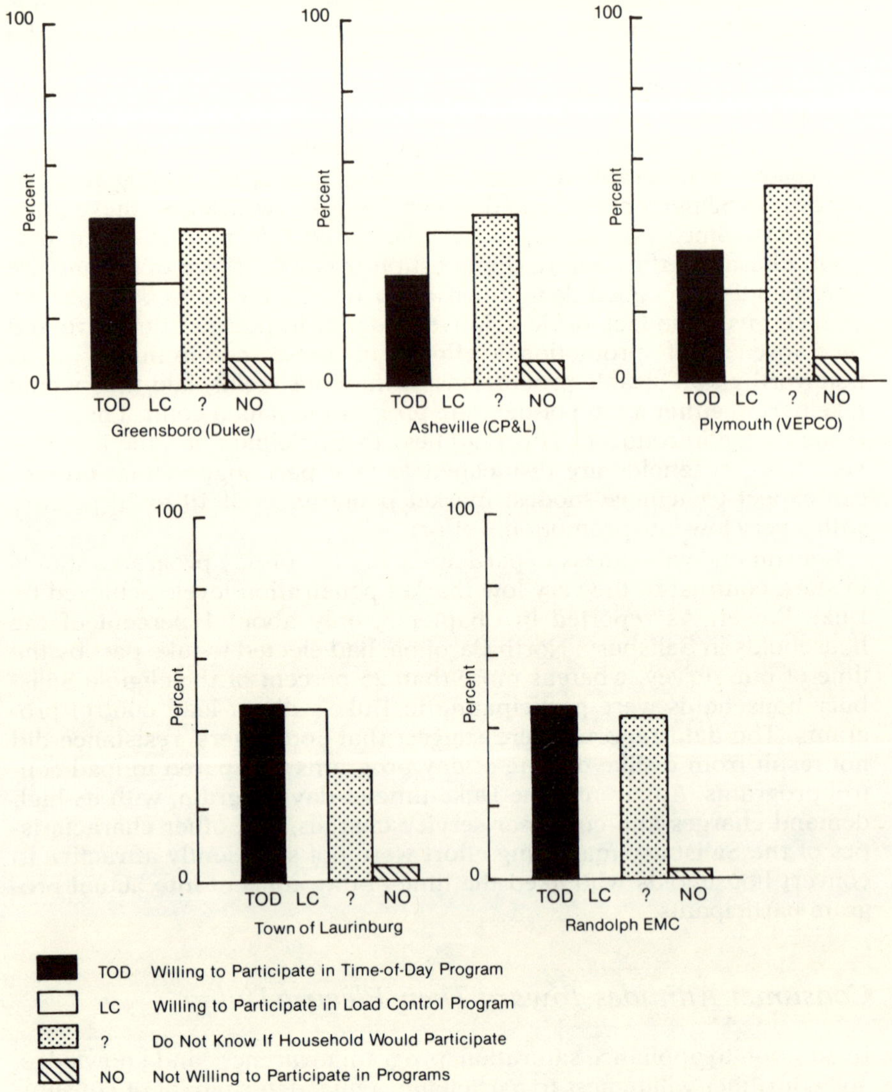

Figure 9.2 Willingness to Participate in Load Management

ship corporation. In each case, a majority of households believe they are paying too much for electricity, and very few believe their utilities are doing all they can to hold down prices.

As reported in Chapter 3, the electric membership corporations and municipal electric systems studied have overcome many problems with their image among utility customers and achieved high rates of program participation. One way they have accomplished that is by shifting the blame for high prices from themselves to the investor-owned gen-

TABLE 9.2

CUSTOMER ATTITUDES TOWARD UTILITY
(percent of households)

Attitude	Future Market Areas (Utility)				
	Greensboro (DUKE)	Asheville (CP&L)	Plymouth (VEPCO)	Town of Laurinburg	Randolph EMC
"We pay too much for electricity"					
Agree	54	76	79	85	83
Not sure	37	19	20	11	14
Disagree	10	5	1	4	3
"Our utility is doing everything possible to hold down rates"					
Agree	17	11	11	16	19
Not sure	51	36	52	27	41
Disagree	37	52	38	57	40
Household rated electric utility one of three most reliable sources of information on ways to save energy	79	69	70	66	72

erating utilities from whom they purchased wholesale power. Since most consumers believe that utilities are reliable sources of information (see Table 9.2), even though they do not like them, they may have been willing to accept this reason for rising prices and to join in load management as a way of getting even.

One possible explanation for the lower market penetration rates achieved by investor-owned utilities, therefore, is their inability to overcome consumers' negative images by finding a plausible scapegoat for rising prices. The analyses reported in Chapter 7 showed that load management programs are one means of improving customers' attitudes toward their electric utilities. Customers taking part in CP&L's and VEPCO's water heater load control programs were less critical of their respective electric utilities than nonparticipants were. The marketing problem is to get customers to enroll in the first place and then to maintain target levels of load management participation.

At least two approaches can be used to overcome investor-owned utilities' poor image with their customers. One that has been used with a great deal of success by Pacific Gas & Electric Company is to use a proxy for the utility in program promotional efforts. PG&E promotional material features a grandmotherly figure, "Mrs. Tooker," who asks people to join her in saving money by taking part in load mangement. While customers may not think highly of PG&E, they are apparently more than willing to follow Mrs. Tooker's advice and enroll in a direct load control program. A second approach, which was demonstrated in the state of New York, is to market load management through a third party. In the New York experiment, each customer served by Consolidated Edison was sent one of three letters with his electric bill asking him to enroll in a load control program. One letter was from Con Ed, the second was from the state public service commission, and the third was from the Cooperative Extension Service at Cornell University. Positive responses from customers were markedly higher, almost double, when the letter enlisting their cooperation did not come from Con Ed (see New York State Department of Public Service 1978).

Summary

Before formulating a mix of marketing tactics, utilities need to assess the potential market for their programs. Market forecasting techniques were discussed in Chapter 8. Additional information that can help utility management assess the market for load control and time-of-day programs has been presented here, based on residential consumer surveys in five market areas where load management programs had not yet been introduced. The results show that market potential will differ from one community to the next, depending on appliance saturation levels, customer awareness and knowledge, their predispositions toward load control and time-of-day programs, and their attitudes toward their electric utilities. For the most part, data from the five communities indicate there is a strong potential market for load management programs. Electric water heater saturation rates tended to be high. Consumer awareness of load mangement programs was remarkably high, even though programs had not been offered in those communities, and many households were predisposed to take part after being given a very brief description of the purpose of load control and time-of-day programs. We also have discussed two potential obstacles to program adoption.

Many households have only a very limited understanding of the purposes of load management programs, and many simply do not like their electric utilities. These obstacles may be reduced, however, through thoughtful marketing designed to increase consumers' understanding of load management and by promotional tactics that either offer consumers a plausible scapegoat for rising electricity prices or substitute a more acceptable person or organization as the source of the program.

MARKET SEGMENTS

Marketing is generally more successful if the total potential market for a product or program can be broken down into different segments that serve as targets for finely tuned promotion and distribution efforts. In the case of residential load management, two market segmentation strategies are often used. One is based on the concept of product diffusion and attempts to isolate characteristics of households who are most likely to be early program participants. By designing a mix of marketing tactics in line with the characteristics of early participants, a utility can accelerate the rate of program adoption substantially. A second market segmentation strategy is based on the fact that motives for participating differ predictably with varying consumer characteristics. Promotional messages will be most effective if they take advantage of that fact and are designed to appeal to specific types of households. The surveys of consumers in areas where load management programs were already being offered and in areas where programs had yet to be introduced provide a number of insights that can help with each of these market segmentation tasks. Segmentation based on the identification of likely early program participants is discussed here; segmentation based on motives for participation is addressed later.

Two approaches are used to identify likely early participants in time-of-day and load control programs. In geographic areas where programs have already been introduced, comparisons of program participants and nonparticipants can be used to provide an indication of early participant characteristics. In areas where programs have not yet been introduced, comparisons of households willing to participate with those who are not willing provide another basis for isolating likely early participant characteristics. The results of an attempt to segment the market for time-of-day and load control programs are illustrated in Table 9.3.

Early adopters are usually defined as the first 10 percent to 15 percent of the market to adopt a new product or join a new program. In order to identify early adopters, program participants were asked to indicate the month and year they had enrolled in a load control or time-of-day program. Unfortunately, most households could not remember and left the answer space blank. As an alternative, households participating in the investor-owned utilities' load management programs were used to help define early adopter characteristics. (See Chapter 5.) These programs had been introduced recently (the oldest had been available for two years at the time of the consumer survey), and only modest market penetration rates had been achieved (at most about one-quarter of those eligible to take part had joined one of the programs). Thus, this group of participants provides a fairly good indicator of early participant characteristics.

Even a cursory review of Table 9.3 will reveal two facts. First, the early participants in time-of-day programs are more sharply differentiated from nonparticipants than is the case for load control programs. Second, in some cases, differences between those who said they would be willing to participate and those who said they would not do not carry over once programs are actually introduced; in fact, differences between actual participants and nonparticipants may be

TABLE 9.3

MARKET SEGMENTATION BASED UPON EARLY PARTICIPATION

Consumer Characteristics	Time-of-Day Programs: Early Adopters[a]	Time-of-Day Programs: Willing Adopters[b]	Load Control Programs: Early Adopters[c]	Load Control Programs: Willing Adopters[d]
Household Characteristics				
1. Type of household	No Children	Children	ND	No Children
2. Education	Higher	Higher	ND	ND
3. Income	Higher	Higher	Higher	ND
4. Race	White	ND	ND	ND
5. Age	Older	Younger	ND	ND
6. Venturesomeness	ND	Higher	ND	ND
Housing Characteristic				
1. Type of dwelling	Single Family	Not mobile Home	Single Family	ND
2. Tenure	ND	Rent	Own	ND
3. Size of dwelling	Larger	Larger	Larger	Smaller
4. Central air conditioning	ND	Yes	ND	Yes
5. All electric	Yes	Yes	ND	Yes
Use/Conservation of Electricity				
1. June electricity bill	Higher	Higher	ND	ND
2. Conservation knowledge	Higher	Higher	ND	Higher
3. Conservation opinion leadership	Higher	Higher	Higher	ND
4. Program knowlege	Higer	Higher	ND	Higher

ND = no difference

[a]Based on characteristics of participants in Duke Power time-of-day program in Salisbury, NC in comparison with nonparticipants.

[b]Based on characteristics of households in areas where programs are not available who indicated they would be willing to participate in a time-of-day program.

[c]Based on characteristics of households who enrolled in Duke Power, CP&L, and VEPCO load management programs in comparison with non-participants. Because of low penetration rates, these households are classed as early adopters.

[d]Based upon characteristics of households in areas where programs are not available who indicated they would be willing to participate in a load control program.

just the opposite of those between households who were willing and those who were unwilling to participate later in areas where programs have yet to be introduced. Thus, some caution is in order in defining market segments based on consumer intentions rather than on actual behavior.

In the case of the time-of-day programs, both early adopters and those who said they would be willing to adopt it in the future had a number of characteristics in common when compared with nonparticipants and those unwilling to adopt the program later. Thus, the early participant segment for time-of-day programs should include households with higher income and educational levels and those living in larger houses and "all electric" homes. In keeping with those characteristics, early participants also tend to have higher electric bills, but they feel better informed about how to conserve electricity. Others come to them for conservation advice. Finally, their knowledge of load management tends to be higher as well.

The early adopter group tended to be older with no children living in the household and to be white. On the other hand, in areas where programs had yet to be introduced, those who said they would adopt the program later tended to be younger families with children. There were no differences among racial groups in willingness to adopt. The differences between the early adopter and willing-to-adopt groups may have resulted from specific characteristics of time-of-day programs. When households learn the degree to which they will have to change their behavior to save money on their electric bills, for example, younger households with children, which might be expected to have less flexible schedules, apparently decided not to take part.

Identification of a clear group of potential early participants is much more difficult for load control programs than for time-of-day programs. As illustrated by the data in Table 9.3, none of the consumer characteristics examined differentiated both the early adopter and willing-to-adopt groups. The early adopters, as reported in Chapter 5, tend to have higher incomes and to be homeowners living in larger, single-family dwellings. They also rank high on electricity conservation opinion leadership. In areas where load control programs have not yet been introduced, however, none of these factors differentiate those who say they would participate in the program from those who say they would not.

PLANNING THE LOAD MANAGEMENT MARKETING PROGRAM

Once target market segments are selected, marketing management must put together a marketing program to achieve penetration objectives within an established time frame. Planning the marketing program requires that management design a program with an optimal combination of product, price, promotion, and distribution characteristics. The following sections discuss the major decisions management must make in formulating a marketing program. The choice of marketing tactics used influences consumers' likely response to the load control program. Therefore, utilities with low penetration objectives over an extended period are likely to choose marketing tactics that are radically different from those chosen by a utility with a high penetration objective to be accomplished over a brief period. Furthermore, the optimal mix of marketing tactics will change as the program objectives change. Once a utility achieves target penetration rates, for example, the marketing task becomes one of maintaining the level of penetration rather than initiating widespread trial and adoption.

PRODUCT DECISIONS

The utility should involve its marketing management in decisions about various characteristics of its load management product as readily as it involves them in promotion decisions. The physical characteristics of the load control devices, capabilities of the system, cycling policy, and program incentives all potentially affect customer acceptance of load management and participation in the program.

Switch and System Characteristics

The location of the load control switch and its physical appearance are issues for many residential consumers. Most consumers are not particularly eager for the switch to be visually evident. In fact, acceptance of the switch itself would probably improve as it were made less visible. It is sometimes possible to hide load control devices completely that mount at the appliance, when an appliance such as the water heater is itself hidden from view. Switches that are mounted on the exterior of the dwelling or on an appliance that is generally located outside, such as most central air conditioning units, are likely to be treated in a manner similar to demand meters and heat pumps. Specifically, most households will be inclined to hide the device with shrubbery if at all possible. Chapter 4 noted some consumer reservations about switches mounted at the water heater even when the water heater is located in an interior closet of the dwelling. Existing switches are not intrinsically attractive and are generally regarded as devices to be hidden away, like demand meters, fuse boxes, and cold air returns.

This general reaction among many consumers is counter to the efforts of some utilities to select a switch system that allows the household to verify whether it is being cycled off or whether its appliances should be operating normally. The switches that include lights to indicate an "off cycle" status may be of some comfort to those households that are anxious about participating in load control. But these same households will be more likely to want the switches hidden from view, regardless of the indicator light feature.

Utilities probably could enhance load control participation by showing pictures of the actual switch that would be installed in the household. However, the switch should be portrayed as being well hidden from view and, indeed, should be installed that way.

An important physical attribute of air conditioner load control switches may be the ability of the household to override the system, should it so desire. Many households have reservations about the loss of control over the water heater and air conditioner in load management programs. If the utility objective is near 100 percent participation, then the possibility of reaching that objective would be enhanced by the addition of a household override switch on the load control device.

Service Interruption Plan

Discomfort is not generally anticipated when households think about water heater direct load control programs. The length of most off-times in service interruption plans studied here resulted in a very low number of complaints from participants in either water heater or air conditioner load control programs. Potential participants are much more anxious, however, about the interruption of the compressor in the air conditioner system. Many households do not really understand how one can stay cool when the air conditioner is "cycled off". They are more comfortable with the idea of cycling off the water heater, since most people can understand that water stays hot for an extended period of time.

The implication of this is that utilities can increase participation in their programs by clearly focusing service interruption plans on water heater interruption as the primary load management tool. It need not address the lack of discomfort anticipated from water heater control. Instead, the service interruption plan should be structured carefully to cycle off air conditioners as a secondary priority, and personal testimony should be offered from satisfied air conditioner control participants, rather than primarily from water heater control participants.

Most of the service interruption plans now in use provide minimal discomfort to residential customers. In fact, many households probably expect to be slightly inconvenienced by load control and are surprised to not experience some inconvenience.

The few exceptions to this have occurred when the load control system itself has malfunctioned. The experience of Four County EMC suggests that a utility should establish a load control system that includes positive checks that the system is operating properly. Chapter 3 described an incident at Four County EMC in which the utility thought the control devices had received the signal to resume normal service, when there had actually been a malfunction in the transmission device and none of the switches was returned to normal service status. Furthermore, the problem was not discovered for several hours, and the situation was complicated further by a delay in getting a service person to repair the damaged electronic component.

The utility system should include control devices mounted near the master panel for verification of cycling episodes. The utility also should have established contingency plans that detail what will be done if various system problems are encountered.

Incentives

There appears to be some segment of a load management market that is not motivated by an economic incentive. This small proportion of the market will participate or refuse to participate regardless of the level of economic incentive offered. A major proportion of the potential market, however, appears to be responsive to economic incentives for program participation.*

In general, the greater the economic incentive offered to a household, the more likely the household is to participate in load management. Several levels of monthly economic incentive were included in the survey of households in areas where no load management programs were being offered. The results were very reliable across the different geographic locations. On average, 17 percent of the households indicated that they would participate in a water heater direct load control program without being offered any economic incentive. An additional 2 percent would participate with a $1 incentive. About 1 percent more would participate for a $2 monthly incentive. A $3 incentive would induce 4 percent more households to participate. About 25 percent more of the households said they would participate if the monthly incentive were $5. An additional 43 percent would participate if the incentive were $10 a month. Finally, about 8 percent of the households reported in the survey that no financial credit (within reason) would be large enough to influence them to participate in water heater direct load control.

This estimated demand curve has some interesting implications for

*The issue of the role and effect of economic incentive in customer participation in load management programs continues to be controversial. Lawrence, Heberlein, and Baumgartner (1984) note the prevailing utility management belief that economic incentives are necessary to achieve any substantial penetration rates. Lawrence, Heberlein, and Baumgartner also suggest, however, that objective evidence is lacking to demonstrate that economic incentives are absolutely necessary for widespread customer acceptance of direct load control programs. Though our findings, based on subjective self-report data, vary somewhat from the Heberlein review in identifying the penetration level goal at which economic incentives will have a positive effect, we converge on the idea that residential customers may be segmented by their likely response or nonresponse to economic incentive.

marketing direct load control. First, a sizable number of eligible households seem quite willing to participate in the program without being offered any direct economic incentive. This is consistent with the experience of Lumbee River EMC, where several thousand load management participation agreements were obtained by the utility in the early months, during which the program included no direct economic incentive to the household. Second, the average holds across all types of utilities: about 17 percent of the market said they would participate without any direct economic incentive, whether the household was in a municipal, electric membership corporation, or investor-owned utility service area. This suggests that utilities that establish modest load control objectives should be able to achieve these objectives with marketing tactics that do not necessarily include any direct economic incentive. The possibility of achieving load control penetration objectives in excess of about 15 percent of the market, however, appears to be enhanced by a product offering that includes some economic incentive.

At the other end of the demand curve, however, is a sizable proportion of the potential market that seems to not respond to economic incentives, even those higher than $10 credit per month. A third implication of the demand curve is that utilities with formal load management objectives of installing as many switches as possible will encounter a customer response barrier at about a 90 percent penetration level regardless of the economic incentive offered. Under a voluntary program with a participation objective of virtually 100 percent, utility marketing management will have to use a tactic other than economic incentives to achieve adoption in roughly the last 10 percent of the potential market.

Between these two extremes, however, the market does appear to respond favorably to increasing levels of economic incentives. A fourth implication of the demand curve is that this estimated consumer response increases sharply at the $5 monthly credit level and again at the $10 level. It appears to make relatively little difference whether the monthly economic incentive offered is $1, $2, or $3.

Economic incentives probably would be more effective if the amount of the credit were advertised at its yearly level rather than at its monthly level. A credit of $24 a year would be more appealing to most households than $2 a month, regardless of how often the credit was actually posted on the electric bill.

The utility also could improve participation by treating the air conditioner and water heater programs as a single program that offers a high (joint) participation billing credit. Packaging the two load control appliances together results in a higher economic incentive, which should increase participation among eligible households. Households that do not qualify for the joint program then can choose to participate in only one of the load control programs at a reduced economic incentive. The greater economic incentive afforded by the combined load control program offering, however, should increase the response from the large segment of residential consumers who are responsive to the bill credits.

Load management participation also would be increased if the product offering included attractive incentives other than strictly financial ones. Some utilities, such as VEPCO and CP&L, have offered water heater insulation wraps as part of their load control programs in some service areas. The extent to which water heater wraps are an attractive incentive is a subject for further consumer research or test marketing. However, the tactic of tying the load management product into other conservation or electrical service offerings—including energy audits and home improvement loan programs—is another approach to using incentives. In fact, to the extent that electrical service to a residence is voluntarily elected by the household, there is the opportunity to tie participation in load management to participation in utility electrical service. Under this incentive arrangement, load control devices or time-of-day meters would become mandatory and would be just as much a part of the electrical service agreement as the traditional demand meter. In fact, that may be the only feasible way that utilities with objectives of 100 percent market penetration can realistically expect to accomplish those objectives.

Installation

A final decision marketing management must make is who will install the load management device. It is clear from the focus group research that most households expect that anything having to do with utility electrical service would be installed by a representative of the utility itself. Thus, most households expect that any wiring or devices would be installed by utility employees and not by subcontractors, regardless of how qualified the subcontractors may be to do the actual installation. Most residential consumers appear to believe that the demand meters are installed by utility personnel and not by private electrical contractors. A similar expectation holds for load management equipment. Many households fear that installation by a private electrical contractor will result in a third party to further complicate any question of who is responsible, should equipment problems be later encountered.

PRICE DECISIONS

A second decision area for marketing management is that of price—what it costs the residential customer to participate in load management. Many of the costs can be expressed in dollars and cents. Other costs have more to do with time and required commitment.

Equipment and Wiring Costs

Marketing management must decide how much of the cost of the load management equipment and supplies for any necessary additional wiring the participating household has to pay. None of the six programs reviewed in Chapter 3 required the household to make a direct payment for the load control switch, for example. Most utilities estimate that each load control switch costs about $100. To require the household to pay an equipment expense would be a disincentive for participation.

Installation Fees

As noted in Chapter 3, Duke Power was the only one of the six utilities reviewed that included the installation fee as a financial price borne directly by the participating household. Such an installation fee is clearly a disincentive for participation in load management, as was shown in Chapter 6. Participation rates should be enhanced if that expense is borne by the utility. Alternatively, utilities that have achieved penetration objectives and changed to maintenance marketing objectives may elect to require installation and equipment fees in further marketing. Four County EMC, for example, achieved penetration rates (reported in Chapter 3) of about 88 percent and 59 percent for water heater and air conditioner direct load control, respectively, by the summer of 1982 and adopted maintenance marketing objectives for its load control programs. Meeting these objectives required only a few new participants each month. Thus, to reduce incremental participation by late adopters, the load management program now includes an installation fee and county electrical inspection fee that is borne directly by newly participating households.

Contracts and Consent Agreements

The load management programs developed by some utilities include signed consent cards or even formal contracts for participation. Households can sign up for other utilities' programs simply by a telephone request or other verbal, informal agreement. The inclusion of a contract or signed consent agreement in the price generally restricts participation in load management. At a minimum, the contract or consent card represents one more price the household must pay to participate. Contracts and consent forms often get misplaced, they take time to read and sign, and they are threatening to many consumers. It is not clear that a unique contract or consent form is needed for participation in load management, even if the household resides in a rental facility.

Contractual Time Commitments for Participation

A formal contract will restrict participation, but longer specified lengths of contract probably will further reduce participation. Long contractual time commitments reduce the trialability of the load management program. Brief initial time commitments make it easier for the household to try the load management program.

Withdrawal Fees

Several of the load management programs mentioned in Chapter 3 included provisions whereby the utilities could charge a participating household a substantial withdrawal fee should the household decide to stop participating after only a year or two. Such a provision probably serves as a disincentive for participation since it represents a financial threat and raises the possibility that the household may not be satisfied with program participation. The clause is particularly irrelevant because utilities with load control programs have had few complaints and requests for removals.

Utilities seeking to keep penetration rates low probably should include high withdrawal fees and removal charges in the marketing program. Withdrawal fees of $50 or more probably would be adequate to discourage households who are uncertain about participation.

Time Costs to Participate

The time a household must spend to qualify for participation in load management is yet another "price" decision for marketing management. Some utilities require households to spend considerable time to qualify for participation in a load management program. Though the group meetings probably are informative and interesting, they require a nontrivial expenditure of household time and effort to attend. Participation in load management programs, then, is likely to be lower where the utility requires households to spend considerable time and effort in order to enroll in load management programs.

PROMOTION DECISIONS

Effective load management marketing requires more than just establishing a well-designed product and making it available at an attractive price. Marketing management also must communicate the availability of load management to households in the target markets, inform those households about the benefits of the programs, and persuade eligible households to participate. Marketing management must consider a number of promotional alternatives to achieve those goals. Promotional tactics should include the use of advertising, publicity, and direct selling. The emphasis of the promotional effort also will change over time within a given market as the utility establishes program awareness and moves on to objectives that require more persuasion.

Communication Source

Most utilities face a difficult problem in communicating with their customers about load management. First, some consumers respond with distrust and suspicion to anything a utility says. Even though the utility is viewed as expert in generating and distributing electricity, as noted in the survey results, many households seem to question the motives behind a persuasive message aired by the utility. Second, households are quite ready to counter-argue utility messages with negative thoughts about exorbitant salaries, lack of productivity incentives, underworked personnel, excessive and lavish buildings, and the like. And third, some consumers do not approve of utilities' spending money for advertising for any reason.

One way to overcome those problems is to use a proxy for the utility. Pacific Gas & Electric Company's use of the "Mrs. Tooker" character was described earlier in this chapter. An alternative to that type of spokesman is a communication source who is highly credible. Walter Cronkite is an example of a highly credible source. In states with highly respected universities, a university faculty member whose area is electrical engineering, environmental planning, or the like might be an appropriately credible utility spokesman.

An alternative would be for load management advertising to be managed and sponsored by a third party, such as (in North Carolina) the state utilities commission or the North Carolina Alternative Energy Corporation. The third party could coordinate region-wide introduction of multiple utility load management programs where the regions would be defined by the areas of dominant influence of the available broadcast media. The utilities in North Carolina for example, owe a debt of gratitude to CP&L and Duke Power for creating considerable load management awareness and basic knowledge throughout most of the state. Media markets overlap utility service areas. Thus, joint promotional cooperatives for load management programs, formed by all utilities within a regional media market and using a single spokesman or third party representative, offer many advantages.

Message Strategies

Optimal promotional message strategies change with the passage of time. Marketing programs must move potential participant households from awareness to basic knowledge and interest in the programs to deciding whether to participate. Messages should be designed to appeal to the motives most consumers have for participating in load management programs.

The focus group discussions described in Chapter 4 and statewide survey reported in Chapters 5 and 6 identified a number of reasons households participate in load management programs. As part of the statewide survey, three different groups of consumers were asked about their motives for participating in load management. First, program participants were asked to tell why they were taking part. Second, nonparticipants living in communities where programs already had been introduced were asked to indicate reasons that might lead them to join. Third, households living in areas where programs had not yet been introduced were asked to indicate reasons that would lead them to join a load control or time-of-day program. Households' characteristics and attitudes were analyzed to identify systematic differences in the types of consumers likely to be motivated by each particular reason for participation. The results are summarized in Table 9.4.

As with the analysis of likely early participation reported earlier in this chapter, factors associated with differences in motives for participation also vary between households who say they intend or do not intend to participate and households that actually did and did not take part in the programs. Nevertheless, some similarities exist across the groups–those who are reporting on future intentions and those whose actual behavior was measured—and can be used to help guide the formulation of promotional messages and the selection of communication channels. Data on motivations of program participants and two groups of nonparticipants, those living where programs were and were not available, are summarized in Table 9.4. Factors differentiating consumer motivations among two or more of the three groups studied, and not contradicted by a significant finding in the opposite direction for a third group, are mentioned briefly below.

1. *Personal savings on the electric bill.* Households who said they were participating or would participate in load management in order to save money on their electric bills were more likely to be families with children living in the home, more highly educated, younger, renters, living in smaller dwellings, and more knowledgeable about load management programs than households who said they were participating (or would) for other reasons. This information can be used in a variety of ways. For example, models and situations used to communicate monetary savings resulting from participation in a load management program could include young families living in a neighborhood of modest homes. Or, the help of school systems might be sought in distributing material about load management in the schools. The material would be most effective if it emphasized the theme of saving money by participating. Themes of saving money also should be emphasized in communicating load management program availability to renters.

2. *Indirect savings when utilities can cut costs.* Households who said they were participating or would participate in load management in

order to help achieve more efficient utility operations and general benefits for utility customers as a whole were more likely to be white, younger, living in single-family dwellings, homeowners, paying higher electric bills, electricity conservation opinion leaders, and more knowledgeable about load management programs than households who said they were participating (or would) for other reasons. This information could be used in formulating situations and choosing models for promotional messages that emphasize general benefits that result from more efficient utility operations. Since electricity conservation opinion leaders are more likely than others to be motivated by this type of appeal, it might be coupled with other conservation messages that are likely to attract the attention of people interested in conservation.

3. *Environmental protection.* Households who said they were participating or would participate in load management in order to reduce the need for new power plants and thereby protect the environment were more likely to be highly educated, white, younger, living in smaller dwellings, paying lower electric bills, electricity conservation opinion leaders, and more knowledgeable about load management programs than households who said they were participating (or would) for other reasons. Again, this information might be used in choosing models and situations in which to emphasize environmental protection messages. Environmental protection themes could be coupled with messages emphasizing more efficient operations, since both reasons for participation are likely to be cited by electricity conservation opinion leaders. Consumers motivated by either reason for participation are also more likely to be white and to be younger households. The primary difference between them is that those citing efficiency tend to live in single-family houses and to be paying larger electric bills, while households likely to be moved by an environmental protection theme tend to live in smaller dwellings and pay correspondingly lower electric bills.

4. *Utility suggestions.* Households who said they were participating or would participate in load mangement at the suggestion of their electric utilities were not consistently different from households who said they were participating (or would) for other reasons on any of the consumer characteristics examined. Of the three groups of consumers examined in Table 9.4, results for program participants seem most consistent with prior expectations. Also, since these households are reporting on their actual behavior rather than a hypothetical situation, they may be the most accurate.

Households who were taking part because their utility suggested that it was a good idea were more likely to be less highly educated, families with lower incomes, families without children living in the home, older homeowners living in single family homes, living in smaller homes, paying lower electricity bills, and more knowledgeable about how to conserve electricity than households who were taking part for other reasons. This market segment might be especially appropriate for door-to-door personal sales.

TABLE 9.4

MARKET SEGMENTATION BASED UPON MOTIVES FOR PARTICIPATION

Motive and Consumer Characteristic	Households Most Likely to Cite Motive: Participant[a]	Non-participant[b]	Household in Future Market Areas[c]
Personal Savings on Electric Bill			
1. Type of household	ND	W/children	W/children
2. Education	Higher	Higher	Higher
3. Income	ND	Lower	ND
4. Race	Nonwhite	Nonwhite	White
5. Age	ND	Younger	Younger
6. Venturesomeness	ND	ND	Higher
7. Type of dwelling	ND	Multi-family	Single family
8. Tenure	Rent	Rent	ND
9. Size of dwelling	ND	Smaller	Smaller
10. Central air	Yes	ND	ND
11. All electric	ND	ND	Yes
12. June electricity bill	Lower	ND	ND
13. Conservation knowledge	Higher	Lower	Lower
14. Conservation opinion leadership	Higher	ND	ND
15. Program knowledge	Higher	Higher	Higher
Indirect Savings When Utility Can Cut Costs			
1. Type of household	ND	Single person(s)	ND
2. Education	Higher	ND	ND
3. Income	ND	Lower	Higher
4. Race	ND	White	White
5. Age	ND	Younger	Younger
6. Venturesomeness	ND	ND	ND
7. Type of dwelling	Single family	Multi-family	Single family
8. Tenure	Own	ND	Own
9. Size of dwelling	Larger	ND	Smaller
10. Central air	Yes	ND	ND
11. All electric	No	ND	ND
12. June electricity bill	Higher	ND	Higher
13. Conservation knowledge	ND	ND	Lower
14. Conservation opinion leadership	Higher	Higher	ND
15. Program knowledge	Higher	Higher	Higher

TABLE 9.4 continued

Motive and Consumer Characteristic	Households Most Likely to Cite Motive: Participant[a]	Non-participant[b]	Household in Future Market Areas[c]
Environmental Protection			
1. Type of household	W/o children	ND	ND
2. Education	ND	Higher	Higher
3. Income	ND	Low/middle	ND
4. Race	ND	White	White
5. Age	ND	ND	Own
6. Venturesomeness	ND	ND	ND
7. Type of dwelling	ND	Multi-family	ND
8. Tenure	ND	ND	Rent
9. Size of dwelling	ND	Smaller	Smaller
10. Central air	ND	Yes	ND
11. All electric	ND	Yes	ND
12. June electricity bill	Lower	ND	Lower
13. Conservation knowledge	Higher	ND	ND
14. Conservation opinion leadership	Higher	Higher	Higher
15. Program knowledge	Higher	Higher	Higher
Utility Suggestion			
1. Type of household	W/o children	W/children	ND
2. Education	Lower	ND	ND
3. Income	Lower	Lower	Higher
4. Race	ND	Black	White
5. Age	Older	Younger	Younger
6. Venturesomeness	ND	ND	ND
7. Type of dwelling	Single family	Multi-family	Mobile home
8. Tenure	Own	Rent	Own
9. Size of Dwelling	Smaller	Larger	ND
10. Central Air	ND	ND	ND
11. All electric	ND	ND	No
12. June electric bill	Lower	ND	Higher
13. Conservation knowledge	Higher	Lower	Lower
14. Conservation opinion leadership	ND	Lower	ND
15. Program knowledge	ND	ND	ND

ND = No difference between households citing reason and not citing reason; chi-square not significant at .10 level and/or gamma less than .10.

[a]Households taking part in load control programs: reason given for participation.

[b]Households living in area where programs are available but not participating: reasons given for possibly participating in future.

[c]Households living in area without program (future market areas): reasons given for possibly participating in future.

Other message strategies can be designed to take advantage of the unique position of municipals and electric membership corporations. As documented in the marketing audits of Chapter 3, those utilities have benefited from an identifiable, plausible villain—the investor-owned generating utility. Previous message strategies have been that participation in load management programs is one specific way to fight back at high demand charges that municipal and EMC utilities must pay for wholesale electricity. The villainous generating utilities have been clearly identified in promotional material. The simple, logical rationale for load management participation and the plausible external villain have been major reasons for high penetration rates enjoyed to date in North Carolina by the municipals and EMCs. If the objective is to achieve a high penetration rate, then municipals and EMCs should take advantage of the ready investor-owned utility villain.

Personal Versus Impersonal Tactics

A number of promotional tactics are available to the utility marketing management staff. Some of the tactics are impersonal and involve the use of mass mailings, bill stuffers, broadcast media, and the like. Other tactics are personal, such as telephone solicitation, door-to-door sales, and lobby intercepts in the utility offices. Impersonal tactics are probably best for the early stages of the promotional campaign, where the promotional objective is to build program awareness. The consumer survey and focus group discussions suggested that most households were aware that load management programs were available and understood the basic logic of load management, even though many households still have some misconceptions about what load management is all about. Thus, most utilities with high penetration objectives should plan promotional efforts dominated by personal types of tactics. Direct selling by utility marketing staff members, other utility employees (perhaps in a sales promotional contest), and load control installation personnel is the best opportunity to secure participation from qualified households. Personal tactics should be supported by occasional impersonal tactics, but it is simply unrealistic for a utility, especially an investor-owned utility, to expect to attain high penetration objectives without a major commitment to direct selling personal promotion tactics that make use of utility personnel, utility agents, or community civic and political leaders. The more employee involvement and community involvement, the higher will be the achieved penetration rates.

DISTRIBUTION CHANNEL DECISIONS

Choosing channels of distribution for the load management program is the final marketing decision utility management must consider. Most utilities have adopted a "zero-step" channel of distribution for their load management program. That is, each utility's personnel have been the selling unit through direct contact with the household customers. The Lumbee River EMC and Four County EMC programs, described in Chapter 3, have been significant exceptions. Those two utilities also used their load control installation contractors to initiate customer contacts and obtain participation in the load management programs. This represents a marketing distribution strategy that is less exclusive and more intensive. In general, penetration rates will be higher with a more intensive distribution strategy. More intensive distribution, however, also reduces the utility's control over the diffusion of load management in the service area and makes it more difficult to control participation rates.

The distribution component of the marketing mix becomes more extensive as more diverse stores and organizations are involved in load management marketing. Given the traditional rationale for load management within the context of an EMC, for example, there is no reason every civic club, gas station, hardware store, grocery store, home improvement store, bank, restaurant, and church within the service area should not be involved in marketing load management. Similar outlets could be used by an investor-owned utility. In either case, the outlet could be offered a variety of economic and non-economic incentives for marketing the program.

Problems of coordination and control increase significantly as distribution becomes more intensive and channels become longer. In more intensive distribution strategies, however, more people come in more frequent contact with potential participants. Penetration rates should be greater and achieved faster than in an alternative distribution approach that uses only a limited number of utility personnel to market load management.

CONTROLLING LOAD MANAGEMENT MARKETING

Regardless of how clearly a utility specifies its penetration objectives within a time frame for a given service area, and regardless of how creatively management puts together a mix of marketing tactics to accomplish those objectives, unexpected developments will occur and revisions in marketing strategy and tactics will be needed. Controlling the marketing program means the utility's plans will be implemented and customer response monitored to identify major problems and make needed marketing adjustments as quickly as possible.

Each utility embarking on load management should have at least one person responsible for marketing the program. In the case of many utilities, the magnitude of the load management program will require several employees plus supporting personnel and special services. The utility load management marketing group should be as careful about implementing and monitoring their plans as they were when they made decisions about product characteristics, price, promotion, and distribution. The more ambitious the program penetration objectives, the more carefully and frequently the marketing group should meet to formally review progress and reconsider strategies and tactics. Weekly status updates and assessment meetings would not be excessive.

Controlling load management marketing also requires that the utility marketing group establish short-term objectives for the program's progress. Performance then can be compared against those immediate objectives. The marketing group also must establish a load management information system to accurately track the program status and help identify problem areas.

SUMMARY AND CONCLUSION

This chapter has provided an overview of the load management marketing process, based on the results of the national survey, marketing audits, focus group discussions, statewide consumer survey, and other research noted in earlier chapters. The suggested marketing process is one that involves three major steps, after formal program objectives and resources have been established by utility management.

Marketing management first must analyze appliance saturation data and consumer awareness and attitudes to identify market segments that are particularly promising. A systemwide objective of 25 percent penetration by the end of 1995, for example, can be accomplished in several forms: for example, through 25 percent penetration in every service area or through much higher market penetration in only a few, large service areas.

After target markets are selected and segments identified, marketing management must establish an appropriate mix of market tactics. Deciding how to mix various tactics requires decisions about product characteristics, price, promotion, and distribution channels. The best mix of marketing tactics for one utility may not be best for a different utility with different penetration objectives and time schedules.

An optimal mix of marketing tactics for a municipal utility or EMC with program objectives of 80 percent penetration within two years might include an unobtrusive load control switch with a customer override feature; a service interruption plan that will not go into effect until virtually all the switches are installed; a $5 per switch monthly bill credit; no installation fee or equipment charge to be borne directly by the household; participation requiring only a verbal request in person or over the telephone; a promotional strategy emphasizing direct selling by all utility employees; clear public identification of an investor-owned generating utility and the demand charges for wholesale power as the source for high electric bills; program awareness established by impersonal advertising and the use of newsletters and publicity; and an intensive distribution strategy that uses other organizations and community groups to market the program. An optimal marketing mix for an investor-owned utility with the same objective might deviate from that mix on several points. For example, the marketing plan might include these differences: a $10 per switch monthly billing credit; use of a highly credible source as a program spokesman in advertising sponsored by the state utility commission; and door-to-door sales in which every eligible household is contacted personally at least twice during the two years.

Marketing efforts for any utility with a less ambitious objective of, for example, no more than 20 percent penetration within three years, would use very different tactics. Given those objectives, the mix of marketing tactics might include a direct load control switch that must be mounted in a somewhat obtrusive location; no customer override capability; some infrequent cycling during the early years; a $2 bill credit per switch per month; no installation or equipment fees; a brief consent agreement to indicate participation; lobby intercepts and telephone solicitation of heavy residential electricity users; frequent supporting advertising materials featuring personal testimony from satisfied local participants; and zero-step distribution handled by the utility.

Finally, the utility must provide the marketing staff to implement and control the load management program. The marketing group must carefully monitor the program and customer response to determine when adjustments in the marketing mix are appropriate.

Selected References

Anderson, C. Dennis, and John D. Claxton. 1982. "Barriers to Consumer Choice of Energy Efficient Products." *The Journal of Consumer Research* 9 (September):163–70.

Argonne National Laboratory. 1980. *Benefits and Cost of Load Management: A Technical Assistance and Resource Material Handbook.* Springfield, Va: National Technical Information Service.

Awad, Ziyad A., Roger H. Johnston, Shel Feldman, and Michael V. Williams. 1982. "Customer Attitude and Intentions to Conserve Electricity." Paper presented at the Annual Meeting of the Consumer Research Association, San Francisco, September.

Barth, Michael, et al. 1974. *The Impact of Rising Residential Energy Prices on the Low Income Population: An Analysis of the Home-Heating Problem and Policy Alternatives.* Washington, D.C.: DHEW.

Bass, Frank M. 1969. "A New Product Growth Model for Consumer Durables." *Management Science* 5 (January).

Battalio, Raymond C., and John H. Kagel. 1976. "Household Demand Responsiveness to Peak Use Pricing: Implications Drawn from Experimental Studies of Consumer Demand Behavior of Both Humans and Animals." *Proceedings of the Third Annual UMR-MEC Conference on Energy.*

Battalio, Raymond C., and John H. Kagel. 1976. "Household Demand Responsiveness to Peak Use Pricing: Implications Drawn from Experimental Studies of Consumer Demand Behavior of Both Humans and Animals." *Proceedings of the Third Annual UMR-MEC Conference on Energy.*

Beck, Paul, Samuel I. Doctors, and Paul Y. Hammond. 1980. *Individual Energy Conservation Behaviors.* Cambridge, Mass.: Oelgeschlager, Gunn & Hain.

Becker, Lawrence J., Clive Seligman, and John M. Darley. 1979. *Psychological Strategies to Reduce Energy Consumption: Project Summary Report.* Princeton: Princeton University, Center for Energy and Environmental Studies.

Berland, A.L., 1980. "Time-of-Day Pricing of Electrical Energy: Does It Promote the Public Interest?" *Energy* 3 (May):779–84.

Berlin, Edward, Charles J. Cicchetti, and William J. Gillen. 1974. *Perspective on Power: A Study of the Regulation and Pricing of Electric Power.* Cambridge, Mass.: Ballinger Publishing Co.

Berry, Sandra H. 1980. "Contacting and Interviewing Residential Electricity Customers." *Papers and Proceedings: Electric Rate Demonstration Conference.* Washington, D.C.: The Onyx Corp.

Bettman, James R. 1979. *An Information Processing Theory of Consumer Choice.* Reading, Mass.: Addison-Wesley Publishing Co.

Blakeley, Edward J. 1976. "Energy, Public Opinion, and Public Policy—A Survey of Urban, Suburban, and Rural Communities." *California Agriculture* 30(8):4–5.

Bloom, Martin, et al. 1975. *The Effect of Rising Energy Prices on the Low and Moderate Income Elderly.* Washington, D.C.: Federal Energy Administration.

Bolt, Gordon J. 1972. *Marketing and Sales Forecasting—A Total Approach.* New York: John Wiley & Sons.

Booz, Allen and Hamilton, Inc. 1980. *Electric and Gas Utility Marketing of Residential Energy Conservation.* Washington, D.C.: U.S. Department of Energy, Economic Regulatory Administration, Office of Utility Systems. April.

Burby, Raymond J., and Mary Ellen Marsden, eds. 1980. *Energy and Housing: Consumer and Builder Perspectives.* Cambridge, Mass.: Oelgeschlager, Gunn & Hain.

Burby, Raymond J., Nicholas M. Didow, Jr., and Mary Ellen Marsden. 1981. *Marketing Load Management Programs: An Assessment of Current Research Needs.* Chapel Hill: Center for Urban and Regional Studies, University of North Carolina at Chapel Hill.

Burns, Barbara A. 1980. *The Relevance of Behavioral and Social Models to the Study of Consumer Energy Decision Making and Behaviors.* Golden, Colo.: Solar Energy Research Institute.

Capehart, Barney L. 1982. "A Survey of Costs and Benefits of Residential Load Management," *Energy Systems and Policy* 6 (2):151–59.

Chambers, John C., Satinder K. Mullick, and Donald D. Smith. 1974. *An Executive's Guide to Forecasting.* New York: John Wiley & Sons.

Cicchetti, Charles J., William J. Gillen, and Paul Smolensky. 1977. *The Marginal Cost and Pricing of Electricity.* Cambridge, Mass.: Ballinger Publishing Co.

Cicchetti, Charles J., and Mo Reinbergs. 1979. "Electricity and Natural Gas Rate Issues." *Annual Review of Energy* 4:231–58.

Claxton, John D., C. Dennis Anderson, J.R. Brent Ritchie, and Gordon H.G. McDougall, eds. 1981. *Consumers and Energy Conservation: International Perspectives on Research and Policy Options.* New York: Praeger Publishers.

Cleary, James P., and Hans Levenback. 1982. *The Professional Forecaster: The Forecasting Process Through Data Analysis.* Belmont, Calif.: Lifetime Learning Publications.

Conference Board. 1978. *Sales Forecasting.* New York: The Conference Board.

Cook, Stuart W., and Joy L. Berrenberg. 1981. "Approaches to Encouraging Conservation Behavior: A Review and Conceptual Framework." *Journal of Social Issues* 37(2):73–107.

Corney, William J., John E. Nixon, and Betty Yantis. 1981. "Centralized Electricity Control." In John D. Claxton, C. Dennis Anderson, J.R. Brent Ritchie, and Gordon H.G. McDougall, eds., *Consumers and Energy Conservation: International Perspectives on Research and Policy Options.* New York: Praeger Publishers. Pp. 224–30.

Craig, Paul P., Joel Darmstadter, and Stephen Rattien, 1976. "Social and Institutional Factors in Energy Conservation." In Jack M. Hollander and Melvin K. Simmons, eds., *Annual Review of Energy,* Vol. 1. Palo Alto, Calif.: Annual Reviews. Pp. 535–51.

Craig, C. Samuel, and John M. McCann. 1977. "Communicating Energy Conservation Information to Consumers: A Field Experiment." *A.M.A. Proceedings.* Chicago: American Marketing Association. Pp. 432–36.

———. 1979–80. "Developing Strategies for Influencing Residential Consumption of Electricity." *Journal of Environmental Systems* 9:175–87.

Cullen, Carman W. 1979. "The Potential for Energy Conservation in the Residential Sector." Unpublished manuscript. Ottawa, Canada: Department of Consumer and Corporate Studies.

Cunningham, William H., and Sally Cook Lopreato. 1977. *Energy Use and Conservation Incentives: A Study of the Southwestern United States.* New York: Praeger Publishers.

Darley, John M. 1977–78. "Energy Conservation Techniques as Innovations, and Their Diffusion." *Energy and Buildings* 1:339–43.

Darley, John M., and James R. Berriger. 1981. "Diffusion of Energy-Conserving Innovations." *Journal of Social Issues* 37(2):150–71.

DeSouza, Glen R. 1981. *Energy Policy and Forecasting.* Lexington, Mass.: Lexington Books, D.C. Heath and Co.

Donnermeyer, Joseph. 1977. "Social Status and Attitudinal Predictors of Residential Energy Consumption." Paper presented at Annual Meeting of the Rural Sociological Society.

Dyer, Robert. 1981. "Direct Control of Household Electricity." In John D. Claxton, C. Dennis Anderson, J.R. Brent Ritchie, and Gordon H.G. McDougall, eds., *Consumers and Energy Conservation: International Perspectives on Research and Policy Options.* New York: Praeger Publishers. Pp. 231–41.

Elrick and Lavidge, Inc. 1977a. "Attitudes and Opinions of Electric Utility Customers Toward Peak Load Conditions and Time-of-Day Pricing: Customer Acceptance Topic 10.1." Elrick and Lavidge for Electric Utility Rate Design Study. January 3.

———. 1977b. "Attitudes and Opinions of Experimental Customers Toward Load Management Alternatives." Elrick and Lavidge for Electric Utility Rate Design Study. August 5.

Evans, John L., J.R. Brent Ritchie, and Gordon H.G. McDougall. 1979. "Energy Use and Consumer Behavior: A Framework for Analysis and Policy Formulation." Unpublished paper. Ottawa, Canada: Department of Consumer and Corporate Affairs.

Farhar, Barbara C., et al. 1979. *Public Opinion about Energy: A Literature Review.* Springfield, Va.: National Technical Information Service.

Faruqui, Ahmad. 1981. "EPRI Perspectives." In Thomas A. Heberlein, *Customer Acceptance of Direct Load Controls: Residential Water Heating and Air Conditioning.* Palo Alto, Calif.: Electric Power Research Institute. Pp. v–viii.

Ferrar, Terry A., Frank Clemente, and Robert G. Uhler. 1979. *Electric Energy Policy Issues.* Ann Arbor, Mich.: Ann Arbor Science Publishers.

Firth, Michael. 1977. *Forecasting Methods in Business and Management.* London: Edward Arnold, Ltd.

Fliegel, Frederick C., and Joseph E. Kivlin. 1966. "Attributes of Innovation as Factors in Diffusion." *The American Journal of Sociology* 72 (November):235–48.

Fourt, L.A., and J.W. Woodlock. 1960. "Early Prediction of Market Success for New Grocery Products." *Journal of Marketing* 25 (October).

Frey, Cynthia J., and Duncan G. LaBay. 1982. "A Comprehensive Study of Energy Consumption and Conservation Across Family Life Cycle." Paper presented at the Annual Meeting of the Consumer Research Association, San Francisco. September.

Gordon, Judith J. 1981. "Market Penetration: Model Perspective." In Avraham Shama, ed., *Marketing Solar Energy Innovations.* New York: Praeger Special Studies. Pp. 64–90.

Gorzelnik, Eugene F. 1982. "Special Report: Utilities Embrace Direct Load Control." *Electrical World* (February):69–84.

Gottlieb, David, and Marc Matre. 1976. *Sociological Dimensions of the Energy Crisis: A Follow-up Study.* Houston, Tex.: The University of Houston Energy Institute.

Green, Robert T., Eric Langeard, and Alice C. Favell. 1974. "Innovations in the Service Sector: Some Empirical Findings." *Journal of Marketing Research* 11 (August):323–26.

Grier, Eunice S. 1976. "Changing Patterns of Energy Consumption and Costs in U.S. Households." Paper presented at the Annual Meeting of Allied Social Science Associations.

———. 1978. "Energy Consumption in American Households." In Raymond J. Burby and A. Fleming Bell, eds., *Energy and the Community.* Cambridge, Mass.: Ballinger Publishing Co.

Groome, Mary Lynn, and Roger D. Levy. 1979. "California Residential Load Cycling Experiment and Attitude Survey, Part I: Statewide Perspective." *Technology for Energy Conservation.* Silver Spring, Md.: Information Transfer.

Harrje, David T. 1978. "The Twin Rivers Experiments in Home Energy Conservation." in Raymond J. Burby and A. Fleming Bell, eds., *Energy and the Community.* Cambridge, Mass.: Ballinger Publishing Co.

Havelock, Ronald G., with Alan Guskin, Mark Frohman, Mary Havelock, Marjorie Hill, and Janet Huber. 1971. *Planning for Innovation Through Dissemination and Utilization of Knowledge.* Ann Arbor: Institute for Social Research, The University of Michigan.

Hayes, Steven C., and John D. Cone. 1977. "Reducing Residential Electrical Energy Use: Payments, Information and Feedback." *Journal of Applied Behavioral Analysis* 10:425–35.

Healy, Robert G., and Henry R. Hertzfeld. 1975. *Energy Conservation Strategies.* Washington, D.C.: The Conservation Foundation.

Heberlein, Thomas A. 1975. "Conservation Information: The Energy Crisis and Electricity Consumption in an Apartment Complex." *Energy Systems and Policy* 1(2):105–18.

———. 1981. *Customer Acceptance of Direct Load Controls: Residential Air Conditioning and Water Heating.* Palo Alto, Calif.: Electric Power Research Institute.

Heberlein, Thomas A., Daniel Linz, and Bonnie P. Ortiz. 1982. "Satisfaction, Commitment, and Knowledge of Customers on a Mandatory Participation Time-of-Day Electricity Pricing Experiment." *Journal of Consumer Research* 9 (June):106–14.

Hellman, Caroline, Temple, Barker and Sloane, Inc. 1980. "Customer Acceptance of Time-Differentiated Rates and Load Controls." (Topic Paper No. 5). Palo Alto, Calif.: Electric Power Research Institute. August 30. (Report to the National Association of Regulatory Utility Commissioners.)

Herndon, Nash. 1981. "Utilities' Loans, Discounts Insulate Consumer Dollars." *Raleigh News and Observer.* October 25.

Hinkle, Charles. 1965. "The Strategy of Price Deals." *Harvard Business Review* 43 (July–August):75–85.

Hisrich, Robert D., and Michael P. Peters. 1978. *Marketing a New Product.* Menlo Park, Calif.: Benjamin/Cummings Publishing Co.

Hutton, R. Bruce. 1977. "Life Cycle Cost: Impact on Consumer Response to New Product Information for Major Home Appliances." Unpublished paper. Denver, Colo.: University of Denver.

Johnson, Craig R. 1979. "Time-of-Day Rate Analysis: A Decision Making Perspective." *Modeling and Analysis of Electricity Demand by Time-of-Day.* Proceedings of EPRI Workshop. Washington, D.C.: Electric Power Research Institute.

Kilkeary, Rovena. 1975. "The Energy Crisis and Decision Making in the Family." Springfield, VA.: National Technical Information Service.

Kohlenberg, Robert, Thomas Phillips, and William Proctor. 1976. "A Behavioral Analysis of Peaking and Residential Electrical Energy Consumers." *Journal of Applied Behavioral Analysis* 9 (Spring):13–18.

Kotler, Philip. 1980. *Marketing Management.* Englewood Cliffs, N.J.: Prentice-Hall.

LaBay, Duncan. 1981. "Attitudes of Near-Adopters of Solar Energy: A Public Policy Perspective." Paper presented at the 1981 Annual Meeting of the Consumer Research Association, Washington, D.C.

LaBay, Duncan, G., and Thomas C. Kinnear. 1981. "Exploring the Consumer Decision Process in the Adoption of Solar Energy Systems." *Journal of Consumer Research* 8 (December):271–78.

Lawrence, A.G., T.A. Heberlein, and R.M. Baumgartner. 1984. *Customer Attitudes and Response to Load Management.* Palo Alto, Calif.: Electric Power Research Institute. July.

Leonard-Barton, Dorothy. 1981. "The Diffusion of Active Residential Solar Energy Equipment in California." In Avraham Sham, ed., *Marketing Solar Energy Innovations.* New York: Praeger Special Studies. Pp. 145–83.

Magat, Wesley A., John W. Payne, Christopher P. Puto, Bart J. vanDissel. 1981. "Improving the North Carolina Conservation Services: Literature Review and Hypotheses." Unpublished paper. Durham, N.C.: Center for the Study of Business Regulation, Duke University.

Mahajan, Vijay, and Eitan Muller. 1979. "Innovation Diffusion and New Product Growth Models in Marketing." *Journal of Marketing* 43 (Fall):55–68.

Malès, René G., and Robert G. Uhler. 1982. *Load Management: Issues, Objectives and Options.* The Final Report to the National Association of Regulatory Utility Commissioners. Palo Alto, Calif.: Electric Power Research Institute.

Marsden, Mary Ellen. 1982. *Attitudes, Knowledge, and Expectations about Alternative Energy Systems: A Review of State and National Surveys.* Chapel Hill: Institute for Research in Social Science, University of North Carolina. August.

McClelland, L., and R.J. Canter. 1981. "Psychological Research on Energy Consumption: Context, Approaches, Methods." In A. Baum and J.E. Singer, eds., *Advances in Environmental Psychology,* Vol III. Hillsdale, N.J.: Erlbaum Associates.

Midgely, David F. 1977. *Innovation and New Product Marketing.* New York: John Wiley & Sons.

Midgely, David F., and Grahame R. Dowling. 1978. "Innovativeness: The Concept and Its Measurement." *Journal of Consumer Research* 4: 236.

Miedema, Allen K., et al. 1980. *North Carolina Rate Demonstration Project: Carolina Power and Light Company Study.* Volume II: Results and Conclusions. Research Triangle Park, N.C.: Research Triangle Institute. September.

Mitchell, Bridger M., and Jan Paul Acton. 1977. *Peak-Load Pricing in Selected European Utilities.* Prepared for the Los Angeles Department of Water and Power. Santa Monica, Calif.: RAND Corporation. Report 4-2031-DWP.

Mitchell, Bridger M., Willard G. Manning, and Jan Paul Acton. 1979. *Peak Load Pricing: European Lessons for U.S. Energy Policy.* Cambridge, Mass.: Ballinger Publishing Co.

Morrison, Bonnie Maas. 1978. "Impacts on Household Energy Consumption: An Empirical Study of Michigan Families." *Sociopolitical Impacts of Energy Use and Policy Contents.* Washington, D.C.: National Academy of Science.

Morrison, Bonnie Maas, and Peter Gladhart. 1976. "Energy and Families: The Crisis and Response." *Journal of Home Economics* 1:15–18.

Morrison, Denton E. 1978. "Equity Impacts of Some Major Energy Alternatives." In Seymour Warkov, ed., *Energy Policy in the United States: Social and Behavioral Dimensions.* New York: Praeger Publishers.

Newman, Dorothy K., and Dawn Day. 1975. *The American Energy Consumer.* Cambridge, Mass.: Ballinger Publishing Co.

New York State Department of Public Service. 1978. *New York: An Examination of the Integrated Effects of Adopting Various Energy Conservation and Load Leveling Policies for the Metropolitan Area of New York City.* Prepared for U.S. Department of Energy. Washington, D.C.: U.S. Department of Energy.

Office of Technology Assessment. 1979. *Residential Energy Conservation.* Vol. 1. Washington, D.C.: U.S. Government Printing Office. Repr. 1983 Totowa, N.J.: Rowman and Allanheld.

Olsen, Marvin E., and Jill A. Goodnight. 1977. *Social Aspects of Energy Conservation.* Seattle, Wash.: Battelle Human Affairs Research Centers, Northwest Energy Policy Project.

O'Neill, Harry W. 1974. "The Effects of Energy Availability and Costs on Consumer Attitudes and Behavior." 5th Annual Proceedings of Association of Consumer Research.

Ostlund, Lyman E. 1972. "Identifying Early Buyers." *Journal of Advertising Research* 12 (April):25–30.

———. 1974. "Perceived Innovation Attributes as Predictors of Innovativeness." *Journal of Consumer Research* 1 (September):23–29.

Palmer, Michael H., et al. 1976. "An Ongoing Experimental Analysis of Electricity Conservation Procedures." *Journal of Applied Behavior Analysis.*

Peck, A.G., and O.C. Doering, III. 1976. "Voluntarism and Price Response: Consumer Reaction to the Energy Shortage." *Bell Journal of Economics* 7(1):287–92.

Perlman, Robert, and Roland Warren. 1975. "Effects of the Energy Crisis on Households of Different Income Groups." Paper presented at the Annual Meeting of Society for the Study of Social Problems.

Pollock, John Crothers. 1982. "Informed Public Decision Making," in *Attitudes, Knowledge and Expectations About Alternative Energy Systems: A Review of State and National Surveys.* Chapel Hill: Institute for Research in Social Science, The University of North Carolina.

Reinbergs, M., and K.M. Harlan. 1980. "Problems with Direct Load Control by Electric Utilities." *Public Utilities Fortnightly.* January 3.

Robertson, Thomas S. 1971. *Innovative Behavior and Communication.* New York: Holt, Rinehart and Winston.

Rogers, Everett M., and Floyd Shoemaker. 1971. *Communication of Innovations: A Cross-Cultural Approach.* 2nd ed. New York: Free Press.

Rogers, E.M., and J.D. Stanfield. 1966. "Adoption and Diffusion of New Products: Emerging Generalizations and Hypotheses." Paper presented at the Conference on the Application of Sciences to Marketing Management, Purdue University.

Rogers, E.M., and P.C. Thomas. 1975. *Bibliography on the Diffusion of Innovations.* Ann Arbor: Department of Population Planning, University of Michigan.

Rohles, Frederick H., Jr. 1981. "Thermal Comfort and Strategies for Energy Conservation." *Journal of Social Issues* 37(2):132–49.

Salzano, F.J., R.J. Hoppe and J. Batey. 1980. "Time-of-Day Pricing of Electrical Energy: Does It Promote the Public Interest? " *Energy* 3(May):779–84.

Seaver, W.B., and A.H. Patterson. 1976. "Decreasing Fuel Oil Consumption through Feedback and Social Commendation." *Journal of Applied Behavior Analysis* 9:147–52.

Seeto, Dewey. 1979. "The California Residential Load Cycling Experiment and Attitude Survey: Customer Attitudes in the PG&E 1977 Air Conditioning Cycling Experiment." *Technology for Energy Conservation.* Silver Spring, Md.: Information Transfer.

Seligman, Clive, and John M. Darley. 1976. "Feedback as a Means of Decreasing Energy Consumption." Paper presented at Annual Meeting of American Sociological Association.

Seligman, Clive, Don Hall, and Joan Finegan. 1982. "Prediction of Home Energy Consumption: An Application of the Fishbein-Ajzen Model." Paper presented at the Consumer Research Association Annual Meeting, San Francisco, Calif., September.

Shama, Avraham. 1981a. "Diffusion of Innovations and Solar Energy: An Overview." In Shama, ed., *Marketing Solar Energy Innovations.* New York: Praeger Special Studies. Pp. 1–26.

________. 1981b. "The Future of Solar Energy Innovations." In Shama, ed., *Marketing Solar Energy Innovations.* Pp. 248–71.

________. 1981c. *Marketing Solar Energy Innovations.* New York: Praeger Special Studies.

Shama, Avraham, and Kenneth Jacobs. 1980–81. "Accelerating the Adoption of Conservation Energy." *Journal of Environmental Systems* 10:353–65.

Sharefkin, Mark. 1974. *The Economic and Environmental Benefits from Improving Electrical Rate Structures.* Washington, D.C.: Office of Research and Development, U.S. Environmental Protection Agency (EPA 600-5-74-033).

Shaw, Whitney. 1981. "Lights Out in 1990? " *Business: North Carolina* 1 (October):15–22.

Shoemaker, Floyd. 1981. "Communication and the Solar Consumer." In Avraham Shama, ed., *Marketing Solar Energy Innovations.* New York: Praeger Special Studies. Pp. 184–207.

Smith, Jim R. 1978. "Socio-Economic Impact of Peak Load Pricing Rates." Atlanta: Georgia Power Company, Rates and Records Department.

Summers, John O. 1971. "Generalized Change Agents and Innovativeness." *Journal of Marketing Research* 8 (August):313–16.

Task Force No. 10, Electric Utility Rate Design Study. 1977. *Customer Acceptance: Topic 10.2.* prepared for Electric Utility Rate Design Study. Palo Alto, Calif.: Electric Power Research Institute. January 4.

"Time of Use Rates." 1981. *Public Utilities Fortnightly* (April):82–88.

Uhl, Kenneth, Roman Andrus, and Lance Poulsen. 1970. "How Are Laggards Different? An Empirical Inquiry." *Journal of Marketing Research* 7 (February):51–54.

Van Liere, K.D., D.R. Ploch, M.S. Kuhn, C.M. Hand, B.W. McConnell, and B.H. Bronfman. 1982. *Public Reactions to Load Management: A Summary of Baseline Community Data for the Athens Automation and Control Experiment.* Oak Ridge, Tenn.: Oak Ridge National Laboratory (ORNL/TM-7961).

Verhallen, Theo M.M., and W. Fred van Raaij. 1981. "Household Behavior and Energy Use." In John D. Claxton, C. Dennis Anderson, J.R. Brent Ritchie, and Gordon H.G. McDougall, eds., *Consumers and Energy Conservation: International Perspectives on Research and Policy Options.* New York. Praeger Publishers. Pp. 32–45.

Walker, Bruce J., and Kenneth A. Coney. 1981. "Consumer Adoption of an Energy Conservation Product." Paper presented at the 1981 American Marketing Association Meeting, Washington, D.C.

Walker, Noland E., and E. Linn Draper. 1975. "The Effects of Electricity Price Increases on Residential Usage by Three Economic Groups: A Case Study." *Texas Nuclear Power Policies.* Austin: University of Texas Center for Energy Studies.

Warkov, Seymour, and Judith W. Meyer. 1982. *Solar Diffusion and Public Incentives.* Lexington, Mass.: D.C. Heath, Lexington Books.

Warner, Kenneth E. 1974. "The Need for Some Innovative Concepts of Innovation: An Examination of Research on the Diffusion of Innovation." *Policy Sciences* 5:433–451.

Warren, E.H. 1980. "Solar Energy Market Penetration Models: Science or Number Mysticism?" *Technological Forecasting and Social Change* 16:105–18.

White, Lawrence T., Barbara A. Curbow, Mark A. Constanza, and Thomas F. Pettigrew. 1982. "Social Psychological Approaches to Promoting Lifestyle and Device-Oriented Conservation Behaviors." Paper presented at the Annual Meeting of the Consumer Research Association, San Francisco, September.

Williams, Terrell G. 1982. *Consumer Behavior: Fundamentals and Strategies.* St. Paul, Minn.: West Publishing Co.

Winnet, R.A., et al. 1978. "The Effects of Monetary Rebates, Feedback, and Information on Residential Electricity Conservation." *Journal of Applied Psychology* 63:73–80.

Winnet. R.A., and M.S. Neale. 1979. "Psychological Framework for Energy Conservation in Buildings: Strategies, Outcomes, Directions." *Energy and Buildings* 2:101–16.

Zaltman, Gerald, and Nan Lin. 1971. "On the Nature of Innovations." *American Behavioral Scientist* 14 (May–June):651–74.

Appendix A

Household Survey Cover Letter and Questionnaire

THE UNIVERSITY OF NORTH CAROLINA
AT
CHAPEL HILL

The Center for Urban & Regional Studies

(919) 962-3074

The University of North Carolina at Chapel Hill
Hickerson House 067 A
Chapel Hill, N.C. 27514

July 20, 1982

Dear

All of us are feeling the rising costs of energy. Gasoline prices, fuel oil costs, and electric bills seem to go up every month. To slow these rising prices, electric utilities are offering people ways of cutting their electric bills. The University of North Carolina at Chapel Hill has been asked to devise ways of making them more useful to you and other people in the state.

I am writing to ask for your help by completing the enclosed questionnaire. Your household is one of a small number which has been selected at random to represent the opinions of thousands of people like you in North Carolina. In order for the results to represent the thinking of people across the state, it is important that each questionnaire be completed and returned.

Your response will be completely confidential. We have placed a number at the top of the questionnaire so that we can check your name off the mailing list when it is returned.

A summary of people's opinions will be given to your electric utility and to the North Carolina Utilities Commission. If you want a copy, write "send copy" on the back of the prestamped return envelope and print your name and address below. Please do not write your name on the questionnaire itself.

I would be very happy to answer any questions you might have. Please write or call. The telephone number is 919/962-3074.

Thank you for your help.

Sincerely,

Raymond J. Burby
Assistant Director

Enclosures

USING ELECTRICITY IN NORTH CAROLINA HOMES 1982

CENTER FOR URBAN AND REGIONAL STUDIES
University of North Carolina at Chapel Hill
Chapel Hill, North Carolina 27514

This survey is designed to provide information that will help to reduce electricity costs in North Carolina. For each question, just circle your answers. If you wish, you can add comments in the margins and on the back of the booklet. Thank you for your help.

YOUR USE OF ELECTRICITY

To start with, we have some questions about your household and energy use.

1. In your household, would you say that conserving electricity is: (circle)

    1 EXTREMELY IMPORTANT
    2 SOMEWHAT IMPORTANT
    3 NOT IMPORTANT AT ALL

2. Do you have an . . .

    a. Electric furnace or heat pump? (circle)

    1 YES
    2 NO

    b. Electric water heater? (circle)

    1 YES
    2 NO

    c. Electric central air conditioner or heat pump? (circle)

    1 YES
    2 NO

    d. Electric stove? (circle)

    1 YES
    2 NO

3. How often do you. . . .

<u>Circle how often you do this.</u> If you do not have an appliance, circle DO NOT HAVE.

Use less water in baths and showers . .	ALWAYS	SOMETIMES	NEVER	DO NOT HAVE
Turn off air conditioner to save money.	ALWAYS	SOMETIMES	NEVER	DO NOT HAVE
Use cold water settings on clothes washer.	ALWAYS	SOMETIMES	NEVER	DO NOT HAVE
Use clothes washer fewer times with larger loads.	ALWAYS	SOMETIMES	NEVER	DO NOT HAVE
Turn off lights	ALWAYS	SOMETIMES	NEVER	DO NOT HAVE
Turn down heat at night	ALWAYS	SOMETIMES	NEVER	DO NOT HAVE

How does your household feel about saving electricity? For each of the following questions, circle the words that best describe how you feel about the statement.

	Please circle one for each statement				
4. Everyone should conserve electricity even if they don't have to worry about the cost . .	STRONGLY AGREE	AGREE	NOT SURE	DISAGREE	STRONGLY DISAGREE
5. We don't mind being uncomfortable if we can save money on electricity	STRONGLY AGREE	AGREE	NOT SURE	DISAGREE	STRONGLY DISAGREE
6. Our electic utility is doing everything it can to hold down the prices it charges for electricity	STRONGLY AGREE	AGREE	NOT SURE	DISAGREE	STRONGLY DISAGREE
7. We pay too much for electricity	STRONGLY AGREE	AGREE	NOT SURE	DISAGREE	STRONGLY DISAGREE
8. We have had difficulty paying some of our electric bills . . .	STRONGLY AGREE	AGREE	NOT SURE	DISAGREE	STRONGLY DISAGREE

9. If you didn't have to worry about the cost, at what temperature would you keep your home when someone is there during the daytime in winter?

__________ degrees [ ] CHECK IF YOU DON'T KNOW

10. During this past winter, at about what temperature did you keep your home during the daytime when someone was there?

__________ degrees [ ] CHECK IF YOU DON'T KNOW

ABOUT YOUR HOME

1. Which of the following best describes your home? (circle)

1 ONE FAMILY
2 DUPLEX
3 MOBILE HOME OR TRAILER
4 CONDOMINIUM
5 APARTMENT BUILDING
6 OTHER (PLEASE DESCRIBE:______________________________)

2. About when was your home built? (circle)

1 BEFORE 1960
2 1960 - 1969
3 1970 - 1974
4 1975 OR LATER
5 DON'T KNOW

3. In what year did you move to your home? (circle)

_________ YEAR

4. Do you own or rent your home? (circle)

1 OWN OR BUYING
2 RENT
3 OTHER

5. How many square feet are there in your home? (circle)

1 Less than 800 SQ. FT.
2 800 - 1,199 SQ. FT.
3 1,200 - 1,499 SQ. FT.
4 1,500 - 1,999 SQ. FT.
5 2,000 - 2,999 SQ. FT.
6 3,000 OR MORE SQ. FT
7 DON'T KNOW

6. Thinking of your home, which of these was there when you moved in and which have you added since then? (For each item, circle ALREADY THERE if it was there when you moved in and circle ADDED if it was added since then. NOTE: you can circle ALREADY THERE <u>and</u> ADDED if both are true.)

	Circle Choices in Each Column		
	Already There When You Moved In	Added Since You Moved In	Don't Have
Storm windows, thermopane glass or plastic sheeting . .	ALREADY THERE	ADDED	DON'T HAVE
Storm doors	ALREADY THERE	ADDED	DON'T HAVE
Insulation in the attic, walls or floor	ALREADY THERE	ADDED	DON'T HAVE
Insulation around the water heater.	ALREADY THERE	ADDED	DON'T HAVE
Insulation around the heating ducts or hot water pipes. . .	ALREADY THERE	ADDED	DON'T HAVE
Caulking or weatherstripping. .	ALREADY THERE	ADDED	DON'T HAVE
Attic or ceiling fan	ALREADY THERE	ADDED	DON'T HAVE
Water heater timer.	ALREADY THERE	ADDED	DON'T HAVE
Wood burning stove.	ALREADY THERE	ADDED	DON'T HAVE

7. Do you plan to do anything else to your home this next year to help cut electricity use?

1 YES (Specify: ______________________________________)
2 NO
3 DON'T KNOW

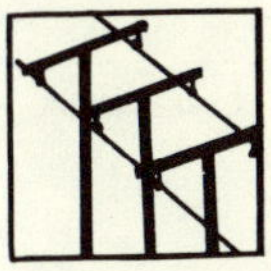

YOUR ELECTRIC UTILITY

The electric utilities have tried to give people more information about the use of electricity. Do you think each of the following statements is true or false?

1. Electrical use by the average household is highest between 10:00 A.M. and 4:00 P.M. (circle)

   1 TRUE
   2 FALSE
   3 DON'T KNOW

2. Electrical use in North Carolina tends to be highest in the summer. (circle)

   1 TRUE
   2 FALSE
   3 DON'T KNOW

3. It costs more to produce electricity during the periods of peak demand than during off-peak hours. (circle)

   1 TRUE
   2 FALSE
   3 DON'T KNOW

4. Electrical load management refers to programs that attempt to level out the peaks and valleys in electrical use. (circle)

   1 TRUE
   2 FALSE
   3 DON'T KNOW

> Electric utilities across North Carolina are developing programs to hold down the costs of electricity. One of these programs is called load control.
>
> Load control uses an automatic switch to turn off electric water heaters and central air conditioners when electricity use throughout the electric utility gets too high. In exchange for letting the water heater or central air conditioner be switched off, households get a credit on the electric bill.

1. Have you read or heard about load control of water heaters and air conditioners from any of the following? (circle all that apply)

   1 PEOPLE AT OUR ELECTRIC UTILITY
   2 INFORMATION WITH THE ELECTRIC BILL
   3 FRIENDS OR RELATIVES
   4 PEOPLE AT WORK
   5 TELEVISION
   6 RADIO
   7 NEWSPAPER
   8 DON'T REMEMBER WHERE I HEARD ABOUT IT
   9 OTHER (PLEASE INDICATE:________________________)
   10 HAVEN'T HEARD ABOUT IT BEFORE

2. Are you taking part in a load control program? (circle)

1 YES--When did you sign up? ________/________ [ ] CHECK IF DON'T REMEMBER
month year

2 NO---Why not? (circle all that are reasons)

1 HAVEN'T HEARD ABOUT IT BEFORE
2 IT'S NOT AVAILABLE HERE
3 WE ARE NOT ELIGIBLE
4 NO ONE EVER ASKED US
5 JUST NOT INTERESTED
6 NEED MORE INFORMATION TO DECIDE ABOUT IT
7 THERE IS AN INSTALLATION CHARGE
8 WE WANT TO CONTROL OUR USE OF ELECTRICITY
9 WE WOULD BE TOO UNCOMFORTABLE
10 WE WERE ON IT AND DIDN'T LIKE IT
11 WE COULDN'T SAVE ENOUGH ON OUR ELECTRIC BILL
12 JUST NOT WORTH THE EFFORT TO CALL AND HAVE IT INSTALLED
13 OTHER (PLEASE INDICATE:________________________________)

Time-of-day programs are also offered by some utilities. These programs are similar to the way long distance telephone calls are charged now. If you call during peak hours, your calls are more expensive, but if you wait and call during the evening, you get a much lower rate. Just like the telephone, you could save money if you shifted more of your electricity use to off-peak hours.

1. Have you read or heard about time-of-day programs? (Circle)

1 YES

2 NO

3 NOT SURE

2. Are you taking part in a time-of-day program? (circle)

1 YES--When did you sign up? ________/________ [ ] CHECK IF DON'T REMEMBER
month year

2 NO---Why not? (circle all that are reasons)

1 HAVEN'T HEARD ABOUT IT BEFORE
2 IT'S NOT AVAILABLE HERE
3 WE ARE NOT ELIGIBLE
4 NO ONE EVER ASKED US
5 JUST NOT INTERESTED
6 NEED MORE INFORMATION TO DECIDE ABOUT IT
7 THERE IS AN INSTALLATION CHARGE
8 TOO HARD TO CHANGE WHEN WE USE ELECTRICITY
9 WE WERE ON IT AND DIDN'T LIKE IT
10 WE COULDN'T SAVE ENOUGH ON OUR ELECTRIC BILL
11 JUST NOT WORTH THE EFFORT TO CALL AND HAVE IT INSTALLED
12 OTHER (PLEASE INDICATE:________________________________)

3. Here are some reasons people have given for taking part in load control and time-of-day programs. If you are not taking part in one of these programs, answer the questions in the <u>left-hand column</u>. If you are taking part in either a load control or time-of-day program, answer the questions in the <u>right-hand column</u>.

If you are <u>not taking part</u> in a load control or time-of-day program, circle any reasons in this column that <u>might lead you to join</u>.

1 SAVE MONEY ON ELECTRIC BILL

2 IF THERE WERE NO INSTALLATION CHARGE

3 WE ALL SAVE IF OUR UTILITY CAN CUT COSTS

4 LESS DAMAGE TO THE ENVIRONMENT IF FEWER POWER PLANTS HAVE TO BE BUILT

5 SOMEONE WE KNOW RECOMMENDS IT

6 SOMEONE FROM OUR ELECTRIC UTILITY SUGGESTS IT

7 OTHER (SPECIFY:________________)

8 NONE OF THE ABOVE

Would you take part in a load control or time-of-day program in the future? (circle)

1 YES, LOAD CONTROL

2 YES, TIME-OF-DAY

3 NO, NEITHER ONE

4 DON'T KNOW

How large would your monthly credit have to be to make it worth your while to take part in a water heater load control program? (circle)

1 NO CREDIT NEEDED

2 $1

3 $2

4 $3

5 $5

6 $10

7 NO AMOUNT WOULD BE ENOUGH

If you are <u>taking part</u> in a load control or time-of-day program, circle all the reasons in this column that explain <u>why</u>.

1 SAVE MONEY ON ELECTRIC BILL

2 THERE WAS NO INSTALLATION CHARGE

3 WE ALL SAVE IF OUR UTILITY CAN CUT COSTS

4 LESS DAMAGE TO THE ENVIRONMENT IF FEWER POWER PLANTS HAVE TO BE BUILT

5 SOMEONE WE KNOW RECOMMENDED IT

6 SOMEONE FROM OUR ELECTRIC UTILITY SUGGESTED IT

7 OTHER (SPECIFY:_______________)

8 NONE OF THE ABOVE

Will you continue to take part in the future? (circle)

1 YES

2 NO

3 DON'T KNOW

How satisfied are you with your load control or time-of-day program? (circle)

1 VERY SATISFIED

2 SOMEWHAT SATISFIED

3 SOMEWHAT DISSATISFIED

4 VERY DISSATISFIED

WHERE YOU GET INFORMATION

1. Would you say that the adults in your household listen to the radio... (circle all that apply)

 1 GOING TO AND FROM WORK IN THE CAR
 2 AT WORK DURING THE DAY
 3 AT HOME DURING THE DAY
 4 AT HOME IN THE EVENING
 5 AT HOME ON WEEKENDS
 6 NONE OF THE ABOVE

2. Would you say that the adults in your household watch television... (circle all that apply)

 1 WEEKDAY MORNINGS
 2 WEEKDAY AFTERNOONS
 3 WEEKDAY EVENINGS
 4 WEEKENDS
 5 NONE OF THE ABOVE

3. Do people in your household read a newspaper? (circle)

 1 YES--Which one(s)? ______________________________

 2 NO

4. Do you read the information sent with the electric bill... (circle)

 1 FREQUENTLY
 2 OCCASIONALLY
 3 SELDOM
 4 NEVER

5. Do you feel that your household is well informed about how to cut electricity costs in your home? (circle)

 1 YES
 2 NO

6. Do people ask for your advice about how to save on electricity costs? (circle)

 1 YES
 2 NO

7. Below is a list of sources of information for ways to save energy. Please circle up to <u>three</u> that you think are the most reliable sources of information.

 1 FEDERAL/STATE/LOCAL GOVERNMENTS
 2 LOCAL OIL COMPANIES
 3 LOCAL ELECTRIC UTILITY
 4 LOCAL NATURAL GAS UTILITY
 5 SCHOOLS AND TECHNICAL CENTERS
 6 LOCAL HEATING/AIR CONDITIONER CONTRACTORS
 7 BUILDING CONTRACTORS

YOUR HOUSEHOLD

In this section we would like to obtain some background information about the people living in your household. The information will be used only to report comparisons among groups of people.

1. Which best describes your household? (circle)

   1 ONE PERSON LIVING ALONE
   2 HUSBAND AND WIFE LIVING ALONE
   3 MARRIED COUPLE WITH CHILDREN
   4 SINGLE HEAD OF HOUSEHOLD WITH CHILDREN
   5 TWO OR MORE UNRELATED INDIVIDUALS
   6 OTHER (PLEASE INDICATE:____________________________________)

2. Please indicate the ages of the males in your household.

   _____ _____ _____ _____

3. Please indicate the ages of the females in your household.

   _____ _____ _____ _____

4. Circle the age(s) above (questions 2 and 3) of the person(s) who completed this questionnaire.

5. How many persons, other than school children, are usually home weekdays during the day time?

   _____ PERSONS, OTHER THAN SCHOOL CHILDREN

6. Please circle the highest grade of regular school completed by you (and another adult if there is one):

   YOU Elementary through high school
   1 2 3 4 5 6 7 8 9 10 11 12

   College
   1 2 3 4 5 6 OR MORE

   OTHER ADULT Elementary through high school
   1 2 3 4 5 6 7 8 9 10 11 12

   College
   1 2 3 4 5 6 OR MORE

7. How much did you spend on your June electricity bill? (circle)

   1 LESS THAN $50 [ ] check if equal billing
   2 $50 - $99
   3 $100 OR MORE
   4 DON'T KNOW

These next questions ask about your race and total household or family income. This information is important in helping to determine how energy costs affect different households. We hope you will answer these questions, but if you do not want to answer, please skip to question 11 below.

8. Are you: (circle)

1 WHITE
2 BLACK
3 INDIAN
4 OTHER (SPECIFY:________________)

9. How many adults (age 18 or over) living in your household are:

_______ WORKING FULL TIME

_______ WORKING PART TIME

_______ WORKING OCCASIONALLY OR SEASONALLY PART TIME

_______ RETIRED OR DISABLED

_______ UNEMPLOYED

10. Considering all sources of income, what was the total amount your entire household received during 1981? (Please circle the amount of your <u>total income before taxes</u>.)

1 LESS THAN $5,000
2 $5,000 - $7,499
3 $7,500 - $9,999
4 $10,000 - $14,999
5 $15,000 - $19,999
6 $20,000 - $24,999
7 $25,000 - $34,999
8 $35,000 - $49,999
9 $50,000 - $74,999
10 $75,000 OR MORE

11. Here is a list of some things that you may have in your home. For each one, please circle if you have NEVER HEARD of it, <u>or</u> you have heard of it but DON'T HAVE it, <u>or</u> you HAVE it.

	Circle one for each item		
Telephone answering device . .	NEVER HEARD OF IT	DON'T HAVE	WE HAVE THIS
Hand-held calculator	NEVER HEARD OF IT	DON'T HAVE	WE HAVE THIS
Microwave oven	NEVER HEARD OF IT	DON'T HAVE	WE HAVE THIS
Home computer.	NEVER HEARD OF IT	DON'T HAVE	WE HAVE THIS
Food processor	NEVER HEARD OF IT	DON'T HAVE	WE HAVE THIS
Video player/recorder.	NEVER HEARD OF IT	DON'T HAVE	WE HAVE THIS
Remote control TV.	NEVER HEARD OF IT	DON'T HAVE	WE HAVE THIS
Large screen video TV.	NEVER HEARD OF IT	DON'T HAVE	WE HAVE THIS
Cordless telephone	NEVER HEARD OF IT	DON'T HAVE	WE HAVE THIS

This last section deals with how households make decisions. Please think about your entire household as you answer each question.

	Please circle one for each statement				
1. Only one person makes the decisions in this household	STRONGLY AGREE	AGREE	NOT SURE	DISAGREE	STRONGLY DISAGREE
2. In this household, specific chores are assigned to each person	STRONGLY AGREE	AGREE	NOT SURE	DISAGREE	STRONGLY DISAGREE
3. People in this household do small favors for one another	STRONGLY AGREE	AGREE	NOT SURE	DISAGREE	STRONGLY DISAGREE
4. Household members work as a team	STRONGLY AGREE	AGREE	NOT SURE	DISAGREE	STRONGLY DISAGREE
5. The people in this household are very close to one another	STRONGLY AGREE	AGREE	NOT SURE	DISAGREE	STRONGLY DISAGREE
6. We have a financial budget. .	STRONGLY AGREE	AGREE	NOT SURE	DISAGREE	STRONGLY DISAGREE
7. One person is clearly the "head of the household" here	STRONGLY AGREE	AGREE	NOT SURE	DISAGREE	STRONGLY DISAGREE
8. We talk to each other a lot in this household	STRONGLY AGREE	AGREE	NOT SURE	DISAGREE	STRONGLY DISAGREE
9. The people in this household help one another with household chores	STRONGLY AGREE	AGREE	NOT SURE	DISAGREE	STRONGLY DISAGREE
10. The decisions in this household are made jointly . . .	STRONGLY AGREE	AGREE	NOT SURE	DISAGREE	STRONGLY DISAGREE
11. There is a lack of communication here	STRONGLY AGREE	AGREE	NOT SURE	DISAGREE	STRONGLY DISAGREE
12. Members of this household cooperate with one another	STRONGLY AGREE	AGREE	NOT SURE	DISAGREE	STRONGLY DISAGREE
13. Everyone has a specific job to do	STRONGLY AGREE	AGREE	NOT SURE	DISAGREE	STRONGLY DISAGREE

WE HOPE YOU FOUND FILLING OUT THIS QUESTIONNAIRE TO BE AN INTERESTING AND ENJOYABLE EXPERIENCE.

IF YOU HAVE ANY ADDITIONAL COMMENTS, PLEASE WRITE THEM ABOVE ON THIS PAGE.

PLEASE RETURN THE QUESTIONNAIRE AT YOUR EARLIEST CONVENIENCE IN THE ENCLOSED SELF-ADDRESSED, STAMPED ENVELOPE.

THANK YOU FOR YOUR HELP AND COOPERATION.

FOR HOUSEHOLDS IN TIME-OF-DAY PROGRAMS

IF YOU ARE TAKING PART IN A TIME-OF-DAY PROGRAM, PLEASE COMPLETE THIS SPECIAL SECTION AND RETURN IT WITH THE QUESTIONNAIRE.

We would like to know your views about the program you are taking part in. Please circle how you feel about each statement.

	Please circle one for each statement				
1. The savings we have received have been worth it	STRONGLY AGREE	AGREE	NOT SURE	DISAGREE	STRONGLY DISAGREE
2. This program has caused discomfort for my household . .	STRONGLY AGREE	AGREE	NOT SURE	DISAGREE	STRONGLY DISAGREE
3. We would still take part even if we did not save on our electric bill	STRONGLY AGREE	AGREE	NOT SURE	DISAGREE	STRONGLY DISAGREE
4. This program has cut our use of electricity	STRONGLY AGREE	AGREE	NOT SURE	DISAGREE	STRONGLY DISAGREE
5. After we signed up for this program, we encouraged several other people to participate	STRONGLY AGREE	AGREE	NOT SURE	DISAGREE	STRONGLY DISAGREE
6. Households that do not take part in a load control or time-of-day program should be charged extra for electricity each month. . .	STRONGLY AGREE	AGREE	NOT SURE	DISAGREE	STRONGLY DISAGREE
7. If our electric utility had asked, we would have signed up even if it didn't save us anything on our electric bill.	STRONGLY AGREE	AGREE	NOT SURE	DISAGREE	STRONGLY DISAGREE
8. Our friends know we are taking part in this program. .	STRONGLY AGREE	AGREE	NOT SURE	DISAGREE	STRONGLY DISAGREE
9. If electricity were less expensive, my household would not participate in this program	STRONGLY AGREE	AGREE	NOT SURE	DISAGREE	STRONGLY DISAGREE

CONTINUE ON THE OTHER SIDE . . .

10. In general, has it been clear or confusing to most of your household which hours are on-peak and which are off-peak? (circle)

1 VERY CLEAR
2 SOMEWHAT CLEAR
3 NOT SURE
4 SOMEWHAT CONFUSING
5 VERY CONFUSING

11. Below is a list of activities done around the home. Please indicate how hard it has been for your household to shift each of these from on-peak to off-peak times.

	Please circle one for each item				
	VERY DIFFICULT	SOMEWHAT DIFFICULT	NOT AT ALL DIFFICULT	WE DO NOT TRY	DOES NOT APPLY
Cooking evening meal. . .	1	2	3	4	5
Dish washing	1	2	3	4	5
Clothes washing	1	2	3	4	5
Clothes drying	1	2	3	4	5
Bathing/showering	1	2	3	4	5
Personal care (hair-drying, etc.).	1	2	3	4	5
Electric heating.	1	2	3	4	5
Electric water heating. .	1	2	3	4	5
Air conditioning.	1	2	3	4	5

12. How useful has the information provided on your electric bill been in helping your household get the most out of time-of-day rates? (circle)

1 VERY USEFUL
2 SOMEWHAT USEFUL
3 NOT SURE
4 NOT USEFUL AT ALL

THANK YOU FOR SHARING YOUR EXPERIENCES WITH YOUR TIME-OF-DAY PROGRAM. NOW PLEASE RETURN TO THE BOOKLET AND CONTINUE ON WITH THE QUESTIONNAIRE. RETURN THIS FORM WITH THE BOOKLET.

Appendix B

National Load Management Marketing Survey: Methodology, Cover Letter and Telephone Survey Questionnaire

SAMPLE AND METHOD

The utilities included in the sample were selected from a national list of utilities made available by the *1980 Survey and Evaluation of Utility Conservation, Load Management, and Solar Land-Use Projects, Volume 3,* January, 1982. From this document, 127 electric utilities offering 158 "load management" programs were identified. A selection criterion based on conceptual and practical reasons narrowed this population to 101 electric utilities across the United States.

The sample was limited to utilities offering their residential customers either direct control of water heaters or air conditioners or those offering differential time-of-day rates. This limiting factor produced a set of programs from which findings would be most useful to the North Carolina utilities participating in this study. Thus, the findings in Chapter Two are based on data from almost all utilities, outside of North Carolina, offering residential customers either water heater or air conditioner control or differential time-of-use rates.

The letter appearing in this appendix was sent to representatives from each utility telling them the goals of the study and requesting their participation in a telephone interview (also in this appendix). During the spring and summer months of 1982, three interviewers telephoned each representative in order to examine how the utility marketed its residential load management programs. Each interview lasted about forty minutes and examined the characteristics, eligibility requirements, and promotional activities of load management programs.

THE UNIVERSITY OF NORTH CAROLINA
AT
CHAPEL HILL

The Center for Urban & Regional Studies

(919) 962-3074

The University of North Carolina at Chapel Hill
Hickerson House 067 A
Chapel Hill, N.C. 27514

April 1982

Dear:

Electric utilities across the nation are adopting direct load control and time of use rate programs to moderate demand in peak power requirements. Utility benefits from these programs are directly tied to the number of customers participating.

A research team from the University of North Carolina is examining ways of promoting and marketing load management programs. This effort, which is described in the enclosure, is supported by the North Carolina Alternative Energy Corporation (AEC). The AEC has a mandate to moderate growth in demand for electrical power.

I am writing to ask for your help in describing how load management programs have been communicated to your residential customers. These programs are relatively new, and we know of no single source describing how utilities across the nation have promoted or intend to promote and market direct load control and time of use rate programs.

A member of our research team (see enclosure) will call you in early May to ask you how you have communicated load management programs to your customers. We would like to ask you about the characteristics of your residential load management programs, the costs and benefits residential customers can expect for their participation, and the ways in which you have informed customers about these programs. We also wish to know what reduction in capacity requirements and other benefits you expect to obtain as a result of residential load management.

We appreciate your help. In exchange for participating in this study we will send you a summary of our national findings regarding utility load management marketing practices.

Sincerely,

Charles F. Hanna
Research Associate

CFH:lm

Enclosure

PHONE SURVEY OF UTILITY MARKETING PRACTICES

Hello, my name is ______________________________ and I'm calling from the University of North Carolina. May I speak with __________________ please? (IF NOT IN, GET TIME TO CALL BACK) ______________________________________

(WHEN RESPONDENT ANSWERS) Good (MORNING, AFTERNOON . . . . BE SURE TO CHECK TIME ZONE), my name is ______________________ and I'm calling from the University of North Carolina. I am very interested in learning more about your load management programs for residential customers. Did you receive a letter from us explaining our project? (PAUSE FOR ANSWER)

(IF YES) Good, then you know that our research team is examining customer participation in direct load control and time of use rate programs. The North Carolina Alternative Energy Corporation is sponsoring our research.

(IF NO) The letter described a study designed to determine why customers participate in direct load control or time of use rate programs. We are also investigating the impact of their participation. This study is sponsored by the N.C. Alternative Energy Corporation.

The reason I'm calling now is to talk with you about your experiences in marketing load management.

PROGRAM CHARACTERISTICS

Let's begin by discussing the characteristics of your load management programs for your residential customers.

1. Does your company offer: [CHECK ALL THAT APPLY]

a. ____Direct Water Heater Control ⟶ When did you introduce this program_____

b. ____Direct Air Conditioner Control ⟶ When did you introduce this program_____

c. ____Time of Use Rates ⟶ When did you introduce this program_____

d. ____Space Heat Control ⟶ When did you introduce this program_____

e. ____Energy Conservation Audits ⟶ When did you introduce this program_____

f. ____Remote Meter Reading ⟶ When did you introduce this program_____

g. ____Any other load management programs (SPECIFY)__________________________

____

____

[IF THEY DO NOT OFFER DIRECT WATER HEATER CONTROL OR DIRECT AIR CONDITIONER CONTROL OR TIME OF USE RATES TERMINATE INTERVIEW AFTER THANKING RESPONDENT]

2. What do you call your a - c programs in promoting them to your customers?

a. Direct Water Heater Control Program__________________________

b. Direct Air Conditioner Control__________________________

c. Time of Use Rates__________________________

d. Have you ever called any of these programs by another official name?

____Yes ⟶ DIRECT WATER HEATER__________________________
____No
DIRECT AIR CONDITIONER__________________________

TIME OF USE RATES__________________________

3A. IS YOUR DIRECT WATER HEATER CONTROL PROGRAM LIMITED TO:

A1. Owner occupied housing?

____Yes
____No

A2. To all electric homes?

____Yes
____No

A3. To customers using a certain amount of kWh?

____Yes ——————→How many kWh? ______________kWh
____No

A4. To customers with a certain size water heater?

____Yes ——————→How many gallons? _________gallons
____No

A5. Are there other eligibility requirements?______________________________

____

____

3B. [IS YOUR DIRECT AIR CONDITIONER CONTROL PROGRAM:]

B1. Limited to owner occupied housing?

____Yes
____No

B2. To all electric homes?

____Yes
____No

B3. Customers using a certain amount of kWh?

____Yes ——————→How many kWh? __________kWh
____No

B4. Customers with a certain size air conditioner?

____Yes ——————→What size is that?____________________
____No

B5. Customers already participating on your water heater program?

____Yes
____No

B6. Are there other eligibility requirements?_________________________________

____

____

3C. [IS YOUR TIME OF USE RATE PROGRAM LIMITED TO:]

C1. Owner occupied housing?

____Yes
____No

C2. All electric homes?

____Yes
____No

C3. Customers using a certain amount of kWh?

____Yes ——→ How many kWh? ____________kWh.
____No

C4. Customers with water heaters of certain size?

____Yes ——→ How many gallons? ____________gallons
____No

C5. Customers with central air conditioning?

____Yes
____No

C6. Are there other eligibility requirements?______________________________

____

____

PROMOTION

[NOW I'D LIKE TO LEARN MORE ABOUT HOW YOU HAVE MARKETED AND PROMOTED YOUR LOAD MANAGEMENT PROGRAMS TO RESIDENTIAL CUSTOMERS.]

4. Have you done any consumer or market research for your load management program(s) to:

4.1 Determine customer eligibility? _______Yes _______No

4.2 Determine customer attitudes and preferences? ________Yes ______No

4.3 Determine what factors might increase customer participation? ____Yes ____No

4.4 Do you offer your staff educational programs so they can learn more about load management? ________Yes ______No

5. Please explain what you did in terms of promotion and research, to introduce:

A. Direct Water Heater Control to residential customers?____________________

____

B. Air Conditioner Control to residential customers?____________________

____

C. Time of Use Rates to residential customers? ____________________

____

D. Do you continue to do this?

____Yes
____No ————→ Because is was not effective?____Yes ____No
Because it was too costly? ____Yes ____No

(OTHER - SPECIFY) ____________________

____

6A. [TO PROMOTE DIRECT WATER HEATER CONTROL HAVE YOU USED:]

A1. Bill inserts in the past year?

____Yes ————→ How many times?____________
____No
Were these bill inserts:
____Very effective in promoting water heater control ?
____Moderately effective ?
____Somewhat effective ?
____Not effective ?

(OTHER) ____________________

____

A2. Mailed letters in the past year?

____Yes ————→ How many times?____________
____No
Were these mailed letters:
____Very effective in promoting water heater control ?
____Moderately effective ?
____Somewhat effective ?
____Not effective ?

(OTHER) ____________________

____

A3. Telephone contacts in the past year?

____Yes ——→ How many times?____________
____No   Were they:
____Very effective in promoting water heater control?
____Moderately effective?
____Somewhat effective?
____Not effective?

(OTHER) ________________________________

____

A4. Personal visits in the past year?

____Yes ——→ How many times?____________
____No   Were these personal visits:
____Very effective in promoting WH control?
____Moderately effective?
____Somewhat effective?
____Not effective?

(OTHER) ________________________________

____

6B. TO PROMOTE DIRECT AIR CONDITIONER CONTROL HAVE YOU USED:

B1. Bill inserts in the past year?

____Yes ——→ How many times?____________
____No   Were these bill inserts:
____Very effective in promoting AC control?
____Moderately effective?
____Somewhat effective?
____Not effective?

(OTHER) ________________________________

____

B2. Mailed letters in the past year?

____Yes ——→ How many times?____________
____No   Were these letters:
____Very effective?
____Moderately effective?
____Somewhat effective?
____Not effective?
(OTHER)________________________________

____

B3. Telephone contacts in the past year?

____Yes ——→ How many times?________
____No Were these contacts:
____Very effective?
____Moderately effective?
____Somewhat effective?
____Not effective?
(OTHER)________________________

____

B4. Personal visits in the past year?

____Yes ——→ How many times?________
____No Were these contacts:
____Very effective?
____Moderately effective?
____Somewhat effective?
____Not effective?
(OTHER)________________________

____

6C. TO PROMOTE TIME OF USE RATES HAVE YOU USED:

C1. Bill Inserts in the past year?

____Yes ——→ How many times?________
____No Were these:
____Very effective in promoting TOU rates?
____Moderately effective?
____Somewhat effective?
____Not effective?
(OTHER) ________________________

____

C2. Mailed letters in the past year?

____Yes ——→ How many times?________
____No Were these:
____Very effective?
____Moderately effective?
____Somewhat effective
____Not effective?
(OTHER)________________________

____

C3. Telephone contacts in the past year?

____Yes ——→ How many times?________
____No Were these:
____Very effective in promoting TOU RATES?
____Moderately effective?
____Somewhat effective?
____Not effective?
(OTHER)________________________

____

C4. Personal visits in the past year?

____Yes ——————> How many times?____________
____No Were these:
____Very effective in promoting TOU RATES?
____Moderately effective?
____Somewhat effective?
____Not effective?
(OTHER) ______________________________________

____

7. What was the most unique aspect of your promotional activities that may be of interest to other utilities?

7.1 Bill inserts:

7.2 Mailed letters:

7.3 Telephone contacts:

7.4 Personal visits:

[INTERVIEWER: REQUEST TEXT OF BILL INSERT, MAILED LETTER, ETC. THAT RESPONDENT BELIEVES IS THEIR BEST. HAVE IT MAILED TO: Promoting Load Management Project, Hickerson House 067A, University of North Carolina, Chapel Hill, North Carolina 27514]

8. [INTERVIEWER: ASK ONLY IF PERSONAL VISIT WAS CHECKED].You mentioned that you visited residential customers about your programs. Who actually made the visit [YOU ARE LOOKING FOR A JOB TITLE]. ______________________________

____

8A. Did this person have training in your load management program?

____Yes
____No

9. Was the visit arranged just to talk about load management? How was the customer informed about the visit? ______________________________

____

____

10A. TO PROMOTE DIRECT WATER HEATER CONTROL HAVE YOU USED:

A1. Radio ads in the past year?

____Yes → How many times?____
____No Were these radio ads:
____Very effective? or
____Moderately effective? or
____Somewhat effective? or
____Not effective? or
(OTHER) ____

____

A2. TV ads?

____Yes → How many times? ____
____No Were these TV ads:
____Very effective? or
____Moderately effective? or
____Somewhat effective? or
____Not effective?
(OTHER)____

____

A3. Newspaper ads?

____Yes → How many times? ____
____No Were these newspaper ads:
____Very effective? or
____Moderately effective? or
____Somewhat effective? or
____Not effective?
(OTHER)____

____

A4. Billboards:

____Yes → How many times?____
____No Were these billboards:
____Very effective? or
____Moderately effective? or
____Somewhat effective? or
____Not effective?
(OTHER)____

____

A5. Public transportation ads?

____Yes → How many times?____
____No Were these?
____Very effective?
____Moderately effective?
____Somewhat effective?
____Not effective?
(OTHER) ____

____

A6. Town meetings, public hearings, focus groups, etc.?

____Yes ——→ How many times?______________
____No Were these:
____Very effective? or
____Moderately effective? or
____Somewhat effective? or
____Not effective?
(OTHER)________________________________

____

A7. Did you try anything else?________________________________

____

10B. TO PROMOTE DIRECT AIR CONDITIONER CONTROL HAVE YOU USED:

B.1. Radio ads in the past year?

___ Yes ——→ How many times?______________
___ No Were these radio ads:

___ Very effective? or
___ Moderately effective? or
___ Somewhat effective? or
___ Not effective?

(OTHER)________________________________

B.2. TV ads:

___ Yes ——→ How many times? ______________
___ No Were these TV ads:

___ Very effective? or
___ Moderately effective? or
___ Somewhat effective? or
___ Not effective?

(OTHER)________________________________

B.3. Newspaper ads?

___ Yes ——→ How many times? ______________
___ No Were these newspaper ads:

___ Very effective?
___ Moderately effective?
___ Somewhat effective?
___ Not effective?

(OTHER)________________________________

B.4. Billboards?

___ Yes → How many times? ____________
___ No   Were these newspaper ads:

___ Very effective?
___ Moderately effective?
___ Somewhat effective?
___ Not effective?

(OTHER) ____________________________

B. 5. Public Transportation ads?

___ Yes → How many times? ____________
___ No   Were these newspaper ads:

___ Very effective?
___ Moderately effective?
___ Somewhat effective?
___ Not effective?

(OTHER) ____________________________

B.6. Town meetings, public hearings, focus groups, etc.?

___ Yes → How many times? ____________
___ No   Were these:

___ Very effective?
___ Moderately effective?
___ Somewhat effective?
___ Not effective?

(OTHER) ____________________________

B.7. Did you try anything else? ____________________________

____

10C. TO PROMOTE TIME OF USE RATES HAVE YOU USED:

C.1. Radio ads in the past year?

___ Yes → How many times? ____________
___ No   Were these radio ads:

___ Very effective?
___ Moderately effective?
___ Somewhat effective?
___ Not effective?

(OTHER) ____________________________

C.2 TV ads?

___ Yes → How many times? ____________
___ No   Were these TV ads:

___ Very effective?
___ Moderately effective?
___ Somewhat effective?
___ Not effective?

(OTHER) ____________________________

C.3. Newspaper ads?

___ Yes → How many times?________
___ No Were these newspaper ads:

___ Very effective?
___ Moderately effective?
___ Somewhat effective?
___ Not effective?

(OTHER)________

C.4. Billboards?

___ Yes → How many times?________
___ No Were these billboards:

___ Very effective?
___ Moderately effective?
___ Somewhat effective?
___ Not effective?

(OTHER)________

C.5. Public Transportation ads?

___ Yes → How many times?________
Were these:

___ Very effective?
___ Moderately effective?
___ Somewhat effective?
___ Not effective?

(OTHER)________

C.6. Town meetings, public hearings, focus groups, etc?

___ Yes → How many times?________
___ No Were these:

___ Very effective?
___ Moderately effective?
___ Somewhat effective?
___ Not effective?

(OTHER)________

C.7. Did you try anything else?________

____

[INERVIEWER: REQUEST TEXT OF RADIO AD, TV AD, ETC. THAT RESPONDENT BELIEVES IS THEIR BEST. HAVE IT MAILED TO: Promoting Load Management Project,
Hickerson House 067A
University of North Carolina
Chapel Hill, N.C. 27514

11. What was the most unique aspect of your promotional activities that may be of interest to other utilities?

Radio ads ______________________________

____

TV ads ______________________________

____

Newspapers ______________________________

____

OTHERS-SPECIFY ______________________________

____

____

12. In general, do you market your load management programs together with other types of CONSERVATION programs or do you market load management separately?

____With other conservation programs?
____Separate from other conservation programs?
____OTHER ______________________________

____

B. Why? ______________________________

____

13. A. Considering all your promotional efforts and disregarding costs, what type of promotion has been:

MOST effective in increasing customer participation? ______________

____

Which is LEAST effective? ______________________________

____

B. If you consider cost, which has been:

MOST Effective in increasing customer participation? ______________

____

LEAST Effective? ______________________________

____

C. What was your typical promotional strategy? Did you use bill stuffers, first, then media or what? ______________________________

____

____

14. As an incentive for customers to participate in your Direct Water Heater Control Program, do you offer:

____An annual lump sum payment? → Average $__________
____A monthly credit? → Average $__________
____A reduced charge per kWh? → Amount reduced $______
____A Water Heater Blanket?
____Free maintenance of water heater?
____Anything else? ______________________________

____

15. As an incentive for customers to participate in your Direct Air Conditioner Control Program, do you offer:

___ An annual lump sum payment? → Average $__________
___ A monthly credit? → Average $__________
___ A reduced charge per kWh? → Reduction $__________
___ Free maintenance of air conditioner?
___ Anything else? ______________________________

____

16. As an incentive for customers to participate in your Time of Use Rates do you offer:

___ An annual lump sum payment? → Average $__________
___ A monthly credit? → Average $__________
___ A reduced charge per kWh? → Reduction$__________
___ Anything else? ______________________________

____

17. Considering all you have done to promote load management (incentive, media, bill inserts, etc.), what would you do now if you had it to do all over again?

____

____

____

____

____

COSTS AND BENEFITS TO CUSTOMERS

You have told me a great deal about your load management programs and how you have promoted them. I have just a few more questions to ask you about the costs and benefits customers can expect from their participation and the benefits your utility derives from load management programs. First, I'd like to know how a potential client for load management becomes an actual participant.

18. What route do most customers follow to become participants?

____Hear it from a friend, then call us.
____Hear it on a media ad, then call us.
____Read letter/bill stuffer, then call.
____We call them
____Other (SPECIFY) ______________________________

____

____

19. What is the customer charged for the controlling device for his or her:

Water Heater?______________

Air Conditioner? $______________

20. What is the customer charged for the metering device?

Time of Use device $______________

Water Heater $______________

Air Conditioner $______________

21. What is the installation charge?

Water heater $______________
Air Conditioner $______________
Time of Use $______________

22. What other charges are there for participating on the __________program?

Water heater (SPECIFY)______________________________
Air conditioner (SPECIFY)______________________________
Time of Use (SPECIFY) ______________________________

23. Do customers have to pay all charges before they can participate?

____Yes
____No ——————→ What % of charges must be paid? ____________%

How is the remainder billed?______________

____

24. For what period of time is a customer required to participate in your:

Water Heater Program?______________Months
Air Conditioner Program?______________Months
Time of Use Rate Program?______________Months

25. [IF CUSTOMER MUST PARTICIPATE FOR SOME PERIOD OF TIME] Does the customer sign a contract or statement of commitment specifying this time period?

____Yes ——————→ What is the penalty for withdrawing from the Program?______________________________
____No

____

26. a. What average monthly savings can Direct Water Heater Control customers expect on their electric bill?

$____________

b. What average monthly savings can Direct Air Conditioner Control customers expect on their electric bill?

$_________

c. What average monthly savings can Time of Use Rate customers expect on their electric bill?

$_________

27. What other important benefits do customers receive by participating in your Direct Water Heater Control Program? ______________________________

____

b. What other important benefits do customers receive by participating in your Direct Air Conditioner Control Program? ______________________________

____

____

c. What other important benefits do customers receive by participating in your Time of Use Rate Program? ______________________________

____

____

UTILITY COSTS AND BENEFITS

Finally, I'd like to find out about the benefits and costs your utility receives as a result of residential customer participation in load management.

28. Approximately what percentage of eligible households are participating on:

Water Heater Programs?__________% → Households?__________
Air Conditioner Programs?__________% → Households?__________
Time of Use Rates__________% → Households?__________

29. What reduction in capacity requirement does your utility obtain as a result of your residential load control and time of use rate programs? [FOR INVESTOR OWNED UTILITIES ONLY].

____

____

30. [FOR EMC's AND MUNICIPAL ELECTRIC UTILITIES]. What reduction in demand requirement does your utility obtain as a result of your residential load control and time of use rate programs?

____

____

31. What percentage of customers do you expect to adopt:

Direct Water Heater Control by the end of 1987?________________%
Direct Air Conditioner Control by end of 1987?________________%
Time of Use rates by the end of 1987?________________%

32. Are there other benefits your utility receives from its:

Water Heater Control Programs?
____Yes ——→What are they?________________
____No

____

Air Conditioner Control Programs?

____Yes ——→What are they?________________
____No

____

Time of Use Rate Programs?

____Yes ——→What are they?________________
____No

____

33. What are the most consistent problems your utility has experienced as a result of its load management programs?

Water Heater Control________________

____

Air Conditioner Control________________

____

Time of Use Rates________________

____

34. Finally, what factors, do you think, affects customers' decisions to participat in load management programs?

____

____

[THANK YOU VERY MUCH. YOU HAVE BEEN VERY HELPFUL. I'M SURE THAT YOUR RESPONSES, ALONG WITH THOSE FROM OTHERS, WILL HELP US TO BETTER UNDERSTAND HOW LOAD MANAGEMENT HAS BEEN COMMUNICATED TO RESIDENTIAL CUSTOMERS.

IF YOU ARE INTERESTED IN RECEIVING A SUMMARY OF OUR FINDINGS, PLEASE GIVE ME YOUR CORRECT MAILING ADDRESS.

____

____

____

____

Appendix C

Market Audit and Focus Group Methods Used in Study

Marketing audits are intended to review each major marketing management decision area. A comprehensive marketing audit should therefore include available information pertaining to product or program characteristics, promotional tactics, price decisions, channels of distribution, and customer response in each residential market segment. A list of load management marketing audit topics summarizes the marketing audit instrument that was sent to a designated key informant at each utility. The instrument provided a list of topic areas and general questions that result in a review of the load management program and its marketing history in the study area. The topic areas included all four marketing management decision areas: product (or program); promotion; price, and, channels of distribution (see pages 267 and 268).

METHODS USED FOR FOCUS GROUP MEETINGS

Focus group discussions were held in five locations across North Carolina. The locations were selected to reflect the current diversity existing in load management programs. The City of Salisbury was selected from the Duke Power service area. Raleigh was selected from the Carolina Power and Light Company service area since it has been the only North Carolina test market for the CP&L load management program. The VEPCO load management program was represented by the selection of the City of Roanoke Rapids. Other locations were chosen to represent municipals and electric membership corporations. The City of Tarboro was selected as a focus group site to represent a municipal's load management program. Finally, the Raeford rural area was selected from the Lumbee River EMC since it provides an example of a load management program available from an electric membership corporation.

Focus group participants in each of the five locations were generally selected at random from the most recent telephone book. Only in the case of the Lumbee River EMC focus group was it necessary to randomly select potential participants from a list other than the telephone book. In this specific instance, participants were randomly selected from the regional EMC membership roster.

Each household selected was sent a personalized letter inviting them to participate in the group discussion. An example of the letter is presented below. The letter was sent to each household on University of North Carolina stationery. The affiliation of the research team was also identified as The University of North Carolina at Chapel Hill. Each household was invited to send an adult to the small group discussion to be held soon in that community. The letter stated that each participating adult would receive a small payment in appreciation for the person's time and travel expenses. Each household was later contacted by telephone to see if an adult would be attending. Reminder cards were mailed to the adult who verbally agreed to attend the session.

About one-third of the originally contacted households were eventually represented by an adult at the group discussion. These adults were quite diverse. While all participants came from areas in which load management programs had been in effect for some time, some adults at the focus group came from households that were participating in load management programs, while others were completely unaware of the load management programs actually available in their service area. The focus group participants were also diverse with respect to demographic characteristics such as sex, race, age, and income. Almost all the participants came from households residing in single family residences. In summary, each adult represented a household that would be considered a prospect by at least one and generally all the utilities that currently offer load management programs within North Carolina.

LOAD MANAGEMENT MARKETING AUDIT TOPICS

Objective

- Monthly history of each residential direct load control and/or time-of-day rate program in selected utility study areas (CP&L: Raleigh; Duke Power: Salisbury; VEPCO: Roanoke Rapids; Municipal: Tarboro; EMC: Lumbee River EMC, Four County EMC).

Product Information

- Description of the load management program offered to residential customers in the service area, including nature and timing of changes in program characteristics.
- Eligibility requirements for participation.
- Service interruption plan for water heater and air conditioner control programs.
- Discount/refund offered to households.
- Residential equipment requirements and installation practices.

Promotion Information

- How was the program promoted to customers? What various promotional activities have been tried by the utility to communicate the availability of the load management program, to encourage participation, and to maintain participation?
- How has the "promotional mix" changed over time?
- Provide examples of various promotional activities, such as bill stuffers, newspaper advertisements, radio ad scripts, and booklets.
- To what extent has direct contact with potential residential customers been tried? Who makes the direct contacts? What do the direct contact personnel say to the customer? How is the program explained?
- What other promotional offers have been tried, such as free hot water heater wraps and the like?

Price

- What does it cost the residential customer to participate in the program(s)?
- How has the cost to potential participants changed over time?
- The cost to the residential customer can be addressed in dollars and in time. What does it cost the residential customer in dollars, such as through equipment and installation fees? To what extent does it cost the customer time to participate? How is a customer's participation secured . . . phone order? written contract?

Channels of Distribution

- Who implements the program for the utility?
- What size staff is available for marketing residential load management programs?
- Has the utility even tried joint distribution of load management programs by combining forces with, for example, local wood stove dealers or energy conservation retail stores?

Customer Response

- What is the history of customer response to each aspect of the direct load control and/or time-of-day rate programs? What is the monthly history of customer sign-ups?
- What is the best estimate of the total possible market in the area, if 100 percent of the eligible households were to participate?
- Can customer response to any of the marketing tactics developed by the utility be documented? For example, if a newspaper ad included a coupon for further information, how many coupons were mailed in following placement of the ads?

THE UNIVERSITY OF NORTH CAROLINA
AT
CHAPEL HILL

School of Business Administration

The University of North Carolina at Chapel Hill
Carroll Hall 012 A
Chapel Hill, N.C. 27514

INVITATION TO FOCUS GROUP DISCUSSION

Dear Mr. ____________:

A research team at the University of North Carolina at Chapel Hill is currently preparing for a statewide study of energy consumption and energy conservation in North Carolina households. This important study will provide useful information for state and local planning officials.

I will be holding several small group discussions at various locations across North Carolina to help the research team prepare for the statewide study. Each of the informal meetings will last about one hour and will consist of casual group discussions of several energy consumption and energy conservation topics in which the other research team members and I have considerable interest.

The purpose of this letter is to invite an adult from your household to attend the small group discussion in Salisbury during Tuesday evening, May 25. The group discussion will begin at 7:30 p.m. and will be held at the Rowan Public Library meeting room, 201 West Fisher Street. The participating adult from your household can attend the group discussion. I do hope that someone from your household will be able to attend at the Rowan Public Library next Tuesday evening at 7:30 p.m.

Sincerely,

Nicholas M. Didow
Assistant Professor

Index